MW00609684

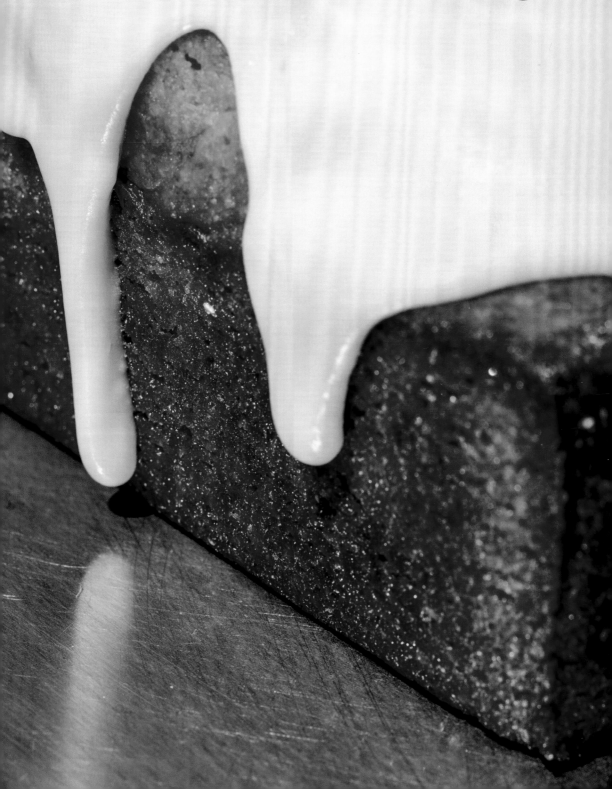

BAKE
CLUB

More!

- - - - - - - - - - - - - - -

Cookbooks

Milk Bar: All About Cookies

Milk Bar: Kids Only

Milk Bar: All About Cake

Milk Bar Life

Momofuku Milk Bar

Kids' Books

Just the Right Cake

Every Cake Has a Story

Book Books

Dessert Can Save the World

BAKE CLUB

& BUTTER TOO

101 Must-Have Moves for Your Kitchen

Christina Tosi

and Shannon Salzano

PHOTOGRAPHS BY HENRY HARGREAVES

ALFRED A. KNOPF

New York   2024

THIS IS A BORZOI BOOK
PUBLISHED BY ALFRED A. KNOPF

Copyright © 2024 by CS Tosi, LLC

Photographs copyright © 2024 by
Henry Hargreaves

All rights reserved. Published in the
United States by Alfred A. Knopf, a
division of Penguin Random House LLC,
New York, and distributed in Canada by
Penguin Random House Canada Limited,
Toronto.

www.aaknopf.com

Knopf, Borzoi Books, and the colophon
are registered trademarks of Penguin
Random House LLC.

Illustrations: (sticky notes) 32 pixels /
Shutterstock; (polaroid frames)
Copperfield1 / Shutterstock; (scissors/
dog) linear_design / Shutterstock

Library of Congress Cataloging-in-
   Publication Data
Names: Tosi, Christina, author. | Salzano,
   Shannon, author. | Hargreaves,
   Henry, photographer.
Title: Bake club : 101 must-have moves
   for your kitchen / Christina Tosi with
   Shannon Salzano ; photographs by
   Henry Hargreaves.
Description: First edition. | New York :
   Alfred A. Knopf, 2024. | Includes index.
Identifiers: LCCN 2024001957 |
   ISBN 9780593802397 (hardcover) |
   ISBN 9780593802403 (ebook)
Subjects: LCSH: Baking. | Desserts. |
   LCGFT: Cookbooks.
Classification: LCC TX763 .T66 2024 |
   DDC 641.7/1—dc23/eng/20240228
LC record available at https://lccn.loc
   .gov/2024001957

Some of the recipes in this book may
include raw eggs, meat, or fish. When
these foods are consumed raw, there
is always the risk that bacteria, which
is killed by proper cooking, may be
present. For this reason, when serving
these foods raw, always buy certified
salmonella-free eggs and the freshest
meat and fish available from a reliable
grocer, storing them in the refrigerator
until they are served. Because of
the health risks associated with the
consumption of bacteria that can be
present in raw eggs, meat, and fish,
these foods should not be consumed
by infants, small children, pregnant
women, the elderly, or any persons
who may be immunocompromised.
The author and publisher expressly
disclaim responsibility for any adverse
effects that may result from the use or
application of the recipes and information
contained in this book.

Cover photographs by Henry Hargreaves
Back-of-cover image: (notepaper)
32 pixels / Shutterstock

Cover design by Chip Kidd

Book design by
Shubhani Sarkar, sarkardesignstudio.com

Manufactured in China
First Edition

To the 3/24/20 originals,
to every newcomer, to the ones
that smile, that choose optimism,
that believe in the power of
a baked good:

Thank you for your kinship,
for cheer, for friendship, for fuel.
Our spirit is always giving and
never ending.

Now turn on that oven,
turn up the tunes,
and let's DO this!

CONTENTS

HIYA/HELLO/WHAT'S UP/WELCOME!   1

INGREDIENTS: YOU HAVE EVERYTHING YOU NEED   3

EQUIPMENT: YOU DON'T NEED MUCH   7

- - - - - - - - - - - - - -

Your DIY Pantry   13

Dropoffable Desserts   63

Baking for Breakfast   103

Daily Bread   137

Cake Every Which Way   173

Snack Aisle   207

Tabletop Desserts   255

- - - - - - - - - - - - - -

SHOUTOUTS   295

INDEX   299

BAKE CLUB

Hiya/Hello/What's Up/Welcome!

I'm really glad you're here. Dare I say PUMPED. Technically, I'm an introvert, and though I originally thought I fell in love with baking because it gave me an excuse to hide out in a kitchen all day and eat dessert for every meal, I've come to realize that the reason I actually love baking is you.

I do what I do because the output becomes a really important part of people's lives. It represents goodness, kinship, solidarity, support, an invitation in, an opportunity, a mechanism for magic.

The power of dessert is pretty cool. Not a one and done, not a fad. If there's one thing I know and learn time and time again, it's that baking will NEVER go out of style. Just like red Chucks, it's always on point. It's powerful, too. Think about it—it's the thing we turn to in good times and bad, celebrations and uncertainty. Cake always has a habit of showing up.

And, no surprise here, it's SO much bigger than me and you, it's ever–growing–reaching–expanding in its limitless potential. There's always an open door with a brilliant influx of curious people, looking to learn, deepen their depth, or try something new on for size amid a few sticks of butter and an 8-by-8-inch pan.

So, without further ado: Welcome to the club! Or, rather, Bake Club (the club AND the cookbook).

Actually, let me rewind the tape a sec. Like many, the first few days of the 2020 pandemic found me wringing my hands a bit, feeling upended by all the uncertainty that surrounded. Historically I combatted moments of unease by losing myself in the creativity of a baking project that once complete I could share, finding a way to lose myself and find myself, but also to be useful. I had always found comfort in the all-encompassing, singular-focused mindset a good bake session brought internally and externally, so naturally I was drawn to my kitchen. Only this was a much trickier time—toilet paper was a commodity, as was flour and other basic pantry staples, as was the loneliness of not being able to see folks, bestow baked goods upon them as I normally would to cope. I took inventory of my pantry and life realities and I realized my community at large may be feeling similarly rudderless, uncertain, lost, but looking. I knew I needed to find a way to show up, to bake, to be useful. With a simple Instagram post—a rushed photo of butter, sugar, flour, and salt—and a note to show up the following day at 2 p.m., Bake Club was born.

With my dog Butter by my side I cranked up the music and (clumsily!) livestreamed my way through my family's go-to cutout cookie recipe. It's the recipe we've always made—for holidays and every days alike—my whole life, together or apart. I told my Instapals to take their own riffs: Play with shape! Whisk up a clever glaze! Let loose! Have fun and forget the world for a moment. And they did. Thousands of home bakers and non bakers alike tuned in and tagged me in proud posts of their creations, excited for the lesson and the excuse to escape. So I did it again the next day. And the next. And the next and the next. People came back, more people peeked in and rolled up their sleeves, showing up, every day at 2 p.m. for 365 days and then weekly after that, with a new recipe and a new playlist and a renewed invitation: bake with me and leave the world behind.

A daily excuse to bake, or make a little mess in the kitchen, time in these pages is sure to enrich life—liven up the ordinary, embrace curiosity, silence the scary, give you a place to go to belong and feel a part of something, give you pride, ownership, creative freedom, and a sense of both newness and accomplishment. Posi vibes VERY much included.

Over the last few years I've met so many members of the Bake Club community and let me tell you, they range from pro-level pastry chefs to never-touched-flour-before novices. Skill level is irrelevant, we are chasing something larger. These pages are YOURS, and it doesn't matter what your age is, or your experience in the kitchen. We're going to cover all categories of the baking universe, from Pop Rocks to Ham and Cheese Puffs (yeah, we get savory). And you're going to crush SO hard. Why? Because you're you.

Also because every recipe in here I've built around dispelling baking misconceptions and the things we tell ourselves: "I don't have enough time," "I don't have the right ingredients," "I don't have a stand mixer," "I'm not a great baker." "Phooey!" as my grandma would say.

Hand on heart: Every recipe in here is meant to lift you up, set you up for success, engage and empower you and anyone else baking alongside you, with concepts and modifications galore; there is no fancy equipment needed. I made them for YOU.

BTW, I KNOW these recipes work, because they are mainstays in my home kitchen—they're the things my fam and friends request on repeat. They are HOW and WHAT I bake at home. They're the starting point to how I approach crafting a killer Milk Bar dessert with the team. They're a collection of what I've learned and loved over decades as a self-taught home cook who eventually started moonlighting as a professional pastry chef.

They're simple and they're special. They represent what's missing in the wild, wonderful world of recipes and the club that builds, fueled by them. That's right, included in each of these gems is a guaranteed best friend or hundred or thousand—maybe a social media buddy just a few streets over, or a digi pen pal on the other side of the country. These recipes connect us and are our conduit for community. So, as you get into the kitchen, get on the #BakeClub socials and start making buds. You'll be amazed how many sweet-toothed soul mates are out there, waiting to cheer you on in the kitchen and show up for you in life at large, so don't forget to tap in.

Welcoming, disarming, unpretentious, yet show stoppingly impressive and insanely delicious, in case you haven't already figured it out, Bake Club recipes are more casual in tone and format, freedom measurements (that's cups and table/teaspoons), grocery store ingredients only. Gettable, bakeable, YOU.

Ready? Here we GOOOOOOO!

BakeClub.com

If you want more TMI, we have a wealth of wacky videos, old and new, teaching you deep dives beyond these pages on recipes, techniques, ingredient swaps, equipment alternatives, and more. Plus, then we can be digi pen pals beyond this book (my selfishly favorite part!).

Ingredients

You Have Everything You Need

The rules for a Bake Club recipe have always been simple: no hard-to-get ingredients and no unnecessary equipment. To make the recipes as accessible as possible, I gut-check with one question: "Can you get all the ingredients at an average grocery store?" So often we box ourselves out of baking by saying we don't have a specific extract or bespoke type of flour or fancy butter and on and on, and that's just pish posh. To help this sink in for you, each recipe has a photo of the ingredients you need to make it, so you can see plain as day just how few items stand between you and something incredible.

The Core Five

The heft of the recipes in this collection can be made with a foundation of butter, flour, sugar, eggs, and salt, with one or two pinch hitters. With these items in your pantry, you're well on your way to greatness.

Butter

Unsalted, by the stick. Save the salted butter for your dinner table. Unsalted butter lets you call the shots on the salt level (and therefore depth of flavor and sharpness)—it's easy to add salt, but impossible to subtract. Butter need not be fancy; the average stuff will get you where you need to go.

"Cold" means cold; "super soft" means leave it out overnight or zap it in the microwave—it's meant to set you up for success when mixing, because super-soft butter whips up much more easily than cold in, say, a dense and fudgy cookie recipe.

Sugar

Granulated sugar is the base sweetener in this book, and a simple bag of it will carry you through.

Light brown and dark brown sugar come in when we are looking for deeper flavor to go with the sweetness.

Confectioners' sugar—aka powdered sugar, aka 10x (because it's granulated sugar ground down ten times)—is used when we want the sugar to dissolve completely into the recipe—think frostings, glazes, etc.

Eggs

Eggs are a real baking MVP, bringing structure, hydration, texture, and flavor in one little compostable package. They come in different shapes. I live and die by large eggs. The ratio of yolk to white is just right, and every egg called for in this book is large. If you like medium or XL, please, by all means, still come to the party! Your end result may be a tad different, but not so much so that anyone will know besides you and me.

Salt

Kosher salt is my preference here—Diamond Crystal to get really specific—because it has larger granules than table salt and sharpens flavors rather than make things taste "salty." Kosher salt is key, not to create a salty taste but more to make a bridge for flavors and to add a dynamism to your bake. If all you have is table salt, bring it! Just reduce every salt quantity by 1/8 teaspoon for every 1 teaspoon called for (smaller granules mean they take up less space).

Flour

All-purpose, if you please. Any brand will do. I don't want to get too pastry-dork on you, but different flours carry different protein contents (bread flour has a higher percentage of protein, and cake flour a lower percentage). Of course, flour type matters when you're really, really zooming in at the top of your professional game, but here, technique will get you to a GREAT place without having to juggle many different flour types (one of my personal pet peeves)!

Whole-wheat is called for at very specific times, when we want more heft, a specific earthy flavor, and structure to our bake—I'm talking graham crackers or cinnamon-toast cereal. If you snag a bag for those recipes, there are loads of others where you can use it as an alt to AP, or to replace half the AP in any recipe you think the flavor could really rock (aka brown-butter chocolate chip muffins or easy, can't-mess-it-up bread).

Bread flour isn't required to make great bread, but if you have a bag or want to take your bread up a notch, I would gladly take it for any recipe in Daily Bread (page 137), especially in something more advanced, like brioche.

Supporting Characters

Outside of the core five, here are some ingredients to help your dream come to life.

Baking powder and baking soda

This dynamic duo is what we refer to as leaveners, primarily controlling the rise, puff, and spread of your bake, but also flavor and color, believe it or not. Double-acting baking powder brings lift and height—acting first when combined with a liquid, and again when it hits the heat of the oven. Baking soda also lifts, but with breadth (if there is an acid in the mix, like buttermilk or lemon juice), and helps with spread. A container of each will last you a while—just watch those expiration dates.

Oil

Neutral, flavorless oil brings moisture when needed and is a great partner for melting chocolate. Remember, it's not about adding flavor, so oil or grapeseed oil works.

Olive oil brings the moisture with a bit of flavor on the side; there are a few recipes that call for it, and you may choose to swap it (or other flavorful oils, like pumpkin-seed or almond or coconut) in when it plays into your flavor story.

Extract

Vanilla extract, the little brown bottle you know and love, brings a depth and a coziness to your bakes. Sure, a fancy one is nice, but a plain-Jane bottle will do just fine.

Don't let your extract game stop at vanilla. Orange, lemon, and peppermint are all called into action here by name, and you may opt to take your own extract flavor journeys when making each recipe your own.

Whole milk

Big fan of milk over here. Milk brings moisture and protein to a recipe, so grab a jug of whole milk when we ask for it. (If yours is a 2-percent or skim household, no judgment—use that in place of whole. Same with alternatives.)

Heavy cream or whipping cream brings a sweeter, thicker dairy moment via a higher fat content. Fat = Flavor. This is your base for whipped cream, crème brûlée, ice cream, fudge sauce, and more—so don't skimp.

Milk powder

Often labeled as "instant nonfat dry milk," milk powder adds depth of flavor, and chew, to any baked good it's a part of. A tablespoon or two of it in your go-to cookie or marshmallow-treat recipe, and your life (and taste buds) will be forever changed.

Yeast

Active dry yeast is what brings every bread creation in this book to life. Technically a leavening agent, yeast gives bread its rise, and open, airy, texture, while also strengthening the dough, giving it an undeniable chew.

Chocolate

Chocolate chips, cocoa powder, cut up your own candy bar. I'm not precious about the chocolate type—nothing fancy needed to get the job done—but chocolate, with its cocoa counterparts, is an important ingredient in flavor, texture, function, and vis when called for.

A note on gluten-free

I get asked often if my recipes can be converted to gluten-free, to which I of course say, "Do YOU!" If you are living a life free of gluten, you know the rules of the road. Substitute your gluten-free flour as you please. And note, there are loads of recipes in here that don't mess with flour at all (page 11), so you've got places to go, regardless.

Let Your Pantry Be Your Guide

You have everything you need. That's what I remind myself every time I go to bake. I've never been one to let something stand between me and dessert, and I think recipes should embolden you to chase down life in a similar manner. The truth is, there is more flexibility in baking than you have been led to believe. Yes, it's a science, in that there are reactions involved, but a swap of ingredients here and there is not going to slow you down. Get to know your core ingredients and the items you keep regularly stocked in your pantry. Get creative in what you bring to the bowl. If you are out of flour, grind down some pretzels and swap them in—no one is mad at that extra flavor. Out of butter? Start whipping up that heavy cream until it takes the shape. Chop up a candy bar in place of chocolate chips, swap cookie butter for peanut butter. Your pantry has the solutions to all your so-called baking problems, so put it to work by knowing what ingredients you have, their role, and how to use them. Experiment and succeed, experiment and fail and learn. Trial and error, instinctual and intellectual ingredient swaps, are where it's at.

Bake every day for a month without a trip to the grocery store. It's how I grew up and learned all of the fun little riffs I carry through in these pages to you. Limitation breeds the highest form of creativity. So stand in that pantry until lightning strikes!

Baking is a form of self expression. You get to create something based on what you are feeling, on what you think sounds delicious, the flavors you are hankering for in that moment. Or even better, for the person you are baking for! I've laid major groundwork in these pages, giving you the simplest roadmap for success, and asking you to add the color. Put your spin on these recipes, make them personal to you. Tinker and taste and riff and jam until you've landed on your own version to call on when the mood strikes! When you see this call out, you'll find examples of my riffs or of the brilliance I have seen Bake Clubbers bring to life, so you can feel inspired and emboldened to chart your own course. This is the NESS of what we do at Bake Club, how we show up in our pantries and cheer one another on. Greatness awaits.

Equipment

You Don't Need Much

A few things are true about the way I like to get down in the kitchen:

1. I aspire to wash as few dishes as possible.
2. I don't believe in unnecessary equipment.

With these two guiding principles, my recipes are pretty lean and mean. I love a one-bowl wonder. I won't have you break out a stand mixer unless it's absolutely necessary. I'll always find a way to make a recipe work with the items you have in your pantry before telling you to purchase a single-purpose tool or ingredient.

Much as with ingredients, you can make do with anything you have in your kitchen. A Ziploc bag can play many roles; so can a used, clean Cool Whip container, ditto a cereal bowl, water glass, and soup spoon.

Non-Negotiables

Though you can MacGyver your way through a lot of recipes, there are a few items I would put on my desert island must-have baking list.

Half sheet pan

A half sheet pan—aka cookie sheet or baking sheet—is that 13-by-18-inch flat piece of metal you can call on for everything from a batch of cookies to a roll-up cake. You don't have to go for broke; it just needs to be sturdy, and even-leveled.

Parchment paper

Available in the paper goods aisle of your grocery store, one roll of this flimsy white paper goes a long way on ease of cleanup, but also on ensuring an even bake for your cookies and cakes. I also love to use a few sheets with my rolling pin when making cutout cookies.

Large bowl

"Larger than you think you need," she yells from the rooftops! A big bowl (one that can act as a helmet over your head) means much less of a mess, giving you the space and freedom you need to get creative. I like to be able to zap it for a few seconds if needed, so microwave-safe is my vote.

Sturdy heat-safe spatula

The best tool around for bringing together doughs and batters, a strong spatula that can stand up to heat will be your most-used tool in the kitchen.

Measuring cups/spoons

When I'm on the Milk Bar clock, I live a life of precise measurements, using a scale to get the exact measurements my recipes call for. At home, I like to live a much more relaxed lifestyle. A simple set of measuring cups and spoons will do you for the recipes in this book; I've worry-proofed them to allow for the range that naturally occurs when measuring at home. You don't even need to worry about a graduated cup for measuring liquids—we live life that far on the edge.

Storage

You didn't spend all that time in the kitchen to have your creations go stale before the crew could dig in. Keeping a few items on hand will give your treats the long life they deserve.

Airtight containers

For ease, I like to order online, in bulk, the kind takeout food arrives in, but the sort you can get at the grocery store work great, too, for keeping moisture in or out.

Plastic wrap

For pies and cakes and trays of cookies, plastic wrapped tight saves on time and dishes.

Disposable pans

The biggest move I have is to do your baking straight in the dish you will store or gift your treats in; it's saved me hours.

Freezer space

Baked goods can last for weeks and weeks in the freezer, so, if you're trying to get down with some serious bulk bakes, freezer space is your BFF. I've got a chest freezer in my garage, and she's always full, and I'm never worried about dessert as such.

The Extended Family

Pans galore

In my opinion, what you bake something in is really just a recommendation. A Bundt can be a loaf, an 8-by-8-inch can be a 9-by-13, a cupcake can be a layer cake, and so on. I give you my rulebook on times and temps on page 178, and here is the cast of characters I keep on hand to chase down my baking visions:

- 8-by-8-inch pan
- 9-by-13-inch pan
- Cupcake/muffin pan with liners
- 9-inch cake pan
- Pie dish, 9- or 10-inch
- Bundt pan (12-cup)
- Loaf pan 8.5-by-4.5-inch is optimal but bigger sizes will do; your loaves will just be shorter and wider

Heavy-bottomed medium-sized pot / heavy-bottomed saucepan / skillet

Whether you're making a caramel, going to soft ball stage (page 220), or baking up sizzling skillet cookies, some of the pots and pans you usually reserve for savory cooking can come into play with baking. Largely, you want something quality with a heavy bottom to make sure the heat spreads consistently so there's no risk of burning.

Blender and sieve

I am not one to get precise when it's not necessary, but I also don't like to phone things in. When you're making a lemon curd or a batch of popovers, a stick blender or traditional blender will give you a smoothness that is key and can't be replicated by hand. Same goes for a sieve when making a batch of ricotta—no matter how hard you try to get the clumps out, a sieve is just the tool for the job!

Rolling pin (with a parchment paper BFF)

A simple wooden dowel, your rolling pin will help you smooth out cookie doughs and croissant sheets. Don't forget the parchment paper—it will save you so much hair pulling.

Stand mixer with attachments for very specific tasks (whisk, paddle, dough hook)

I told you I would never ask you to get more than you need, except for very specific uses; this is an essential. I've never whipped egg whites by hand successfully into a meringue, and if you're going to mixer town, good news is it works for a drop cookie, too.

Cookie scoop . . . but also just a dinner spoon

If you're in the business of cranking out loads of drop cookies, a cookie scoop is nice for consistency (equal scoops mean equal bake)—I like a 2¾-ounce scoop. But I've made zillions of beautiful cookies with a dinner spoon as my instrument, too!

Cookie cutters

When you're slicing up wafer cookies or getting fancy with graham crackers, it's nice to have a few sizes of cookie cutters . . . but a water cup turned upside down will get you where you need to go.

Know Your Oven

Listen, you can't always trust the dial on your oven, but it's your oven, and you must know her kind of well by now. Her hot spots, her cold spots, where she gives your baked goods more color versus less. If she's always burning the bottom of your lasagna, move the rack much higher up before you bake your PB s'mores bars, and if you know she likes it when you rotate your sheet pan of cookies from back to front mid-bake for an even golden brown, honor her. Leverage your relationship, and work within the facts you've already gathered for any of these recipes.

Cheat Sheet

Dealing with some special diets? No prob! Here are a few of my fave Bake Club recipes that fit the bill.

Gluten Free

Chewy Oat Bars

Lemon Crinkle Cookies

Chewy Granola Bars

PB Cups

Puppy Chow

Marshmallow Treats

Caramel Apples

Gummy Bears

Fudge

Turtles

Peppermint Patties

Macarons

Crème Brûlée

Pudding

Soft Caramels

Peanut Butter Nougat

Gluten Free & Vegan

Chocolate Peanut Butter Crunch Pie

Lemon Ice

Granola

Chocolate Shell

Marshmallows

Pop Rocks

Potato Chips

YOUR DIY
PANTRY

Fancy Butter   16

The Caramel Sauce of Your Dreams   21

Fudge Sauce   22

Choose Your Flavor Whipped Cream   24

Fruit Jam   27

Citrus Jam   28

Brown Sugar Wafers   32

Chocolate Wafers   33

Graham Crackers   37

Granola   38

Sprinkles   40

Ice Cream Cones   43

Chocolate Shell   44

Marshmallows   47

Soft Caramels   50

Pudding   52

(Any) Fruit Curd   55

Ricotta   56

Hot Chocolate   58

Toffee   61

@samsfoodventure

@willguidara

@jessmakesfoods

#bakeclub

@timross41

@flutterbypay18

#bakeclub

@europeanstylebutter

@elmendez

There are a few reasons I'm starting the book with this chapter, aside from the fact that I am a notorious pantry snacker (a handful of granola in passing or a graham cracker between Zoom calls goes a long way in keeping me chugging). As you'll hear me say on repeat in the pages to come, my hope with this book is that you remove your barriers to baking, so that you start to view it as something you can do on a whim, with whatever time and ingredients you have on hand.

First off, I want to set the record straight on what baking IS. Yes, a gorgeous layer cake is baking. Yes, a perfectly placed lattice-topped apple pie is baking. As is a tray of Grandma's oatmeal cookies. But baking is a universe beyond these finished beauties, too. Baking can be the bits and bobbles that you whip up with creativity in your kitchen to dress up the other moments of life, like making a deep caramel sauce for store-bought vanilla ice cream on a Tuesday night, or a batch of fluffy marshmallows ready to be s'more-ified on a weekend. So— reason one for this chapter: understanding that baking is all around you.

Beyond that, I want to instill in you that baking is a very useful skill. By "skill" I don't mean it is something you need to spend hours perfecting. No, what I mean by skill is that it's useful. Baking is something you can deploy, a cool trick to have in your back pocket to make things happen, to find solutions, to create something tangible out of the intangible. I hope that, with a few recipes under your belt, you'll start to see the world through a lens of "Can I bake _____ myself?" As someone with hours of DIYing under her own belt, I am here to tell you: yes. An awesome side effect of this hands-on approach to life is the extreme sense of satisfaction that comes with announcing something as "homemade."

And my third goal in encouraging you to get baking is to help you to realize that ingredients are things you can create yourself. Want to make a batch of birthday blondies but don't have sprinkles? NBD. Trying to make an icebox cake, but someone ate all your cookies or crackers? No worries! Out of pudding mix, but need a parfait in your life? Come here. This chapter is your cheat-code section. If you're looking to bake but some key items are missing from your ingredient list, get after it. No excuses, and absolutely nothing in your way. You can literally stock your own pantry shelves: FLEX.

So what the heck are you waiting for? Let's go!

FANCY BUTTER

Makes 1 stick

1 stick (8 tablespoons)
    unsalted butter, at room
    temperature
Any combo of one or more
    flavors and seasonings
    (see page 19)

Also known as compound butter, this recipe lets you use butter as your canvas. You can take any flavor and spice up, purée down, or whip in to butter. Do I brown it, bringing out its nuttiness? Should I smoke it, to give it a campfire essence? Butter is the shape shifter of shape shifters and fancy butter is my go-to way to church up a laminated pastry like a Croissant (page 133), a fun way to make grilled-cheese night more intriguing, or, long before butter boards were a thing, to slather onto a great piece of bread (page 140). It also makes mashed potatoes or corn on the cob come to life in a whole new way.

⇨ I don't mess around here. Though you can certainly make compound butter by hand, I like to make it in a stand mixer to ensure a fully combined mixture.

1. In the bowl of a stand mixer fitted with the paddle attachment, mix the butter on medium speed for 1 minute, or until it is soft and fluffy.

2. Start to add in whatever flavor(s) you are rooting for. Paddle for 30 seconds, until the ingredient is well dispersed. Taste, and adjust as needed. Scrape down the sides of the mixing bowl with a sturdy spatula. Repeat until you reach your target flavor-story taste. In an airtight container in the fridge, fancy butter will keep up to 1 month.

You can totally make your own butter

In a stand mixer with a whisk attachment, or in a large jar with the lid tightly on, whip or shake heavy cream until it turns into . . . butter. It will whip up, then start to curdle and separate a bit, then become a pretty solid mass in a pool of liquid (butterfat in a puddle of buttermilk), and then, finally, become butter. The timing varies, based on how much heavy cream you want to make into butter and your method. If you want super-yellow butter, form your butter mass into a ball and rinse and wring it in ice-cold water, changing the water two or three times as you go, every time it gets cloudy. One cup of heavy cream produces about 8 tablespoons of butter. (And, yes, you can use the liquid left behind in any recipe that calls for buttermilk!)

- DO YOU -
BAKE CLUB

Scribble down every measurement in a notebook so that you can come back to it later (when you want to make the same compound butter again).

This is a great place to apply flavor-sharpening techniques, using different sugars, salts, and acids to amp up and round out any flavor.

Salt and Pepper Butter

1 stick (8 tablespoons)
  unsalted butter, at room
  temperature
1 tablespoon sugar
1 1/2 teaspoons kosher salt
1 teaspoon black pepper

Old Bay Butter

1 stick (8 tablespoons)
  unsalted butter, at room
  temperature
1 tablespoon + 1 teaspoon
  sugar
2 teaspoons Old Bay
  Seasoning
1/4 teaspoon sherry vinegar

Strawberry Jam Butter

1 stick (8 tablespoons)
  unsalted butter, at room
  temperature
1/3 cup Strawberry Jam
  (page 27)
Pinch of kosher salt

Coffee Butter

1 stick (8 tablespoons)
  unsalted butter, at room
  temperature
1/4 cup confectioners' sugar
3/4 teaspoon instant coffee
1/4 teaspoon kosher salt

Cinnamon Sugar Butter

1 stick (8 tablespoons)
  unsalted butter, at room
  temperature
1/2 cup confectioners' sugar
1 tablespoon maple syrup
2 teaspoons cinnamon
1/4 teaspoon kosher salt

Mustard Butter

1 stick (8 tablespoons)
  unsalted butter, at room
  temperature
2 teaspoons sherry vinegar
1 teaspoon yellow mustard
1/2 teaspoon
  Worcestershire sauce
2 tablespoons sugar
1 teaspoon kosher salt

Kimchi Butter

1 stick (8 tablespoons)
  unsalted butter, at room
  temperature
1/2 cup puréed kimchi
1/2 teaspoon kosher salt
1/4 teaspoon black pepper

Curry Butter

1 stick (8 tablespoons)
  unsalted butter, at room
  temperature
1 tablespoon + 2 teaspoons
  honey
2 1/2 teaspoons curry powder
1/2 teaspoon kosher salt

➔ If you want your caramel thicker, use
1–2 tablespoons less liquid; if you want your caramel
thinner, add 1–2 tablespoons more liquid.

➔ When warm, your caramel will be thinner and
more fluid; cold, your caramel will be thicker.

THE CARAMEL SAUCE
of YOUR DREAMS

Makes 2 cups

Outright, caramel is a star on top of a plain-Jane scoop of ice cream, but don't you dare stop there. Deploy it as a spreadable filling in a layer cake. Slather it as a base layer in your apple pie. Sandwich it between two cookie wafers for a sammy. The possibilities are endless. Straightforward caramel flavor is a classic for a reason, but bring a flavored liquid to the party and you open up a whole new world—upgrading this icon to legend status.

- -

1 cup sugar

²/₃ cup flavored liquid (apple juice, cola, chocolate milk, heavy cream, etc.)

1 stick (8 tablespoons) unsalted butter

1 teaspoon vanilla extract

1 teaspoon kosher salt

1. **Make a dry caramel:** In a heavy-bottomed medium-sized saucepan, heat the sugar over medium heat. As soon as the sugar starts to melt, use a sturdy heat-safe spatula to move it constantly around the pan—you want it to melt and caramelize evenly. Cook and stir, cook and stir, until the caramel is consistently smooth, translucent, and a deep amber color, 3–5 minutes from when the sugar first starts to melt.

2. Once the caramel has reached the target color and opacity, remove the saucepan from the heat. Very slowly and very carefully, pour in the liquid. The caramel will bubble up and steam; stand away until the steam dissipates. Use the heat-safe spatula to stir the mixture together.

3. Add the butter, vanilla, and salt, and continue stirring. If the sauce is at all lumpy, or if there are any clumps of hardened caramel present, put the saucepan back over medium heat and warm it, stirring constantly, until it's smooth. Use the caramel sauce while it's warm, or cool it down, depending on your vision for it. In an airtight container in the fridge, the caramel will keep fresh for 1 month.

> **- DO YOU -**
> ## BAKE CLUB
>
> Swap 1 teaspoon of the vanilla extract with any other flavor that supports the main flavor liquid (think chocolate milk plus mint extract, strawberry milk plus banana extract, coconut milk plus coconut extract, etc.).

FUDGE SAUCE

Makes 2 cups

My love for fudge sauce is an inherited one; my mother—Greta, or GG for those in the know—is a fudge fanatic. When she is around, no scoop of ice cream is safe from its chocolatey-rich path. I get it: fudge sauce is incredible. Homemade fudge sauce is the ultimate flex, and its applications go far beyond a hot-fudge sundae. Try it drizzled into a cup of coffee for a mocha moment, smoothed into a layer cake for a deeply fudgy, soulful tune, or blended into a milkshake for the ultimate take down. Thanks, Mom!

⇨ The cream of tartar gives your fudge sauce shine and a flavor edge. If you don't have any, your sauce will survive, it just won't be quite as shiny or flavorful.

⇨ If you don't have heavy cream, substitute 6 tablespoons milk and 4 tablespoons unsalted butter for the heavy-cream-and-water combo.

⇨ When it's warm, your fudge will be thinner and more fluid; cold, your fudge will be thicker.

²/₃ cup sugar
¹/₂ cup heavy cream
¹/₄ cup water

¹/₂ cup chocolate chips
¹/₄ cup cocoa powder
Pinch of kosher salt
Pinch of cream of tartar

1. In a heavy-bottomed medium-sized saucepan, heat the sugar, heavy cream, and water over medium heat, stirring intermittently with a sturdy heat-safe spatula, until the mixture comes to a boil, 2–3 minutes.

2. As the liquid is heating up, measure the chocolate chips, cocoa powder, salt, and cream of tartar into a medium bowl. The moment the dairy mixture boils, pour it over the contents of the bowl and let this sit for 1 full minute, so the heat of the liquid can begin melting the chocolate and hydrating the cocoa powder.

3. Slowly, slowly, begin to whisk the mixture, increasing the vigor of your whisking every 30 seconds, until the mixture is glossy and silky-smooth. This will take 2–3 minutes, depending on your speed and strength. Use the fudge sauce while it's warm, or cool it down, depending on your vision for it. In an airtight container in the fridge, the sauce will keep fresh for 1 month.

- DO YOU -
BAKE CLUB

If you're looking for a fudge brownie sauce:

¹/₂ cup sugar
¹/₄ cup milk
4 tablespoons
   unsalted butter

6 tablespoons cocoa
   powder
Pinch of kosher salt
Pinch of cream of
   tartar

CHOOSE YOUR FLAVOR WHIPPED CREAM

Makes 3 cups

I'm the type of person who wants the most out of life. I cannonball into the pool, I don a themed outfit on Halloween, and I always take the scenic route. Stands to reason I expect a lot out of my desserts, and I believe every element that ends up on the plate has an obligation to bring something to the flavor story. So why wouldn't I spruce up whipped cream? Adding a flavor element takes whatever it lands on up a hundred notches. Cinnamon-toast-crunch whipped cream on your waffles, pretzel whipped cream on your Hot Chocolate (page 58), cookies-and-cream whipped cream on your ice cream sundae—now you're really living.

And never underestimate a bowl of fruit with a fun flavored whipped cream: A bowl of apples with caramel whipped cream! Blueberries with pie crust whipped cream!

4 cups something with awesome flavor (cereal, pretzels, donuts, carrot cake pieces, etc.)

2 cups heavy cream

1/3 cup confectioners' sugar Pinch of salt

▷ Dairy-free heavy whipping cream is welcome here; use a one-for-one substitution.

▷ You can use a stand mixer with the whisk attachment here, but I prefer to whip cream by hand, which means I always get it to just the right consistency.

▷ Whipped cream should always be whisked fresh. If you're working ahead, stop at Step 3 and transfer your unwhipped flavored cream to an airtight container. In the fridge, the unwhipped flavored cream will keep fresh for 1 week.

1. Decide whether your awesome thing will taste better—deeper—in flavor slightly toasted. If so, heat the oven to 300°F. If not, skip Step 2. (For example: fruity cereal should not be toasted—it won't get any more fruity as it toasts—but donuts *should*—more caramelization will bring out more donut flavor.)

2. Spread the awesome-flavored thing on an unlined half sheet pan, and toast it for 15 minutes, until it has slightly darkened in color and your kitchen smells awesome toasty. Cool it completely on the pan.

3. Transfer your awesome thing to a medium bowl. Pour the cold heavy cream over the top, and stir while steeping for 2 minutes. Strain out the awesome thing, pouring the heavy cream into a large bowl.

4. In the same large bowl, with a whisk, whip the flavored heavy cream until soft peaks form, about 2 minutes; then add the sugar and salt. Whip the cream to medium peaks, about a minute more. Serve immediately.

- DO YOU -

BAKE CLUB

Skip the steeping process and swap ½ cup heavy cream for a killer sour cream or yogurt. Tang is the new spice of life.

Layer in ¼ teaspoon of a spice or an extract to add to the flavor story.

Swap the sugar for light brown sugar, dark brown sugar, honey, molasses, etc., as long as it enhances the flavor story.

After you've strained it out of the cream (see Step 3), you can turn whatever awesome-flavored ingredient you used into a crispy snack by drying it out in a 300°F oven for 30–45 minutes. I dry out my pretzels anew and dip them in honey mustard, or toast them with some blue cheese sprinkled on top!

FRUIT JAM

Makes 2 cups

2 pounds hearty fruits,
cored or pitted and
roughly chopped,
OR 2 pints (1 pound) of
your favorite berries
1 cup sugar
4 teaspoons lemon juice
(from 1 lemon)
Pinch of kosher salt

Jamming with fruit is one of my favorite things to do as an adult, probably because I always pity the bruised and overripe fruit at the grocery, the farmers' market, or in my own fridge—in fact, it's sweeter and more delicious than ever, just needs a makeover. Plus, jam is so darn colorful, punchy, and worthy—the flavor base of a No-Churn Ice Cream (page 274) or star of a Pie Bar (page 272) or layered onto a Crepe and rolled up, to my kids' delight (page 113).

- -

➪ Looking to rock some citrus instead? See Citrus Jam (recipe follows).

➪ Frozen fruit is TOTALLY permitted here in place of fresh.

➪ Get a discount at the farmers' market by asking for "seconds," the bruised, super-ripe, and fragrant fruit that makes the best jam but isn't much to look at un-jammed.

➪ When you're choosing berries, the smaller and truer the color (red, blue, black, etc.), the better.

➪ In a pinch, substitute 2 teaspoons water and 2 teaspoons vinegar for the lemon juice.

- -

1. In a heavy-bottomed medium-sized saucepan, stir together all the ingredients, and warm them over medium-low heat, stirring intermittently with a sturdy heat-safe spatula for 3–4 minutes, until the mixture comes to a gentle boil.

2. Reduce the heat to a low simmer, set a timer for 15 minutes, and check in every 5 minutes or so, moving the mixture across the pan with the spatula to prevent any burning and to gauge the viscosity. You're looking to thicken the fruit mixture while also reducing its volume by half, and breaking the fruit down into a smaller and translucent state. This can take as little as 15 minutes for smaller, less hearty berries, like blues or raspberries, or up to 45 minutes for cherries (the intensity of the heat will also slow down / speed up the time). If the jam becomes too dry and thick before the fruit pieces become translucent, add a splash of water or two and continue cooking.

3. Spoon the jam into a jar or other airtight, heatproof container while it's still warm, and let it cool completely at room temperature. In the fridge, jam will keep fresh for 1 month.

- DO YOU -
BAKE CLUB

Combine like fruits (berries with other berries or peaches, plums and cherries, mango and pineapple, apples and pears . . . you get the idea).

CITRUS JAM

Makes 2½ cups

3 large oranges, or
  5 lemons, or 2 medium
  grapefruits
1½ cups sugar

Technically more of a citrus preserve or marmalade, depending on how chunky you leave your citrus rinds, citrus jam is a quick way to use up the rinds of an already squeezed lemon or orange, or grapefruit, or the untouched citrus that has lingered a little too long in that bowl on your counter. It's perfect spread on a thick slice of toast with a dollop of Ricotta (page 56), but don't limit yourself: this jam works anywhere you might use fresh citrus—to doll up a plain seltzer or cocktail, or shaken up in a salad dressing or marinade.

⇨ Looking to rock a fruit other than citrus? See Fruit Jam (page 27).

⇨ This recipe scales up and down like a dream, depending on how much citrus you have on hand.

⇨ Citrus fruits in all states are welcome—already zested and/or juiced, or untouched.

⇨ Lime is good but not great as jam alone: it loses its green hue during cooking, though it does give a joyful twist when cooked with lemon.

1. On a cutting board, with a chef's knife, cut the citrus into quarters (for smaller fruits) or eighths (for larger); you want 3–4 cups overall of roughly chopped fruit. Place the citrus chunks in a food processor fitted with the steel blade, and sprinkle the sugar atop. Secure the lid, and pulse the citrus and sugar together until no pieces larger than a garbanzo bean remain.

2. Transfer the mixture to a heavy-bottomed medium-sized pot, and cook over medium heat, stirring intermittently with a sturdy heat-safe spatula, until the jam is translucent and thick enough so that when you drag the spatula through it, it takes 1–2 "Mississippi"s before the jam falls in the spatula's path, about 10 minutes. If the jam becomes too dry and thick before the fruit pieces become translucent, add a splash or two of water, and continue cooking.

3. Spoon the jam into a jar or other airtight, heatproof container while it's still warm, and let it cool completely at room temperature. In the fridge, jam will keep fresh for 1 month.

Chocolate Wafers, page 33

BROWN SUGAR WAFERS

Makes 12

1 stick (8 tablespoons)
  unsalted butter,
  super soft
¼ cup light brown sugar

1 cup + 2 tablespoons flour
¼ teaspoon kosher salt

- DO YOU -
BAKE CLUB

Spruce these wafers up
with Any Flavor Glaze
(page 34).

Add cinnamon or ginger
or curry powder, etc., to
take these cookies in a
spice-forward direction.
Or add ½ teaspoon of
any extract you please
to give them a whole
new flavor identity.
@timross41 and Lil
show off their Gluten
Free cup4cup flour
in both these wafer
recipes regularly!

I'm not a gambling person—unless you count a friendly wager on who will win *The Bachelorette*—but good money says this recipe will become one of your favorites. Made with just four simple ingredients, these wafers may sound plain, but don't let them fool you—they're a 100/10. Completely crushable on their own, used in place of ladyfingers in your next tiramisù, or rolled thin for cutout cookies, these wafers are endlessly usable, though it won't surprise me if they never quite make it into your pantry, because they're so darn delicious right off the sheet pan.

⇨ If you're feeling more playful than functional, ditch the round and use any shape cookie cutter. Adjust the bake time: longer for larger shapes and shorter for smaller shapes.

1. In a large bowl, using a sturdy spatula, mix together the butter and sugar until they are fully combined, about 1 minute.

2. Measure the flour and salt into the mixing bowl. Toss together only the dry ingredients on top with the spatula first, before truly stirring them into the wet ingredients below. Then mix all until they are just combined.

3. With a rolling pin on the counter, flatten the dough between two pieces of parchment to ¼-inch thickness.

4. Using a cup or a 3-inch round cookie cutter, cut dough circles as close together as possible. Refrigerate or freeze the entire sheet of dough until it's firm, about 5 minutes.

5. Heat the oven to 350°F. Pan-spray a half sheet pan, or line it with a fresh sheet of parchment paper.

6. Pop your chilled rounds off the parchment and transfer them to the sheet pan, spacing ¼ inch apart (they don't spread in the oven!), and bake at 350°F for 8–10 minutes, until the edges are golden brown. Cool the rounds completely on the pan.

7. Reshape your dough scraps into a ball, roll it out, chill it, and bake it. In an airtight container at room temperature, the wafers will keep fresh for 2 weeks.

CHOCOLATE WAFERS

Makes 12

Good wafers—both brown sugar and chocolate—are essential in my home, ready to be adorned with a dab of peanut butter when the blood sugar drops too low, or dunked in a glass of milk at Sonny's snack time. A crisp, thin, flat, light go-to cookie gives me something to fashion into an ice cream (or frosting, pudding, or curd) sammy on the fly. It can be crumbled into ice cream or as a textural moment in my next cookie dough. You just never know when inspiration (or company) might knock.

- -

1 stick (8 tablespoons)
  unsalted butter,
  super soft
²/₃ cup sugar
2 tablespoons honey
¹/₂ teaspoon vanilla extract

1 cup flour
²/₃ cup cocoa powder
¹/₂ teaspoon kosher salt
¹/₂ teaspoon baking soda

1. In a large bowl, using a sturdy spatula, mix together the butter, sugar, honey, and vanilla until they are fully combined, about 1 minute.

2. Measure the flour, cocoa powder, salt, and baking soda into the mixing bowl. Toss only the dry ingredients on top together with the spatula first, before truly stirring them into the wet ingredients below. Then mix all until they are just combined.

3. With a rolling pin on the counter, flatten the dough between two pieces of parchment to ¹/₄-inch thickness.

4. Using a cup or a 3-inch round cookie cutter, cut dough circles as close together as possible. Refrigerate or freeze the entire sheet of dough until it's firm, about 5 minutes.

5. Heat the oven to 350°F. Pan-spray a half sheet pan, or line it with a fresh sheet of parchment paper.

6. Pop your chilled rounds off the parchment and transfer them to the sheet pan, spacing ¹/₄ inch apart (they don't spread in the oven!), and bake at 350°F for 8–10 minutes. Set a timer— they're chocolate so you won't see them turning golden brown! Cool the rounds completely on the pan.

7. Reshape your dough scraps into a ball, roll it out, chill it, and bake it. In an airtight container at room temperature, the wafers will keep fresh for 2 weeks.

Any Flavor Glaze

Makes about ¼ cup

1½ cups confectioners'
sugar
1 tablespoon milk, or any
other flavored liquid
Food coloring, optional

In a small bowl, whisk the milk and confectioners' sugar together, mixing until smooth, about 30 seconds. Add a drop or two of food coloring, if you want. If you want your glaze to be thicker, whisk in more confectioners' sugar; if you want your glaze to be thinner, add a splash of milk.

⇨ Want crackers that are more playful than functional? Ditch the rectangle and use any shape cookie cutter. Adjust the bake time: longer for larger shapes and shorter for smaller shapes.

⇨ Whole-wheat flour gives you the true graham cracker look and taste. You can make this recipe with all-purpose flour, but the vis and flavor will be a bit more shallow. Plus, whole-wheat flour is also the secret weapon for Cinnamon Toast cereal (page 106). Read up on flours on page 4.

⇨ You can mix by hand to make this dough, but I find that the power and intensity of the stand-mixer paddle help bring this dough together more uniformly and therefore with better quality.

GRAHAM CRACKERS

Makes 6

4 tablespoons unsalted
  butter, super soft
1/3 cup confectioners' sugar

2 tablespoons milk
2 tablespoons honey

1 cup whole-wheat flour
1/2 teaspoon kosher salt
1/2 teaspoon cinnamon

I can reverse-engineer a taco seasoning mix when we run out of the packaged stuff. I like to whip up a fresh tray of Buns (page 145) when the weather calls for a grill outside. When I've been wowed by a dessert while dining out—R&D when you run a bakery biz is a wonderful thing—my mind won't rest until I've re-created it at home. A whole new phase of my life started when I realized I could make graham crackers from scratch. (I actually think they're leaps and bounds above what you get in the store!) You'll never need to push a cart down the cracker aisle again.

- -

1. In the bowl of a stand mixer fitted with the paddle attachment, combine the butter and sugar on medium speed until they are fully combined, about 1 minute. Add the milk and honey, and mix on low speed until they are combined, about 1 minute. Measure the flour, salt, and cinnamon into the bowl and, on low speed, mix until everything is just combined, about 1 minute, scraping down the sides of the mixing bowl as needed.

2. With a rolling pin on the counter, flatten the dough between two pieces of parchment the size of your baking sheet. Roll the dough to 1/2-inch thickness, about twice as thick as your standard wafer or cutout cookie.

3. Peel back the top sheet of paper, and carefully, using a chef's knife, bench scraper, or pizza roller, cut the dough into six 2.25-by-5-inch rectangles. Prick the dough with a fork, and score each rectangle length- and width-wise to mimic the classic graham cracker vis. Transfer the dough, scraps and all, to a half sheet pan. Refrigerate or freeze the entire sheet of dough until it's firm, about 5 minutes.

4. Heat the oven to 325°F.

5. Carefully, transfer the half sheet pan of dough to the oven and bake at 325°F for 18–20 minutes, until the entire surface of the crackers is a deep golden brown and some edges are a tad toasty. Remove the hot sheet pan from the oven to a safe place to cool, and while the crackers are still very warm, use the same cutting device as before to retrace the lines of the large rectangles, to ensure clean lines and easy release.

6. Cool the crackers completely on the sheet pan. I snack on the baked scrap pieces! In an airtight container at room temperature, the crackers will keep fresh for 2 weeks.

GRANOLA

Makes about 4 cups

If you read the word "granola" and instantly fell asleep, listen, I get it. Historically, granola is a bit of a snoozer, but hearty, lightly sweetened, with an element of excitement, granola has the potential to be a pretty incredible snack. Or breakfast. Or sundae topping. Or cookie-dough mix-in. This base will give you a solid starting point to invite your creativity in—bring your favorite nuts or seeds to the mix, or plus it up with some dried fruit. And no one's mad at chocolate chips. Call your mix whatever you want, but don't you dare call it boring.

⇨ Triple-check that you've got rolled or old-fashioned oats at the ready (NO instant oats allowed anywhere near this recipe!).

⇨ The better the quality and flavor of the olive oil and maple syrup you put into this recipe, the more delicious the granola—please don't skimp.

⇨ If you use pre-salted nuts, omit the salt.

1½ cups old-fashioned rolled oats
½ teaspoon kosher salt

¼ cup olive oil
¼ cup maple syrup

1 cup big things that will taste better toasted (think walnuts! pecans! pretzels! cornflakes!)
¼ cup little things that will taste better toasted (think shredded coconut! sunflower seeds! sesame seeds!)
½ cup big *and* little things that will taste best untoasted (craisins! butterscotch chips! banana chips!)

1. Heat the oven to 300°F, and pan-spray a half sheet pan.

2. In a large bowl, using a sturdy spatula, quickly toss together the oats and salt to combine. Mix in the oil and syrup, stirring to coat all of the salted oats evenly in a syrupy glisten, about 1 minute. Toss in 1¼ cups of big and little things that will taste better toasted, stirring to distribute them evenly across the mixture, about 30 seconds.

3. Spread the mixture thinly and evenly across the greased sheet pan, and bake at 300°F for 30–35 minutes; pop into the oven every 10 minutes or so to toss the granola around with a clean spatula so the clusters get even heat distribution and caramelization while baking. Cool the granola completely on the sheet pan, by which point it should have become crunchy (it will still seem wet and mushy when warm). Scatter over it your ½ cup of things that will taste better untoasted, toss them with the granola, and transfer it to a jar or other airtight container. At room temperature, the granola will keep fresh for 1 month.

- DO YOU -
BAKE CLUB

Bring citrus zest or juice to the mix if you're feeling wild, or 1–2 teaspoons of an extract of your choice. Add these in alongside the oil and syrup.

Play around: swap different oils (even melted butter) for the olive oil, but remember that the quality and flavor of your fat will elevate or tank your granola.

@kathleen.kelly rocked her granola using lemon zest, juice, honey, avocado oil, pistachios, sunflower, pumpkin & chia seeds, dried cranberries, and chopped fresh rosemary. YEAH, MAMA!

SPRINKLES

Makes 1 cup

1 egg white
¼ teaspoon vanilla extract

1¾ cups confectioners'
  sugar + more for rolling
¼ teaspoon kosher salt
Food coloring, as many
  colors as you want

If you've set foot into a Milk Bar bakery, you've seen sprinkles by the truckload. A colorful fleck of sugar can really go a long way visually, but don't underestimate the flavor, texture, and celebratory spirit a sprinkle brings, too. One heck of a parlor trick, yes, they're also a spectacular way to get a two-year-old excited about toast for breakfast or broccoli for dinner (yes, sometimes I'm that desperate, or life is just *that* fun).

1. In a large bowl, use a whisk to mix together the egg white and vanilla until they're combined, about 30 seconds. Whisk in 1 cup confectioners' sugar and the salt, and mix until a smooth paste forms, about 1 minute.

2. Switch mixing tools: use a sturdy rubber spatula to mix in the remaining ¾ cup confectioners' sugar until a smooth ball forms, about 1 minute.

3. Divide the ball into as many small bowls as the different colors of sprinkles you intend to make.

4. Drop a little food coloring into each bowl, one color in each, and, with the spatula, mix until the hue is evenly distributed, adding more drops of color as you go if you want the sprinkles to be deeper in color. If your ball becomes sticky and wet, add confectioners' sugar a tablespoon at a time until it reaches the right consistency. Pick up one of the balls; when you've reached your target sprinkle color, it should also be dry enough to roll in the palms of your hands without sticking. Set it aside, and repeat with the remaining bowls.

5. As you conquer each color, microwave the bowl of colored mass in 10-second spurts to heat the mixture and zap the hydration into a pliable, roll-able state.

6. Dust a clean, dry counter or ungreased half sheet pan with powdered sugar, and roll out each colored paste into several long, thin ropes, the diameter of your ideal sprinkle size. It's a learned technique; don't freak out. If your rope breaks or is uneven, just start over. Sprinkles are meant to bring lightness, not stress—they're also SUPER forgiving.

7. Leave the ropes to dry out slightly on the counter, uncovered, for 10 minutes; then, using a butter knife, cut them into your ideal sprinkle length. Leave the sprinkles to sit out uncovered for another 20 minutes or up to overnight before transferring them to an airtight container. At room temperature, the sprinkles will keep fresh for 1 month.

ICE CREAM CONES

Makes 4

Why do we only eat ice cream in a cone when we're desserting out? Probably because you can't buy a great one at the grocery, and we haven't yet programmed ourselves to think, "I'll just make one!" Until now. You don't need much at all. I rock mine on a baking sheet in the oven, and though this recipe works great in a pizzelle or other cookie or ice-cream-cone iron, they're not necessary unless you already have one. I have attempted making ice cream cones in a waffle maker to no avail—they do have a limit!

1 egg white
¼ cup sugar
2 tablespoons milk
1 tablespoon unsalted
  butter, melted
¼ teaspoon vanilla extract

⅓ cup flour
Pinch of kosher salt

1. Heat the oven to 300°F, and pan-spray or line a half sheet pan with parchment.

2. In a large bowl, using a whisk, mix together the egg white, sugar, milk, butter, and vanilla for about 1 minute, until they are fully combined.

3. Measure the flour and salt into the mixing bowl. Toss together only the dry ingredients on top with the whisk first, before truly stirring them into the wet ingredients below. Then whisk everything together until the batter is smooth.

4. With a small spatula, spread 1½ tablespoons batter into a thin, even layer on the prepared sheet pan, roughly 6 inches around. Repeat with the remaining batter, spacing the discs ½ inch apart. Bake at 300°F for 10–12 minutes, until the discs are golden brown.

5. Remove the pan from the oven, and while they're still very warm, lift one disc and QUICKLY roll from the bottom of the cone to shape it. Pull at the top to make a wider cone, and hold it seam side down for 1–2 minutes, or until the cone cools and hardens. Pop the sheet pan back into the oven and heat for 1–2 minutes, to warm up the rounds that have cooled; the warmer they are, the more pliable and shapeable they'll be. This entire process becomes less awkward as you make more cones.

6. In an airtight container at room temperature, the cones will keep fresh for up to 3 days.

- DO YOU -
BAKE CLUB

Dip the tops of the cones in melted chocolate or butterscotch, and cover them in nuts or sprinkles; or dip, then stand it in a glass to cool until the chocolate hardens.

The ultimate, unreasonably hospitable move is to fill the bottom of your cones with mini-marshmallows, or to pour in a little melted chocolate and let it set, to seal the bottom and keep ice cream from melting into someone's lap!

CHOCOLATE SHELL

Makes 1 cup

Though we often splurged on ice cream when I was growing up, we never got to splurge on the sundae fixin's, especially not chocolate shell. Getting a chocolate-dipped sundae at home seemed far out of reach until I came into my own and figured out what a cinch chocolate shell is to make and keep on hand in my own home pantry. Ripe for innovation (white chocolate chamomile! chocolate–peanut butter! strawberry–dark chocolate!), you'll practically be able to start your own chocolate-shell business after dreaming up a few batches.

1 cup baking chips
3 tablespoons vegetable oil

1. In the microwave, in a small, heatproof bowl, melt the chocolate and oil together. Work in 30-second spurts, stirring with a sturdy heat-safe spatula in between blasts until the mixture is smooth, 1–2 minutes.

2. Spoon the shell over ice cream, or add ice cream to the bowl with the chocolate shell. In an airtight container in the fridge or pantry, the chocolate shell will keep fresh for 1 month. Warm it slightly before use.

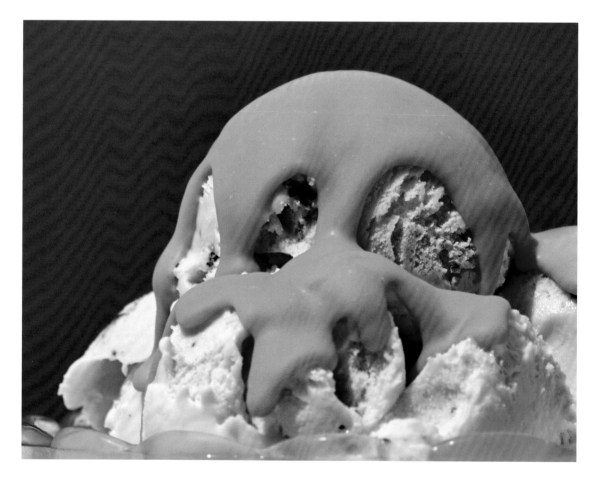

⇨ For a thinner chocolate shell, add 1 tablespoon vegetable oil; for a thicker one, add 2 tablespoons chocolate chips.

- DO YOU -
BAKE CLUB

Add any extract, syrup, or spice, or ground coffee or tea, or a pinch of salt, if you so please. Stir in 1–2 teaspoons of such flavorings once the chocolate and fat have come together.

Push beyond the humble chocolate chips and swap in butterscotch chips, white chocolate cut into chunks, leftover candy bars, or a combo or all of the above.

Speaking of fat, swap vegetable oil for a more flavorful fat—pumpkin-seed oil, lemon oil—heck—even some peanut butter—as long as it adds to the flavor story of your chocolate shell.

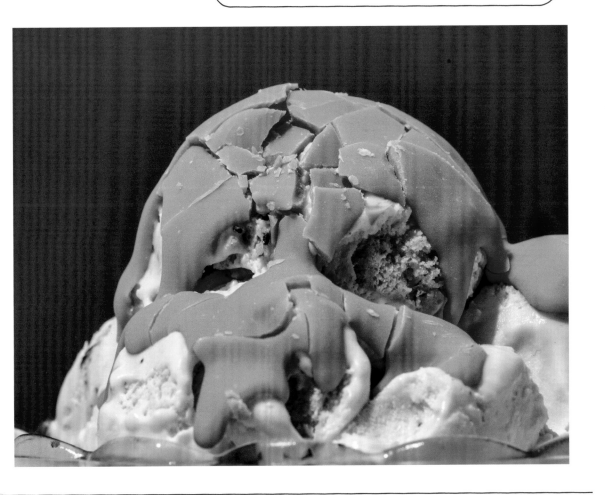

MARSHMALLOWS

Makes 16

There are few recipes that I feel are straight-up magic, and this is one of them. The transformation of just four ingredients—sugar, corn syrup, vanilla, gelatin—into marshmallows leaves me wonderstruck. Ask your squad the next time they're over "Hey—do you want to make marshmallows" and count how many squeals your q yields. On their own, folded into a batch of brownies, or as part of the obvious s'more flex, they're great in ANY form. Just promise me you won't tell anyone how simple they are to make, a magician never reveals their secrets.

▷ This recipe is a stand-mixer affair. Do not attempt this recipe by hand!

▷ Read up on Blooming Gelatin (page 48).

▷ Read up on soft ball stage sugar and water (page 220).

---

5 teaspoons (2 envelopes) unflavored gelatin

2 teaspoons vanilla extract

1 cup sugar
2/3 cup light corn syrup

- DO YOU -
BAKE CLUB

Swap 1/2 cup water with 1/2 cup of Fruit Jam (page 27) of any kind (blueberry, strawberry, and peach marshmallows live on repeat in my house).

Omit the vanilla extract if you want to amp up the berry flavor.

Increase gelatin to 7 1/2 teaspoons or 3 envelopes total for a taller mallow.

Swap the vanilla extract with any extract you like—mint! almond! banana! Feel free to add food coloring as your imagination takes off!

1. Lightly pan-spray an 8-by-8-inch baking pan, and set it aside.

2. To the clean, dry bowl of a stand mixer, add 1/2 cup water, sprinkle the gelatin evenly over it, and then add the vanilla. Lock the stand-mixer bowl into the machine, and engage the hook; let it sit for 5 minutes to allow the gelatin to bloom.

3. In a heavy-bottomed, medium-sized saucepan, combine a splash of water, sugar, and corn syrup. On medium, without stirring whatsoever, heat the mixture to soft ball stage (technically 235°F), or when your bubbles are approximately the same size across your mixture and when you dip a spoonful of it into ice water you get a . . . soft ball of sugar. Though never mixing, you can swirl the saucepan around with the flick of your wrist if the mixture seems like it is uneven in temperature.

4. Turn the mixer on at low speed, and carefully but quickly pour the sugar syrup into it. The heat will liquefy the gelatin mixture on contact. When all the syrup has been added, increase the speed to medium, and whip it for 2 minutes to cool the mixture down. Once all the steam has subsided, increase the mixer speed to its highest level, and whip for 7–8 minutes, until a glossy, fluffy, marshmallow mixture forms.

5. With a sturdy spatula, transfer the marshmallow to the prepared baking pan, and spread it evenly into the corners— smooth and flat or with dramatic peaks, your call. Let it sit out at room temperature to cool completely for 2 hours. Use clean scissors to cut it into four rows of four, giving sixteen squares. In an airtight container at room temperature, the marshmallows will keep fresh for 1 week.

Blooming Gelatin

We love gelatin for the structure it gives some of our favorites, from gummy bears to marshmallows. In order for gelatin to do its work, it needs to be bloomed, or hydrated in cold water and softened. We do this by sprinkling gelatin powder over cold water (warm or hot water will melt the gelatin before it's hydrated, rendering it useless) and letting it sit for 5–10 minutes to perk up into a bouncy state. If it's still dry and brittle after 5 minutes, try stirring it into the liquid below, or adding the tiniest bit of liquid on top. Once it's bloomed—soft and bouncy—we always need to heat or "melt" the bloomed gelatin to a liquid state before adding it to the recipe or setting it into the mold, for our ideal end result.

SOFT CARAMELS

Makes 50

One 14-ounce can sweetened
  condensed milk

1/4 cup sugar

4 tablespoons
  unsalted butter

4 tablespoons
  unsalted butter

1/2 teaspoon kosher salt

Soft caramels are an all-around knockout—and they are pretty fun to make, too. If you do a bit of digging into soft-caramel recipes, you'll quickly learn that they can call for all sorts of wild ingredients. So I got to work on finding a simpler way. The resulting recipe is a combination of sweetened condensed milk, sugar, and butter—so you know it's gonna be a goody. (Spoiler alert: it is, in fact, a goody.)

1. Pan-spray an 8-by-8-inch baking pan, and set it aside.

2. In a heavy-bottomed medium-sized saucepan, combine the sweetened condensed milk and sugar, and stir intermittently with a sturdy heat-safe spatula over medium heat for 2–3 minutes, until the mixture comes to a boil.

3. Carefully stir in 4 tablespoons butter. If your mixture starts to color quickly, reduce the heat to medium-low. Continue stirring for another 6–8 minutes, a bit more aggressively in the final 2–3 minutes, as your mixture dries out and takes on color. Think of these final minutes as babysitting your mixture so it takes on depth evenly—not too dark, but with enough camel tones (think trench coat or winter coat color) to let you know your color will equal flavor.

4. Off heat, gently stir in the remaining 4 tablespoons butter and the salt until a smooth caramel mixture forms. Pour it into the prepared baking pan, and pop it into the fridge to cool down for about 1 hour.

5. When it's completely cool, your caramel slab should be set, but still pliable. Pop the caramel out onto a clean counter, and pinch or cut it into your desired sizes and shapes. Roll your caramels on the counter to form a tootsie-roll-like shape, or cut them into small squares or rectangles. In an airtight container in the fridge, or at room temperature, the caramels will keep fresh for 1 month.

- DO YOU -
BAKE CLUB

Add 1 1/2 teaspoons of any spice, or 2 teaspoons of any extract, to personalize your next batch.

For a seasonal twist, add in 1/3 cup canned pumpkin and 1 1/2 teaspoons cinnamon off the heat, with the final 4 tablespoons of butter and salt.

➪ Wrap the caramels in little pieces of waxed paper for the true candy-store experience.

PUDDING

Makes 2 cups

1 cup milk

¹/₂ cup sugar

3 egg yolks

1 tablespoon + 1 teaspoon
   cornstarch

1 teaspoon vanilla extract

4 tablespoons unsalted
   butter, cold

¹/₂ teaspoon kosher salt

Of all the many things nostalgic to me as a kid born to Midwestern families and sensibilities, pudding isn't one of them. Maybe because store-bought just isn't that fly, I didn't fall in love with pudding until pastry school. The French crèmes (anglaise [thin], patisserie [thick], légère [with whipped cream]) were a deep dive into dairy-forward custardy delights. Pudding is the milk-based cousin to the Curd (page 55), and you'll note very quickly that the process for making the two desserts is nearly the same. Me? I love to eat this pudding in a cup, sometimes half frozen, unless I'm transforming it into a chocolate, butterscotch, coconut, or banana ditty.

⇨ For a stiffer, pastry-cream-like pudding, use 2 full tablespoons of cornstarch.

⇨ A blender is the foolproof tool for making velvety-smooth pudding every time. It's an old pastry-chef technique, which I use in the home kitchen to set myself and you up for success. Don't fear the blender bubbles at the beginning; they will subside as your pudding cooks.

- DO YOU -
BAKE CLUB

Add ¹/₄ cup mini–chocolate chips to your pudding for a little texture and fun.

For banana pudding: Add two incredibly ripe (nearly brown) bananas and six drops of yellow food coloring to the blender alongside the milk–sugar–egg-yolk–cornstarch mixture. Increase cornstarch to 2 tablespoons plus 1 teaspoon cornstarch. Increase salt to ³/₄ teaspoon salt.

For chocolate pudding: Remove ¹/₄ cup sugar, and add ¹/₂ cup chocolate chips to the blender with the butter and salt.

For butterscotch pudding: Reduce sugar to 2 tablespoons total, and add ³/₄ cup butterscotch chips to the blender with the butter and salt.

For coconut pudding: Substitute coconut milk for the milk, and coconut extract for the vanilla extract. If you want to go vegan, substitute coconut cream for heavy cream, too!

For rice pudding: If there's leftover rice from the night before, it can always have a second life, along with 1 teaspoon cinnamon.

1. In a blender, measure the milk, sugar, egg yolks, cornstarch, and vanilla. Secure the lid, and blend on low speed until you have a light-yellow mixture, about 30 seconds. You're aiming for a homogeneous mixture, not an intensely bubbly, aerated one.

2. Transfer the mixture to a heavy-bottomed medium-sized pot. Clean the blender base and lid, measure into it the cold butter and salt, and set it aside.

3. Heat the milky mixture over low heat, whisking regularly for 2–3 minutes, until it comes to a gentle boil. As it heats up, the mixture will begin to thicken because of the cornstarch and egg yolks; keep a close eye on it so it doesn't cook unevenly or, worse, overcook. Once it's at a boil, reduce the temperature to low, and whisk regularly for the next 1–2 minutes, until the mixture doesn't thicken anymore (meaning the cornstarch is fully hydrated and activated). Remove the mixture from the heat, and pour it into the blender, over the butter and salt. Secure the lid, and blend the mixture anew on low speed until the pudding is thick, shiny, and super smooth.

4. Pour the mixture into an airtight, heatproof container while it's still warm, and let it cool completely at room temperature. In the fridge, pudding will keep fresh for 2 weeks.

- DO YOU -
BAKE CLUB

Swap the fresh citrus juice for ⅓ cup of any acidic fruit juice—I'm partial to passion fruit purée or fresh pineapple juice.

(ANY) FRUIT CURD

Makes about 1½ cups

¹/₃ cup juice (and some zest, if you have it) of any citrus fruit

¹/₃ cup sugar

4 eggs

1 stick (8 tablespoons) unsalted butter, very cold

½ teaspoon kosher salt

The American dessert scene needs to catch up on the glory and wonder of curd—a spread or topping usually made from citrus, because its tart acidity lends well to being the star flavor of this creamy delight. Fruit curd is a less milky, brighter, and more buttery cousin to the pudding; I adore it in all its forms, from lemon to grapefruit to passion fruit; layered in a pie, tart, or cake; swirled into ice cream; or used in place of whipped cream in an icebox cake creation. The more tart the fruit juice you use, the more successful the curd.

- -

⇨ Make a half-batch of Citrus Jam (page 28) with the "used" lemon halves!

⇨ A blender is the foolproof tool to make velvety-smooth curd every time—no curdling here. It's an old pastry-chef technique, which I use in the home kitchen to set myself and you up for success. Don't fear the blender bubbles at the beginning; they will subside as your curd cooks.

- -

1. In a blender, measure the citrus juice, zest if you have it, sugar, and eggs. Secure the lid, and blend on low speed until you have a bright-yellow mixture, about 30 seconds. You're aiming for a homogeneous mixture, not an intensely bubbly, aerated one.

2. Transfer the mixture to a heavy-bottomed medium-sized pot. Clean the blender base and lid, measure into it the cold butter and salt, and set it aside.

3. Heat the citrus mixture over low heat, whisking regularly for 2–3 minutes, until it comes to a gentle boil. As it heats up, the mixture will begin to thicken because of the eggs; keep a close eye on it so it doesn't cook unevenly or, worse, overcook. Once it's at a boil, remove the mixture from the heat and pour it into the blender, over the butter and salt. Secure the lid, and blend the mixture anew on low speed until the curd is thick, shiny, and super smooth.

4. Pour the mixture through a fine-mesh sieve to remove any zest, and into an airtight, heatproof container while it's still warm, and let it cool completely at room temperature. In the fridge, curd will keep fresh for 2 weeks.

RICOTTA

Makes 1 cup

2 cups milk

¼ cup heavy cream

½ teaspoon kosher salt

1 tablespoon fresh lemon
   juice (from ½ lemon)

Dolloped on Pizza (page 156), spread onto my morning toast with Fruit Curd (page 55), mixed with mascarpone for a baller cannoli filling, baked in with noodles for lasagna night, ricotta wears many important hats, both sweet and savory. Mastering ricotta at home might not have been on your vision board, but once you realize how easy it is, you'll be looking for any excuse to get a batch happening.

➡ The lemony liquid that remains is all yours—I like to use it in place of milk in my Pancakes (page 109) for a surprising, delicious twist!

➡ No cheesecloth? Me, too, sometimes. Stack two wire-mesh sieves inside one another for the same result.

➡ Make some Citrus Jam (page 28) with that leftover lemon and rind!

➡ This recipe doubles, triples, quadruples easily!

1. Line a large sieve with a layer of cheesecloth, and place it over a large bowl.

2. In a heavy-bottomed medium-sized pot, whisk together the milk, cream, and salt over medium heat, and stir intermittently for 3–4 minutes to bring the mixture to a rolling boil without scorching.

3. Whisk in the lemon juice; then reduce the heat to low, and simmer the mixture for 2–4 minutes, stirring intermittently, until it curdles.

4. Carefully pour the hot mixture into the lined sieve, and let it drain for 1 hour. In an airtight container in the fridge, the cheese will keep fresh for 2 weeks.

HOT CHOCOLATE

Makes 4 mugs

4 cups (1 quart) milk
⅓ cup sugar

⅔ cup chocolate chips
2 tablespoons cocoa
   powder

I grew up on hot-chocolate mix. It wasn't until I traveled abroad as a teenager to meet my dad's family that I had a cup of REAL hot chocolate. You know, the kind that makes you feel like you've been living your whole hot-chocolate life in black and white, then the light flickers, and all of a sudden you're drinking hot chocolate in full color. The secret? Make it from scratch, and add some proper chocolate to the mix—the rest is for you to decide.

⇨ All milks and alternative milks are welcome here. Remember, the closer to whole milk or alternative whole milk, the richer and rounder the mouthfeel and viscosity.

⇨ Combine the sugar, chocolate, and cocoa, then divide into four giftable baggies, and share them with friends, instructing the recipients to add 1 cup scalding milk, let the mixture sit for 1 minute, then whisk until their *à la minute* hot-chocolate dreams come true.

⇨ The more chocolate you add, the thicker and more flavorful the hot chocolate will be. The less chocolate you add, the thinner.

1. In a heavy-bottomed medium-sized pot, whisk together the milk and sugar over medium heat, and stir intermittently for 2–3 minutes, to scald the mixture and dissolve the sugar, bringing the mixture just to the brink of boiling.

2. In a medium-sized heatproof bowl, measure the chocolate chips and cocoa together. Pour the hot milk mixture over the bowl of chocolate, and let it sit for 60 seconds so the heat penetrates all the ingredients; then slowly whisk it to hydrate the cocoa powder and melt the chocolate into a ganache. Continue whisking gently until the entire mixture comes together as smooth, flavorful hot chocolate.

3. Divide evenly among four mugs, and drink it immediately. If prepping for a snow day ahead, store this mixture in an airtight container in the fridge for 1 week.

- DO YOU -
BAKE CLUB

Swap in fancy chocolate, candy bars cut into small pieces; even a combo of chocolate forms works here. I rarely make the same hot chocolate twice.

Add as little as ½ teaspoon of an extract or as much as 2 tablespoons of, say, peanut butter or caramel sauce, or add a shot of espresso to really redefine your hot-chocolate game.

Garnish as you please—Marshmallows (page 47), Toffee (page 61), cookies! You're in charge.

TOFFEE

Makes 1 cup of bits

I just found out that my mom is not a butterscotch fan. What the what?! She loves to make a cinnamon butterscotch cookie but always substitutes Heath Bits, only she can't make the cookies unless she goes to the store to buy the bits. So I made this toffee recipe for her home pantry.

⇨ Double this recipe and use a greased 9-by-13-inch baking pan. Spread 1 cup chocolate chips, melted on the top and 1 cup chocolate chips, melted on the bottom for a real candy-shoppe toffee moment.

1 stick (8 tablespoons) unsalted butter
½ cup sugar
Pinch of kosher salt

1. Pan-spray an 8-by-8-inch baking pan, and set it aside.

2. In a heavy-bottomed medium-sized saucepan, stir together all ingredients over medium heat to combine. Stir intermittently with a sturdy heat-safe spatula for 2–3 minutes, until the butter has melted completely and the toffee has begun taking on color around the edges.

3. Cook for an additional 1–2 minutes, still stirring intermittently, until the mixture is a medium amber color. Carefully, pour the hot toffee mixture into the prepared baking pan, and let it sit at room temperature to cool completely, about 1 hour. Your toffee will become a shade darker, because it will continue to caramelize as it cools.

4. Once it's fully cool, break it into sizable pieces and transfer them to a large Ziploc bag. Break up the toffee by alternating between using the edge of a rolling pin to shatter it, and rolling the rolling pin over the bag to break the toffee into smaller bits. In an airtight container at room temperature, toffee will keep fresh for 1 month.

> **- DO YOU -**
> ## BAKE CLUB
> No one's mad at a little nuts in their toffee—scatter ½ cup toasted nuts in or atop.

DROPOFFABLE DESSERTS

Go-To Chocolate Chip Cookies   67

THE Biscuits   70

Bugle Bars   73

Brownies As You Like   74

Birthday Blondies   77

Chewy Oat Bars   78

What's-in-Your-Pantry
Marshmallow Cookies   81

Maple Pecan Crispies   82

Sunshine Bars   84

Coconut Oatmeal Cookies   87

Lemon Bars   88

Super Chocolate Cookies   91

Mint Chip Sammies   92

Lemon Crinkle Cookies   97

Sugar Cookies   98

Frosted Gingersnaps   100

#bakeclub

@carpedolce

@drhousewife_

@prestons.kitchen

- OFFICIAL MAIL -
BAKE CLUB
TO: AYSHA
XO, TOSI
#bakeclub

@carpedolce

BELIEVE
@jessmakesfoods

@smmonson

woohoo
Big. Birthday. Blondie. Energy.
@rachiesbakes

Most people think bakers fall in love with their pursuit because they love sweets (ahem, guilty as charged). But as anyone who has ever spent a few hours scooping cookie dough and mixing cake batter can tell you: it is much more about giving than receiving.

At its core, baking is an altruistic practice, something you do with others in mind because you know the magic it brings into the world. Many of us fall for dessert for its ability to connect us, heart to heart, with those around us. Yes, it's always nice to have something to share, but when that something is made with your hands and with no ulterior motive, it creates a very rare moment of lightness in this world. Maybe that is why most recipes yield a dozen cookies or enough cake for eight servings, too much for even the most trained sweet tooth to keep to themselves.

This chapter is brimming with items I like to deploy in my quest to bake for everyone in the world (yes, an actual goal!). You want a shareable dessert to be sturdy—stable at room temperature and/or stackable. I find that cookies (in drop-cookie form, bar form, or otherwise) and their cousins brownies are the best vehicle for taking your dessert game on the road. Trust me, I've clocked some serious hours mastering the art of the "ding-dong drop," and live to light up someone's mailbox with a handcrafted care package. These recipes are now yours to do the same. Try creating some community with the wink-wink that is a killer Chocolate Chip Cookie (page 67) and a little note that says, "Hope you slayed the day," left on the stoop of your neighbor three doors down. Or tape up a box full of Bday Blondies (page 77) using a blown-up balloon as padding and drop it in the mail for your pen pal on the other side of the country. No matter your move, get ready to start living your life through the lens of what we call "Dropoffable Desserts."

Please Don't Leave Me Alone with All These Baked Goods

So much of the reason I love baking is the act of giving away what I create. As big of a dessert maniac as I am, even I can't take down all the cakes and cookies and pies I like to bake up, so over the years I've perfected the art of "ding-dong ditching" desserts and shipping care packages to sweet-toothed soul mates all over the country. Here's how I get it done.

- **Padding is forever your friend.**

  Crinkled newspaper, bubble wrap, reused packing peanuts from your most recent online order, whatever cushiony stuff you have lying around the house will help your treats stay safe in transit.

- **"Dropoffable Desserts" says it all.**

  Though some recipes in other chapters (items that are stored at room temperature and are not at all delicate—like Granola!) would love to be left in a mailbox or a doorstep, the more finicky and temp-sensitive prefer to stay on your tabletop as a treat.

- **Choose the right size container for your baked goods.**

  The best things come in small packages, and what I mean by that is your baked goods will show up at their best if they are packed with little room to move around. If you're hand-dropping, a small package is also more likely to fit into a mailbox or through a mail slot.

- **Give a gift, not a chore.**

  No one wants to sweat how and when to return the dish a pie came in, and you don't want to be chasing someone down for your fave pie plate. Give your goods away in disposable bakeware and keep it stress-free.

- **Hey, Picasso!**

  No matter if it's a reused Amazon box or a fresh white cardboard diddy, decorate the box! Getting your arts and crafts on lets you personalize the experience; I mean, it's called a care package for a reason.

GO-TO CHOCOLATE CHIP COOKIES

Makes 18

I've long believed each individual has their own relationship with this classic, which is why we don't sell a standard "chocolate chip cookie" at Milk Bar. Maybe your grandma made them to perfection. Or you baked batches with your babysitter after school. Or you zapped globs of store-bought dough in your dorm-room microwave when you got homesick. How could we compete with that connection? But that doesn't mean I don't have my own beloved chocolate chip cookie recipe to add to the conversation. Maybe, someday, it will be yours, too.

⇨ I like a cookie pulled from the oven a minute or two early, for a fudgy center, every time.

⇨ Why do my cookies always look so great? Because, before baking the entire batch of cookies, I always bake a tester cookie—one from the batch I just mixed, to triple-check that the time, temperature, and mixture are exactly what I want them to be before baking the rest of the dough. That is one of the coolest things about a cookie—you still have control over the mixture, compared with cake or bread, so take advantage, and test that cookie before going full force into the oven.

⇨ If those brilliantly baked cookies need a great storage home, my go-to is to stack them in an airtight container with a slice of bread, to keep the soft and fudgy cookies soft and fudgy.

⇨ And, unless otherwise noted, everyone much prefers a freshly baked cookie, so freeze the dough (or baked cookie) and defrost and bake (or eat) if you're baking ahead.

⇨ Milk powder brings a secret depth of flavor and a slight chew to this classic cookie (see page 5).

2 sticks (16 tablespoons)
  unsalted butter,
  super soft
3/4 cup light brown sugar
1/2 cup sugar

1 egg
2 teaspoons vanilla extract

13/4 cups flour
2 tablespoons milk powder
11/4 teaspoons kosher salt
1/2 teaspoon baking powder
1/4 teaspoon baking soda

2 cups (one 12-ounce bag)
  chocolate chips

- DO YOU -
BAKE CLUB

This is not only my go-to chocolate chip cookie recipe, it's also my (and now your) jumping-off point. Incorporate your own fun ingredients, points of inspiration, and seasonal moods. Swap the chocolate chips for any other flavor baking chip you have (or a combo).

Want a crunchy chocolate chip cookie? Flatten the domes of your scoops and bake the cookies at 315°F for 25 minutes.

Want a chipless wonder? Leave out the chocolate chips and keep the rest.

Feeling s'more-y? Add 1/2 cup mini-marshmallows and 1/4 cup graham crackers crushed into bite-sized pieces.

Add 1 tablespoon cinnamon! Brown the butter before mixing!

1. Heat the oven to 350°F, and pan-spray two half sheet pans or line them with parchment.

2. In a large bowl, using a sturdy spatula, mix together the butter and sugars, flexing your muscles for about 2 minutes, until they are fully combined. Add the egg and vanilla, and stir until everything is combined and fluffy, about 1 minute.

3. Measure the flour, milk powder, salt, baking powder, and baking soda into the mixing bowl. Toss together only the dry ingredients on top with the spatula first, before truly stirring them into the wet ingredients below. Mix until everything is just combined. Stir in the chocolate chips.

4. Scoop or roll your dough into balls (⅓ cup or 2¾-ounce ice cream scoop in size), and place them 2–3 inches apart on your prepared sheets. Bake at 350°F for 8–10 minutes, until the edges of the cookies are golden brown. Cool them on the trays. In an airtight container at room temperature, the cookies will keep fresh for up to 1 week.

THE BISCUITS

Makes 12

2 sticks (16 tablespoons)
  unsalted butter, melted
1¹/₃ cups confectioners'
  sugar
3 tablespoons light brown
  sugar

3 egg yolks

1³/₄ cups flour
Scant ¹/₂ teaspoon
  kosher salt

It may not come as much of a surprise that a show about the power of optimism and the meaning of teamwork would strike a chord with my relentlessly glass-half-full personality. One episode of *Ted Lasso* and I was all in. I fell even deeper when Ted deployed his secret recipe for homemade biscuits—really a shortbread-type cookie—to win over his hard-to-crack boss, a move right out of my mother's Kill Them with Kindness playbook, for sure. When the show asked me to re-create the coach's recipe to help promote its second season, it was game on. Yes, these are THE biscuits.

⇨ The melted butter in this recipe delivers a dense, almost sandy biscuit, which is key.

⇨ Make some Peanut Butter Nougat (see page 228) with those whites!

1. Heat the oven to 325°F, and pan-spray one 8-by-8-inch baking pan.

2. In a medium bowl, using a sturdy spatula, mix together the butter and sugars, flexing your muscles for about 2 minutes, until they are well combined. Add the egg yolks, and stir until everything is combined and glossy, about 1 minute.

3. Measure the flour and salt into the mixing bowl. Toss together only the dry ingredients on top with the spatula first, before truly stirring them into the wet ingredients below. Mix until everything is just combined. The less you mix the dough, the more posi vibes your biscuits will have.

4. Press the dough into an even layer in the pan, and bake at 325°F for 40–45 minutes, until a thin golden-brown layer forms on top.

5. Cool it completely in the pan before cutting it into two even columns and six even rows. In an airtight container at room temperature, the biscuits will keep fresh for 1 week.

BUGLE BARS

Makes 9

I've worked in every type of kitchen, from rustic country inns to Michelin-starred fine dining. I've served dessert to folks from all walks of life, and one thing remains consistent: the most unassuming, quick-to-pull-together desserts are oftentimes the most beloved. Enter Bugle Bars, my ultimate salty-sweet pantry hack. Scratching every itch, they are wildly gooey on the bottom, yet wildly crunchy on top. I love when opposites attract—tension, that teeter-totter, is so important in a great creation, especially a dessert. Every tray of these bars that I bake up is gone in a flash, with requests for seconds. They are also infinitely adaptable, so you can customize them with your audience (or your pantry's snack supply) in mind—no matter who (or what) they may be.

⇨ If you want to forgo store-bought and make your own cookie dough, flip to the Go-To Chocolate Chip Cookies recipe (page 67) and use three-quarters of the dough (12 cookies' worth).

⇨ I love to use leftover sweetened condensed milk to fancy up my coffee or oatmeal!

One 14-ounce package store-bought cookie dough, at room temperature

12 Ritz crackers, broken down into pieces about ¼ the original size
12 bite-sized crunchy cookies
¼ cup mini-marshmallows
2 cups original Bugles

⅓ cup sweetened condensed milk (about ¼ of a 14-ounce can)

1. Heat the oven to 325°F, and pan-spray an 8-by-8-inch baking pan.

2. Use your hands to press the cookie dough evenly into the base of the pan.

3. Scatter the cracker pieces, cookies, and mini-marshmallows over the dough. Scatter the Bugles to cover the top of the pan.

4. Drizzle the sweetened condensed milk evenly over the Bugles, using a zigzag formation, and bake at 325°F for 30–35 minutes, or until the edges of the Bugles are golden brown. I like to bake my bars on a lower rack, so the cookie base bakes a bit longer while the Bugles get candy-coated slow and low without burning.

5. Cool the dough before cutting into three rows of three squares and serving. At room temperature, covered with a lid or plastic wrap, the bars will keep fresh for 1 week.

- DO YOU -
BAKE CLUB

Swap in any type of dough, cracker, cookie, salty snack, or other fun pantry item. These bars are meant to be a salty-sweet textural adventure, and you get to design the road map.

BROWNIES AS YOU LIKE

Makes 9

1 stick (8 tablespoons)
  unsalted butter
1/2 cup chocolate chips

1 cup sugar

2 eggs
1½ teaspoons vanilla extract

1/3 cup flour
1/4 cup cocoa powder
1/2 teaspoon kosher salt

Everyone needs a great back-pocket fudgy brownie recipe that they can edge up or down, depending on what chocolatey ingredients they have on hand, or whatever mix-ins they like—peanut-butter swirl! Cream cheese dollops! Bejeweled with extra chocolate chips! Use this brownie recipe as a base to get wild. Me, I love walking on the wild side, but I make this recipe weekly just as is. They're that good. They also scale up like a dream—brownies for the masses!

⇨ No cocoa powder? No problem, increase the amount of chocolate chips to 1¼ cups, and flour to ²/3 cup.

⇨ No chocolate chips? No problem, increase the cocoa powder to ¹/2 cup, and the flour to ¹/4 cup.

⇨ Though I'm typically a fan of the "nicer the ingredients, the better the result" mentality, classic semisweet grocery aisle chocolate chips and cocoa powder can go toe-to-toe with any fancier chopped chocolate or cocoa powder you might want to sub in here (which you're welcome to do!).

⇨ The vanilla in this recipe helps give the chocolate company, and flavor context. Whenever I'm making something with chocolate, I always buttress it with a little vanilla and a healthy amount of salt.

⇨ The sign of a great brownie is the paper-thin layer of what brownie experts call "flint." Drop that into your next baking convo and see whose head turns.

⇨ Believe it or not, a plastic knife is the best way to cut brownies. Plastic knives are naturally nonstick and won't tear the brownies as you slice, while the fudgy center of a brownie clings to metal knives.

- DO YOU -
BAKE CLUB

I'm a purist when it comes to a dense, fudgy brownie, but take this and run with it—layer, swirl, stud to your heart's desire.

@samkrayons adds a little instant coffee with her dry ingredients and tops them with espresso frosting. Game on. @tiffanybrittdesigns tops hers with Pop Rocks (page 218) for a masterclass in FUN.

1. Heat the oven to 325°F, and pan-spray an 8-by-8-inch baking pan.

2. In the microwave, in a large heatproof bowl, melt the butter and chocolate chips together. Work in 30-second spurts, stirring with a sturdy heat-safe spatula in between blasts, until the mixture is smooth, about 2 minutes.

3. **Switch mixing tools:** Whisk in the sugar, and use the whisk to stir until it's combined, about 30 seconds. Whisk in the eggs and vanilla, and stir until the mixture is smooth and glossy, about 30 seconds.

4. Measure the flour, cocoa powder, and salt into the mixing bowl. Switch back to the spatula, and toss together only the dry ingredients on top first, before truly stirring them into the wet ingredients below. Mix until everything is just combined.

5. Pour the batter into the prepared pan, and bake at 325°F for 25 minutes, just until the flint forms and the brownie starts to set. (The gooier the better, if you ask me.)

6. Cool the batter a tad in the pan before slicing into three rows of three squares and serving. Or cool it entirely—it's brownies as YOU like! At room temperature, covered with a lid or plastic wrap, the brownies will keep fresh for 1 week.

- DO YOU -
BAKE CLUB

Swap the clear vanilla extract out for any other flavor you might
be into, and swap the rainbow sprinkles for whatever other vis
follows suit.

BIRTHDAY BLONDIES

Makes 9

These sugar-cookie-esque bars are a lesson in Flavor 101. When developing Milk Bar's signature birthday layer cake, I had to get real down and dirty with extracts. I spent a few initial rounds of testing using the classic brown-bottled McCormick vanilla extract—a must-have for any vanilla-forward dessert, right? Not so fast. Though dark vanilla extract helps sing the deeper, more soulful vanilla notes—think your favorite chocolate chip cookie—birthday calls for something else. Enter: clear vanilla extract. Easily findable online, this extract can transform any plain vanilla recipe into a celebration.

- -

⇨ Some blondies are actually just vanilla bar cookies. But, if you ask me, a blondie should be a lighter, white chocolate take on a brownie; hence the white chocolate chips in this recipe.

- -

1 stick (8 tablespoons)
  unsalted butter
1/3 cup white chocolate
  chips

2/3 cup sugar
1/4 cup light brown sugar

1 egg
1 teaspoon clear
  vanilla extract

3/4 cup + 1 tablespoon flour
1/2 teaspoon kosher salt
1 tablespoon rainbow
  sprinkles

1. Heat the oven to 325°F, and pan-spray an 8-by-8-inch baking pan.

2. In the microwave, in a large heatproof bowl, melt the butter and chocolate chips together, working in 30-second spurts, stirring with a sturdy heat-safe spatula in between blasts, until the mixture is smooth, about 2 minutes.

3. Mix in the sugars, and stir until everything is combined, about 30 seconds. Mix in the egg and vanilla, and stir until the mixture is smooth and glossy, about 30 seconds.

4. Measure the flour and salt into the mixing bowl. Toss together only the dry ingredients on top with the spatula first, before truly stirring them into the wet ingredients below. Mix until everything is just combined.

5. Pour the batter into the prepared pan, and spread it evenly across the surface. Scatter the sprinkles over the top. With a butter knife, swirl the sprinkles into the surface of the blondie, or leave them as a topping. Bake at 325°F for 40–45 minutes, until the edges are golden brown and the bull's-eye center is set.

6. Cool the batter in the pan before cutting it into three rows of three squares and serving. At room temperature, covered with a lid or plastic wrap, the blondies will keep fresh for 1 week.

CHEWY OAT BARS

Makes 9

Sometimes, what I really want is a hearty bite, a baked good that is sturdy and filling enough to be considered breakfast or a great midday snack. I love a good oatmeal cookie, but always want to push the limits of the oats. "What if I use two times—*three* times—the oats called for in a recipe?" I wonder. Enter these brilliant bars, literally All About Oats. Accidentally gluten free and not super sweet, they are a mainstay in my kitchen. I know they're not much to look at, but I promise, you'll keep them in your rotation.

- -

⇨ Triple-check that you've got rolled or old-fashioned oats (NO instant oats allowed anywhere near this recipe!).

- -

2 sticks (16 tablespoons) unsalted butter, super soft
²/₃ cup light brown sugar
¹/₃ cup sugar

1 egg
2 teaspoons vanilla extract

1¹/₂ cups rolled oats

1 teaspoon kosher salt
¹/₄ teaspoon baking soda
¹/₈ teaspoon baking powder
3 cups rolled oats

1. Heat the oven to 350°F. Pan-spray an 8-by-8-inch baking pan.

2. In a large bowl, using a sturdy spatula, mix together the butter and sugars, flexing your muscles for about 2 minutes, until they are fully combined. Add the egg and vanilla, and stir until everything is combined and fluffy, about 1 minute.

3. In a food processor or blender, grind 1¹/₂ cups rolled oats down into a flourlike consistency, 30–60 seconds.

4. Transfer the oat "flour" to the mixing bowl, then measure the salt, baking soda, and baking powder in, as well. Add the remaining 3 cups rolled oats, and mix together the dry ingredients on top with the spatula first, before truly stirring them into the wet ingredients below. Mix until everything is just combined. The dough will be a slightly fluffy, fatty mixture, in comparison with your average cookie dough.

5. Transfer the dough to the pan, and spread it evenly across the surface. Bake at 350°F for 20–30 minutes, until the dough has risen in height, the edges and surface are a deep golden brown, and the bull's-eye center is set.

6. Cool the dough in the pan before cutting it into three rows of three squares and serving. At room temperature, covered with a lid or plastic wrap, the bars will keep fresh for 1 week.

- DO YOU -
BAKE CLUB

If you're not into grinding oats down into a flour, skip that step and sub in 1 cup of your favorite flour (whole-wheat! rye! all-purpose!).

These bars love some chocolate chunks, if you're game. A little spice, if that's your thing. Dare I even suggest ½ cup of Caramel Sauce (page 21) or Fruit Jam (page 27)?

BAKE @350
8-10 MINS
EAT WARM :)

WHAT'S-IN-YOUR-PANTRY MARSHMALLOW COOKIES

Makes 18

Marshmallows are a bit of a shape-shifter in the baking tool kit. Straight from the bag, these little white puffs don't pack much of a punch, but bake them into a cookie or toast and fold them into a layer cake and you're in business. A creamy vanilla essence that helps build a flavor bridge, and a bouncy chew that creates a bit of complexity. This recipe puts marshmallow's superpowers to work, playing matchmaker between a buttery, fudgy cookie dough and whatever textural goodies your pantry might have in store.

⇨ Because every pantry selection will be a different size, I highly recommend baking a tester cookie first (page 67).

⇨ This is my favorite cookie dough to ding-dong-drop in a Ziploc bag with baking instructions. A warm, gooey marshmallow moment is the best gift you could give someone to enjoy on their own time!

2 sticks (16 tablespoons) unsalted butter, super soft

1½ cups sugar

1 egg

½ teaspoon vanilla extract

2¼ cups flour

1½ teaspoons kosher salt

½ teaspoon baking powder

¼ teaspoon baking soda

1½ cups crunchy pantry goodies/cereal

1 cup mini-marshmallows

1. Heat the oven to 350°F. Pan-spray two half sheet pans, or line them with parchment.

2. In a large bowl, using a sturdy spatula, mix together the butter and sugar, flexing your muscles for about 2 minutes, until they are fully combined. Add the egg and vanilla, and stir until everything is combined and fluffy, about 1 minute.

3. Measure the flour, salt, baking powder, and baking soda into the mixing bowl. Toss together only the dry ingredients on top with the spatula first, before truly stirring them into the wet ingredients below. Mix until everything is just combined. Stir in the pantry haul and marshmallows, and mix until they're just combined.

4. Scoop or roll your dough into balls (⅓ cup or 2¾-ounce ice cream scoop in size), and place them 2–3 inches apart on your prepared sheets. Bake at 350°F for 8 to 10 minutes, until the edges of the cookies are golden brown. Cool them on the trays. In an airtight container at room temperature, the cookies will keep fresh for up to 1 week.

- DO YOU -
BAKE CLUB

Change up your sugar, depending on the mix-ins you use. Pretzels make me think dark brown sugar, Cracklin' Oat Bran screams light brown sugar, Golden Grahams signal honey to me, and so on. You can sub up to ¾ cup of sugar with light brown sugar or dark brown sugar or honey if your selections inspire it.

MAPLE PECAN CRISPIES

Makes 24

1 cup pecan pieces

1 stick (8 tablespoons)
   unsalted butter,
   super soft
²/₃ cup sugar
¹/₃ cup maple syrup

¹/₂ teaspoon vanilla extract

1 cup flour
1 teaspoon kosher salt
¹/₄ teaspoon baking powder
¹/₄ teaspoon baking soda
1 cup Rice Krispies

I became obsessed with super crunchy cookies when we were recipe testing ideas to bring Milk Bar to grocery aisles. Marrying a classic pecan sandy with my Nonna Trudy's move of hiding Rice Krispies in her cookie dough, these cookies were what I'd rush home to recipe-test on my own time. They use less flour than your average cookie, and I love the way these crispies take what a cookie can be to the outer limits, spreading into a lacy, almost toffeelike state, yet still a cookie in my book!

⇨ These are naturally egg-free; we omit the water and protein of an egg to lean deeper into the crunch delivered by the sugars, cereal, and nuts.

⇨ A longer bake on these cookies guarantees a super-crunchy, crispy cookie all the way through.

1. Heat the oven to 350°F. Pan-spray two half sheet pans, or line them with parchment. As the oven heats up, spread the pecans on one of the half sheet pans and toast them for 10–15 minutes, until you can smell the warm nuts and they are a deep golden brown under the skin.

2. In a large bowl, using a sturdy spatula, mix together the butter, sugar, and maple syrup, flexing your muscles for about 2 minutes, until they are fully combined. Add the vanilla, and stir until everything is combined and fluffy, about 1 minute.

3. Measure the flour, salt, baking powder, and baking soda into the mixing bowl. Toss together only the dry ingredients on top with the spatula first, before truly stirring them into the wet ingredients below. Mix until everything is just combined. Stir in the cereal and toasted nuts, and stir until they're well combined.

4. Scoop or roll your dough into 2-tablespoon-sized balls (half the size of a Ping-Pong ball), and place them 1–2 inches apart on your prepared sheets. Bake at 350°F for 12 minutes, until the cookies have baked and spread into a flat, lacy state, and caramelized into a deep golden-brown color all around. Cool them on the trays. In an airtight container at room temperature, the cookies will keep fresh for up to 1 week.

- DO YOU -
BAKE CLUB

Swap the pecans for whatever nuts you got. Same with the vanilla extract. Coconut and coconut, I'm in! Almond and almond, or hazelnut and orange . . . The possibilities are endless!

SUNSHINE BARS

Makes 9

I like to think dessert has the power to make any bad day better and any good day great—and these light and fluffy bars are living proof. There is something undeniably cheerful about a citrusy-flavored baked good covered in Creamsicle-esque glaze—I mean, the tart brightness almost forces your face into a smile! A few grated carrots give these slices of UV some texture and a little boost of vitamins, to make them even more of a powerhouse. They are just begging to be shared, so consider making a double batch.

⇨ Use your leftover oranges to make Citrus Jam (page 28).

1 stick (8 tablespoons)
   unsalted butter,
   super soft
¾ cup sugar
¼ cup light brown sugar

1 egg
2 teaspoons vanilla extract

¼ cup vegetable oil

1½ cups flour
1½ teaspoons kosher salt
½ teaspoon baking powder

1 cup Microplaned carrots
Grated zest of 2 oranges

1 recipe Sunny Glaze
   (recipe follows)

1. Heat the oven to 350°F, and pan-spray an 8-by-8-inch baking pan.

2. In a large bowl, using a sturdy spatula, mix together the butter and sugars, flexing your muscles for about 2 minutes, until they are fully combined. Add the egg and vanilla, and stir until the mixture is combined and fluffy, about 1 minute. Add the oil, and stir until everything is combined and super glossy, about 1 minute.

3. Measure the flour, salt, and baking powder into the mixing bowl. Toss together only the dry ingredients on top with the spatula first, before truly stirring them into the wet ingredients below. Mix until everything is just combined. Stir in the carrots and orange zest until they're well combined.

4. Pour the batter into the prepared pan, and spread it evenly across the surface. Bake at 350°F for 30 minutes, until the top and edges are golden brown and the bull's-eye center is set.

5. Cool the batter completely in the pan before getting your Jackson Pollock on and drizzling the glaze across the surface. Let the glaze set for 30 minutes before cutting into three rows of three squares and serving. At room temperature, covered with a lid or plastic wrap, the bars will keep fresh for 1 week.

Sunny Glaze

Makes enough for one batch of Sunshine Bars

½ cup confectioners' sugar
1 tablespoon orange juice
Zest of 1 orange

Because kitchen humidities differ, when you're making the glaze, add more confectioners' sugar (1 tablespoon at a time) to thicken it, or a very, very small splash of OJ to thin it out.

In a small bowl, using a spoon or small spatula, stir together the confectioners' sugar, OJ, and zest, stirring until thick and smooth, 1–2 minutes. Use the glaze immediately, or store it in an airtight container in the fridge for up to a week.

COCONUT OATMEAL COOKIES

Makes 18

14 tablespoons (1 stick +
6 tablespoons) unsalted
butter, super soft
3/4 cup light brown sugar
1/3 cup sugar + more for
rolling

2 eggs
2 teaspoons vanilla extract

2 cups old-fashioned oats
1 1/2 cups flour
1/2 cup sweetened
shredded coconut
1 teaspoon kosher salt
1 teaspoon cinnamon
1 teaspoon baking soda

1 cup confectioners' sugar,
for rolling

My grandma's oatmeal cookie recipe was the first cookie dough I ever ate—and also the first cookie I ever learned how to make. Long story short, she caught me eating more than my fair share and cut me off, so I had to learn how to fight for myself—natural selection at its finest! I never dare compete with the sacred intersection of nostalgia and dessert, so, rather than attempt Grandma's legendary cookies in my own kitchen, I honor my favorite parts of her recipe and twist the rest into a sharper, chewier, nuttier moment by bringing sweetened shredded coconut to the mix.

⇨ Triple-check that you've got rolled or old-fashioned oats at the ready (NO instant oats allowed anywhere near this recipe!).

⇨ The secret to the best powdered-sugar-dusted cookie is to roll your dough ball first in granulated sugar, then in confectioners' sugar.

⇨ Grandma loved to store her oatmeal cookies back in the oatmeal container with a slice of bread to keep them fresh.

1. Heat the oven to 375°F. Pan-spray two half sheet pans, or line them with parchment.

2. In a large bowl, using a sturdy spatula, mix together the butter and sugars, flexing your muscles for about 2 minutes, until they are fully combined. Add the eggs and vanilla, and stir until everything is combined and fluffy, about 1 minute.

3. Measure the oats, flour, coconut, salt, cinnamon, and baking soda into the mixing bowl. Toss together only the dry ingredients on top with the spatula first, before truly stirring them into the wet ingredients below. Mix until everything is well combined.

4. Scoop or roll your dough into balls (1/3 cup or 2 3/4-ounce ice cream scoop in size). Make one small bowl of granulated sugar, and another small bowl of confectioners' sugar. Roll each dough ball in granulated sugar, then in confectioners' sugar.

5. Place all the sugared dough balls 2–3 inches apart on your prepared sheets. Bake at 375°F for 7–9 minutes, until the edges of the cookies are golden brown. Cool them on the trays. In an airtight container at room temperature, the cookies will keep fresh for up to 1 week.

LEMON BARS

Makes 9

The best part of being a baker is being able to transform a recipe from what's written on the page into your ideal version. Maybe it's shaving a few minutes of bake time off a pan of brownies so they are 10 percent gooier. Or swapping some white sugar for dark brown sugar in a cookie, to get a deeper, more soulful flavor. When it came time to tackle the much-beloved lemon bar for Bake Club, I dreamed of something different from the typical graham cracker crust—merging together gooey butter cake with bright lemon flavors.

⇨ These bars are tall, which I love, but if you're yearning for thinner, shorter bars, they bake just as nicely in a 9-by-13-inch pan at 350°F for 20–25 minutes total.

For the Crust

One standard box lemon
  cake mix
1 stick (8 tablespoons)
  unsalted butter, melted
1 egg

For the Filling

4 ounces block cream
  cheese, softened

1¼ cups confectioners'
  sugar + more for dusting

1 egg
2 lemons, zested and juiced
  (about ¼ cup juice)

1. Heat the oven to 350°F, and pan-spray one 8-by-8-inch baking pan.

2. **Make the crust:** In a large bowl, using a sturdy spatula, mix together the cake mix, butter, and egg until they are fully combined, about 1 minute. Measure out ¾ cup of this dough and set it aside. Press the remaining dough evenly into the base of the pan.

3. **Make the filling:** In the same mixing bowl, with the same spatula, mix together the reserved ¾ cup dough with the softened cream cheese, flexing your muscles for about 2 minutes, until they are smooth and fully combined. Stir in the confectioners' sugar, and mix until it's all smooth and fully combined, about 2 minutes. Stir in the egg, lemon juice, and grated lemon zest, and mix until everything is smooth and fully combined, about 1 minute.

4. Pour the batter into the prepared pan, and spread it evenly across the surface. Bake at 350°F for 25 minutes, until the top has puffed slightly, is golden brown, and is beginning to crack. Reduce the oven temperature to 325°F, and continue baking another 10–15 minutes, until the bull's-eye center is set.

5. Cool the dough completely in the pan before cutting into three rows of three squares and serving. At room temperature, covered with a lid or plastic wrap, the bars will keep fresh for 1 week.

- DO YOU -
BAKE CLUB

Swap the lemon cake mix with strawberry or any other fruit flavor cake mix (pineapple! orange!) and sub lemon zest and juice in for any other citrus or fruit juice you like.

SUPER CHOCOLATE COOKIES

Makes 18

An ode to my favorite baked good of all time, the fudgy brownie, this cookie means business—and is also a great jumping-off point for any chocolate cookie-base creation you might dream up. My nieces and I wrapped the dough around scoops of dulce de leche during our most recent sleepover, and no one got mad at it. I've also made these into thumbprint cookies with wells of peanut butter baked in, to say "I'm sorry," and I can say that I am still happily married because of it.

⇨ The honey in this recipe is a flavor bridge of both sweetness and acidity for the chocolate and cocoa. It also ensures that the dough will stay fudgy when baked and is pliable.

⇨ The vanilla in this recipe helps give the chocolate company, and flavor context. Whenever I'm making something with chocolate, I always buttress it with a little vanilla and a healthy amount of salt.

⇨ Though I'm typically a fan of the "nicer the ingredients, the better the result" mentality, my grocery aisle, classic semisweet chocolate chips and cocoa powder can go toe-to-toe with any fancier chopped chocolate or cocoa powder you might want to sub in here (which you're welcome to do!).

---

2 sticks (16 tablespoons) unsalted butter
1/3 cup chocolate chips

1 1/2 cups sugar
1/4 cup honey

1 egg
1/4 teaspoon vanilla extract

1 1/4 cups flour
3/4 cup cocoa powder
1 3/4 teaspoons kosher salt
3/4 teaspoon baking powder
1/4 teaspoon baking soda

1. Heat the oven to 350°F. Pan-spray two half sheet pans, or line them with parchment.

2. In the microwave, in a large, heatproof bowl, melt the butter and chocolate chips together, working in 30-second spurts, stirring with a sturdy heat-safe spatula in between blasts, until the mixture is smooth, about 2 minutes. Add the sugar and honey, and mix until everything is combined, about 1 minute. Add the egg and vanilla, and mix until they're combined, about 1 minute.

3. Measure the flour, cocoa powder, salt, baking powder, and baking soda into the mixing bowl. Toss together only the dry ingredients on top with the spatula first, before truly stirring them into the wet ingredients below. Mix until everything is well combined.

4. Scoop or roll your dough into balls (1/3 cup or 2 3/4-ounce ice cream scoop in size), and place them 2–3 inches apart on your prepared sheets. Bake at 350°F for 8–10 minutes. These cookies will puff, crackle, and spread. It's kind of impossible to gauge when a cookie this chocolatey is done, so bake a tester cookie (page 67) to nail your preferred bake time. Cool them on the trays. In an airtight container at room temperature, the cookies will keep fresh for up to 1 week.

MINT CHIP SAMMIES

Makes 12

Mint chip remains one of my all-time favorite ice cream flavors, and a combo I'm always trying to re-create in cake, pie, or, in this case, cookie form. These chocolate chip cookie wafers are dangerously delicious on their own, and, when sandwiched with this Oreo-like mint filling, make a dropoffable duo sure to make magic on anyone's doorstep, back porch, or mailbox.

⇨ The confectioners' sugar in this recipe brings sweetness but also structure and snap; it's technically granulated sugar pulverized into a powderlike state with a little cornstarch, perfect for a cookie we know we want to roll out and bake.

1 stick (8 tablespoons)
   unsalted butter, melted
¼ cup sugar
¼ cup confectioners' sugar

1 egg yolk
1 teaspoon vanilla extract

1 cup flour
½ teaspoon salt

⅓ cup mini–chocolate
   chips

1 recipe Mint Filling (recipe
   follows)

1. In a large bowl, using a sturdy spatula, mix together the butter and sugars until they are fully combined, about 1 minute. Mix in the egg yolk and vanilla, and stir to combine, about one minute.

2. Measure the flour and salt into the mixing bowl. Toss together only the dry ingredients on top with the spatula first, before truly stirring them into the wet ingredients below. Mix until everything is just combined. Stir in the chocolate chips.

3. With a rolling pin on the counter, flatten the dough between two pieces of parchment to ½-inch thickness, or approximately the height of a mini–chocolate chip.

4. Using a chef's knife, cut twenty-four dough rectangles 1½ by 2 inches. (You're welcome to cut 2-inch rounds if you don't like right angles!) Refrigerate or freeze the entire sheet of dough until firm, about 5 minutes.

5. Heat the oven to 325°F. Pan-spray a half sheet pan, or line it with parchment paper.

6. Pop your chilled rounds off the parchment and transfer them to the half sheet pan, spacing them ¼ inch apart (they don't spread in the oven!), and bake at 325°F for 10–12 minutes, until the edges are golden brown. Cool the rounds completely.

7. Reshape your dough scraps into a ball, roll it out, chill it, and bake it.

8. Using a butter knife, the back of a spoon, or an offset spatula, sandwich as much or as little mint filling as you want between two chocolate chip wafers. In an airtight container at room temperature, the cookies will keep fresh for up to 1 week, or in the freezer for up to a month. (I quite like them right out of the freezer during the summer months :).)

- DO YOU -
BAKE CLUB

Not a mint fan? My feelings aren't hurt! Swap the mint filling for Caramel Sauce (page 21), Curd (page 55), Citrus Jam (page 28), Fudge Sauce (page 22)! Or Frosting (page 269)!

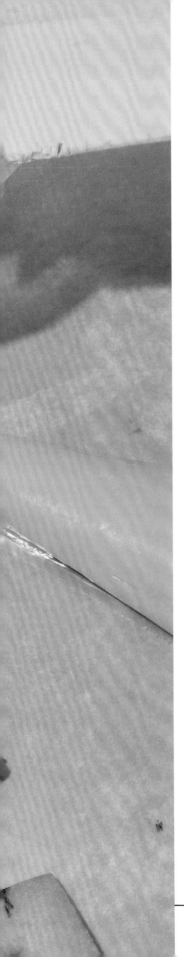

Mint Filling

Makes enough for 1 batch of Mint Chip Sammies

2 tablespoons Crisco shortening
$1/4$ cup corn syrup

$1/4$ teaspoon peppermint extract
$1/4$ teaspoon vanilla extract
1 drop green food coloring

1 cup confectioners' sugar
$1/8$ teaspoon kosher salt

In a small bowl, using a sturdy spatula, mix together the shortening and corn syrup until they are fully combined, about 1 minute. Mix in the extracts and coloring, and stir to combine everything into one mint-green mass with no streaks, about 1 minute. Add the confectioners' sugar and salt, and stir until the combination is smooth and one consistent color, about 3 minutes. Use it immediately, or store it in an airtight container at room temperature for up to 1 week.

LEMON CRINKLE COOKIES

Makes 12

These bright babes are gluten-free, but don't let that fool you into thinking they are less-than in any way. Like many of my favorite gluten-free recipes, these are that way by way of accident. The almond flour helps give the cookies a chewier texture and a flavor that makes the perfect landing pad for lemon. Drop them off with your CrossFit friends to give them a punch of protein—muscle buffs need cookies, too.

⇨ The secret to the best-looking crinkle is to roll your dough ball in granulated sugar first, then in confectioners' sugar.

3 egg whites
¼ cup sugar + more for rolling

6 drops yellow food coloring
1 teaspoon lemon extract
Zest of 1 lemon

2 cups almond flour
2 cups confectioners' sugar + more for rolling
¼ teaspoon kosher salt
¼ teaspoon baking powder

1. Heat the oven to 300°F. Pan-spray two half sheet pans, or line them with parchment.

2. In the bowl of a stand mixer fitted with the whisk attachment, whip the heck out of the egg whites on high speed until they form soft, foamy peaks. Sprinkle in the granulated sugar little by little, and mix for another minute, until you have glossy but soft peaks.

3. Detach the mixer, and remove the whisk attachment. With a sturdy spatula, mix the food coloring, extract, and zest into the egg whites, stirring until everything is one consistent yellow color, no streaks, about 2 minutes.

4. Measure the almond flour, confectioners' sugar, salt, and baking powder into the mixing bowl. Toss together only the dry ingredients on top with the spatula first, before truly stirring them into the wet ingredients below. Mix until everything is well combined; this will result in a much firmer dough.

5. Scoop or roll your dough into balls (⅓ cup or 2¾-ounce ice cream scoop in size). Make one small bowl of granulated sugar and another small bowl of confectioners' sugar. Roll each dough ball in granulated sugar, then in confectioners' sugar.

6. Place all the sugared dough balls 2–3 inches apart on your prepared sheets. Bake at 300°F for 18 minutes, during which time the cookies will puff and crackle but remain dense, rich, and fudgy in the center. The edges will take on little to no color. Cool them on the trays. In an airtight container at room temperature, the cookies will keep fresh for up to 1 week.

- DO YOU -
BAKE CLUB

Swap the yellow and lemon elements for orange, or even another flavor (and color if you like) altogether.

SUGAR COOKIES

Makes 18

When I was growing up, the ultimate luxury of our week or month, for me and my mom, was going to the fresh bakery section of the grocery store and buying a giant "Smiley Cookie"—essentially a giant sugar cookie—to split. Yet in my three (. . . four?!) decades as a baker, I'd never attempted a classic sugar cookie myself. This one is not too sweet, combining confectioners' sugar and cream of tartar for a little structure and a little bite; you only have to roll this cookie around in Sugar in the Raw, or in colored sprinkles, and watch, er, taste it come to life.

⇨ Milk powder will bring a secret depth of flavor and a slight chew to this classic cookie (see page 5).

2 sticks (16 tablespoons)
   unsalted butter,
   super soft
1½ cups confectioners'
   sugar

1 egg
1 teaspoon vanilla extract

2 cups flour
1 tablespoon milk powder
1 teaspoon kosher salt
1 teaspoon baking soda
1 teaspoon cream of tartar

Sugar (granulated sugar,
   Sugar in the Raw, colored
   sugar, etc.), for rolling

1. Heat the oven to 350°F. Pan-spray two half sheet pans, or line them with parchment.

2. In a large bowl, using a sturdy spatula, mix together the butter and sugar, flexing your muscles for about 2 minutes, until they are fully combined. Add the egg and vanilla, and stir until everything is combined and fluffy, about 1 minute.

3. Measure the flour, milk powder, salt, baking soda, and cream of tartar into the mixing bowl. Toss together only the dry ingredients on top with the spatula first, before truly stirring them into the wet ingredients below. Mix until everything is just combined.

4. Scoop or roll your dough into balls (⅓ cup or 2¾-ounce ice cream scoop in size), roll them in sugar, and place them 2–3 inches apart on your prepared sheets. Bake at 350°F for 10 minutes, until the edges of the cookies are golden brown. Cool them on the trays. In an airtight container at room temperature, the cookies will keep fresh for up to 1 week.

Cookie Monster

Cookies adhere to a size/baking time ratio. Scale any recipe up/down, scoop any recipe smaller than called for, or make any cookie recipe into a cookie pie.

- **Smaller, mini-cookies:** 6–8 minutes, 350°F
- **Medium-sized, ⅓ cup dough round cookies:** 10–12 minutes, 350°F
- **Larger cookies:** 12–16 minutes, 350°F
- **Cookie pie:** (aka all the cookie dough smooshed into a greased 9-inch cake pan or pie plate) 20–25 minutes, 350°F

FROSTED GINGERSNAPS

Makes 24

1¹⁄₂ sticks (12 tablespoons) unsalted butter, super soft

¹⁄₂ cup light brown sugar

¹⁄₄ cup sugar

¹⁄₂ cup molasses

2 cups flour

2 tablespoons milk powder

1 tablespoon + 1 teaspoon ground ginger

2 teaspoons baking soda

1 teaspoon cinnamon

³⁄₄ teaspoon kosher salt

1 recipe Frosted Glaze (recipe follows)

As we started dreaming up this book, we made a list of all the recipes we wanted to bring to its pages. As fans of collaboration, we asked our cookbook team, "What essential recipes are we missing?" Our brilliant editor, Lexy, chimed in, "I live in a house filled with molasses-ginger cookie lovers," and so we knew we needed to conquer the spice and chew of the classic snap, opting to dunk it in a light frosting to make it irresistibly ours. Now yours. And your neighbors'. And your cousin's. And your doorman's.

⇨ This recipe is naturally egg-free; we omit the water and protein of an egg to keep the cookie flatter and snappier as it bakes.

⇨ Milk powder will bring a secret depth of flavor and a slight chew to this classic cookie.

⇨ This is a stickier dough—don't freak out! But if it is too sticky to handle, cool it in the fridge for 30 minutes, then come back to it.

1. Heat the oven to 350°F. Pan-spray two half sheet pans, or line them with parchment.

2. In a large bowl, using a sturdy spatula, mix together the butter and sugars, flexing your muscles for about 2 minutes, until they are fully combined. Add the molasses, and stir until everything is combined, about 1 minute.

3. Measure the flour, milk powder, ginger, baking soda, cinnamon, and salt into the mixing bowl. Toss together only the dry ingredients on top with the spatula first, before truly stirring them into the wet ingredients below. Mix until everything is just combined.

4. Scoop or roll your dough into 2-tablespoon-sized balls (half the size of a Ping-Pong ball), and place them 2–3 inches apart on your prepared sheets. Bake at 350°F for 8–10 minutes, until the cookies puff and crackle and the edges become a dark golden brown. (Bake the cookies a minute less if you like chewier cookies, or a minute more if you like the snappier variety.) Cool them on the trays, where the cookies will collapse in height a bit.

5. Dip a cookie, face-down, into the bowl of frosted glaze. Allow some of the glaze to drip off before putting the cookie, frosted side up, back on the baking tray. Repeat until all the cookies are frosted. Let them sit, uncovered, for 1 hour, to allow the frosting to harden. In an airtight container at room temperature, the cookies will keep fresh for up to 1 week.

Frosted Glaze

Makes enough for 1 batch of Frosted Gingersnaps

½ cup confectioners' sugar
2 tablespoons milk

Because kitchen humidities differ, when you're making the glaze, add more confectioners' sugar (1 tablespoon at a time) to thicken it, or a very, very small splash of milk to thin it out.

- -

In a small bowl, using a dinner spoon, stir together the confectioners' sugar and milk, mixing until they're smooth, about 1 minute. You want a runny (not thick) consistency. Use it immediately, or store it in an airtight container in the fridge for up to 1 week.

BAKING FOR
BREAKFAST

- -

Cinnamon Toast Cereal	106
Silver Dollar Pancakes	109
Brown Butter Chocolate Chip Muffins	110
Crepes	113
Old-Fashioned Donuts	114
Cinnamon Buns with Brown Sugar Goo	117
Quiche	120
Biscuits	124
Bagels	127
English Muffins	130
Croissants	133

@carpedolce

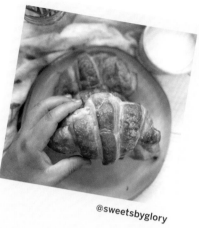

@sweetsbyglory

@rachies.bak

#bakeclub

@rachies.bakes

@missjiahebakes

Poppy Seed

Jalapeno Bacon Cheddar

Asiago Parmesan

@azcookielove

@cpg1203

#bakecl

By definition, dessert is an opt-in course, which has the side effect of making desserts inherently joyful. But joy doesn't have to stop there. I like to test the boundaries of just how joyful the more "mandatory" meals can be as well. The so-called most important meal of the day, breakfast can be every bit as fun and playful and delicious as dessert, when you apply the same rules, bringing into it your POV, your: YOU.

To me breakfast is a state of mind. It can be at 1:00 p.m. on a Sunday, while I'm nursing my cold cup of coffee and trying to read the paper between feeding bites of crepe to my littlest one. Or Tuesday night, when I pull out a stack of English muffins to serve as cheeseburger buns. Or Friday night, when donuts make an appearance as the perfect movie-time snack. Or Breakfast for Dinner (or Brupper—breakfast-supper—as my mom, Greta, calls it) any day of the week.

I'm of the opinion that the different traditional meal classifications—breakfast and lunch and dinner—are simply a rough draft. They're just occasions we create to keep our blood sugar above board, and any food group is allowed. Sweet riffs like cereal or muffins or cinnamon buns or donuts let us feel like we're blurring the lines of the food pyramid, and living life on our own terms. When I unleashed my baking curiosity on the more square-meal-related staples in my life, I unearthed them as a jumping-off point for individuality—and for fun. Tell me quiche is stuffy, I dare you. There are no rules when it comes to mealtime. Try it on for size. It keeps the spirit alive, the who'd'a would'a should'a could'a at bay.

#bakeclub

@ whitneyjweiss

CINNAMON TOAST CEREAL

Makes 4 cups

We have entered into the next dimension: the one where you make your favorite breakfast cereal at home, from scratch. A cereal obsessive, I had a ton of time on my hands in the early mornings the years between the pandemic and motherhood. I made cornflakes *and* sugary cornflakes *and* sugary corny cereal *and* crispy rice cereal *and* sweet graham cracker cereal. But of all my loves, this was my favorite—perhaps because it also makes a killer cereal Marshmallow Cookie (page 81), cereal marshmallow Skillet Cookie (page 258), on-the-fly pie crust to fill with ice cream, or epic late-night munchie.

- -

⇨ Whole-wheat flour gives you the true cereal look and taste. You can make this recipe with all-purpose flour, but the vis and flavor will be a bit more shallow. Plus, whole-wheat flour is the secret weapon to Graham Crackers, too (page 37). Read up on flours on page 4.

⇨ You can mix this dough by hand, but I find the power and intensity of the stand-mixer paddle help bring it together more uniformly, and therefore with greater quality.

- -

For the Cinnamon Sugar

2 tablespoons sugar
1/4 teaspoon cinnamon

For the Cereal

6 tablespoons unsalted butter, super soft
1/3 cup sugar
1/3 cup confectioners' sugar

2 tablespoons milk

3/4 cup flour
1/2 cup whole-wheat flour
1 teaspoon cinnamon
1/4 teaspoon kosher salt

2 tablespoons unsalted butter, melted

1. **Make the cinnamon sugar:** In a small bowl, toss together the sugar and cinnamon. Set this aside.

2. **Make the cereal:** In the bowl of a stand mixer fitted with the paddle attachment, combine the butter and sugars on medium speed until they are fully combined, about 1 minute. Add the milk, and mix on low speed until it is combined, about 1 minute. Measure the flours, cinnamon, and salt into the bowl and, on low speed, mix until everything is just combined, about 1 minute, scraping down the sides of the mixing bowl as needed in between additions.

3. With a rolling pin on the counter, flatten the dough between two pieces of parchment the size of your baking sheet. Roll the dough to 1/4-inch thickness, as you would a wafer or a cutout cookie. The dough will cover nearly the entire surface.

4. Peel back the top sheet of paper, and carefully, using a chef's knife, bench scraper, or pizza roller, cut the dough into as many 1/2-inch squares as possible. Transfer the parchment with all the dough (squares and scraps alike) to a half sheet pan. Refrigerate or freeze the entire sheet of dough until it's firm, about 5 minutes.

5. Heat the oven to 325°F. Brush the surface of this thin dough with the 2 tablespoons melted butter; then evenly sprinkle the cinnamon sugar over the top.

6. Carefully, transfer the half sheet pan of cinnamon-sugar-dusted dough, scraps and all, to the oven, and bake at 325°F for 18–20 minutes, until the entire surface of the cereal is golden brown and some edges are a tad toasty. Remove the hot sheet pan from the oven to a safe place to cool, and while the cereal is still very warm, use the chef's knife, bench scraper, or pizza roller to retrace the lines of the cereal squares, to ensure clean lines and easy release.

7. Cool the cereal completely on the sheet pan. (I snack on the baked scrap pieces!) In an airtight container at room temperature, the cereal will keep fresh for 2 weeks.

SILVER DOLLAR PANCAKES

Makes 18

Nothing against the traditional pancake stack, but I prefer a silver dollar tower. Better butter-to-syrup ratio. And you don't have to do so much knife-and-forking for yourself or any nearby toddlers. This recipe brings in milk powder (page 5) and a drop of vanilla extract to turn the dial up on the pancake base. And, no surprise, the pancakes are just the starting-off point for glam— take your butter game (page 16) out for a spin, or sprinkle a little cinnamon sugar (page 106) into the pan before adding your batter, to give it a crackly, caramelized snickerdoodle exterior.

- -

1 cup flour

¹/₄ cup sugar

2 tablespoons milk powder

1 tablespoon + 1 teaspoon
   baking powder

¹/₂ teaspoon kosher salt

²/₃ cup milk

1 egg

3 tablespoons unsalted
   butter, melted

1 teaspoon vanilla extract

1. In a medium bowl, whisk together the flour, sugar, milk powder, baking powder, and salt to combine them evenly. Whisk in the milk, egg, butter, and vanilla, and stir until the batter is smooth, about 1 minute.

2. Pan-spray a heavy-bottomed medium-sized griddle or nonstick pan, and warm it over medium heat. Pour or scoop 1 tablespoon pancake batter into the pan. Cook until the pancake batter has set on the bottom and bubbles appear on the top, about 1 minute. Flip it carefully with a spatula, and cook the other side until it's golden brown, about 1 minute more. Move the pancake to a plate and repeat, making as many silver dollars as will fit in the pan at a time, allowing 2–3 inches between each, spraying the pan between the rounds. Remember, the first pancake never works; consider it a christening of the pan—and the universe's snack gift to you. The second pancake will make you proud.

3. Remove the mini-pancakes from the pan with a heat-safe spatula, and serve them in an adorable stack. Dress them with butter, syrup, jam, whatever you please; just promise to serve them warm.

BROWN BUTTER CHOCOLATE CHIP MUFFINS

Makes 6

A good muffin is a real a.m.-to-p.m. power player. Muffins can be a meal on the go or a little something sweet on the side—and as with a killer cookie or brownie, everyone needs a great muffin recipe in their back pocket to call on when the time comes. This recipe toes the "undercover dessert" line, bringing in the classic cookie move of browning your butter and folding in creamy chocolate chips, to make it my ideal handheld meal.

⇨ If you want to forgo the brown butter because it doesn't fit your flavor story, omit it altogether and add a total of ¹/₂ cup vegetable oil.

⇨ Fun fact: Muffins and pound cakes bake best on Day 2, once the batter is fully relaxed and hydrated. If you're in a hurry, you can bake immediately after mixing, but your muffins will be a bit more dense and tense.

1 egg
²/₃ cup dark brown sugar
¹/₄ cup sugar
²/₃ cup milk
2 teaspoons vanilla extract

¹/₄ cup vegetable oil

1¹/₃ cups flour
2¹/₂ teaspoons baking
   powder
³/₄ teaspoon kosher salt

1 stick (8 tablespoons)
   unsalted butter, browned
   (see box)
²/₃ cup chocolate chips

1. Pan-spray a muffin pan or fill it with muffin liners.

2. In a large bowl, whisk together the egg, sugars, milk, and vanilla until they're well combined; then whisk in the oil, and mix until it's glossy and everything is well combined, about 1 minute total.

3. Measure the flour, baking powder, and salt into the mixing bowl. Toss together only the dry ingredients on top with the whisk first, before truly stirring them into the wet ingredients below. Mix until everything is just combined. Stir in the brown butter and chocolate chips.

4. Using a measuring cup or ice cream scoop, spoon ¹/₃ cup of batter into each muffin cup or liner. The batter should reach just under the lip of the cup or liner (but shouldn't go over!). Cover the muffin pan with plastic wrap, and refrigerate it overnight.

5. Heat the oven to 375°F, and remove the muffin batter from the fridge.

6. Bake for 18–20 minutes, until the muffin tops pouf and brown slightly and a toothpick, when inserted, comes out clean. Let the muffins cool slightly before digging in. In an airtight container on the counter, the muffins will keep fresh for 5 days.

- DO YOU -
BAKE CLUB

Sub other fats and mix-ins in: 1 cup fresh blueberries plus ½ cup white chocolate chips, 1 cup butterscotch chips plus 1 tablespoon cinnamon and on!

Brown Butter Is a Way of Life

At home, browning butter is a snap; here is my foolproof method.

In a large heavy-bottomed saucepan over medium-high heat, melt 1 stick of butter. Turn down the heat to medium-low, and keep an eye on the butter until it reaches a deep brown color and gives off a nutty aroma, about 5 minutes. Don't hesitate—this is no time to be bashful! Color equals flavor, so let that butter go until you see truly brown bits on the bottom of the pan. Once you've got them, transfer the butter to a heatproof bowl and stir to distribute the caramelized milk solids (the brown bits!) evenly. Cool it completely (the remaining fat will solidify, like leftover bacon grease does) before using it in a recipe. Store it in an airtight container in the fridge for up to 1 month.

Use brown butter in place of some or all the butter in any recipe where you think its depth of nuttiness will do you right.

- DO YOU -
BAKE CLUB

In a pinch (out of flour and sugar and eggs) fun fact: you can make crepes with pancake mix! Use 1 cup pancake mix, 1½ cups milk, ½ teaspoon salt. A splash of vanilla extract if you're making sweet crepes. Same procedure, same yield, same party.

You can totally get on the crepe cake trend by layering 2 tablespoons of (Any) Fruit Curd (page 55) between the crepes as you stack them up high to the sky!

My ideal spread of sweet fillings: apple slices with cinnamon sugar, Nutella with strawberries or bananas, raspberries with flavored Whipped Cream (page 24), blueberries with Greek yogurt and honey, all the jams/jellies on the fridge door, cream cheese, guava paste, Sugar in the Raw, Caramel Sauce (page 21), Fudge Sauce (page 22), Marshmallow (my nieces go crazy for this one; page 47).

My ideal spread of savory fillings: sunny-side-up eggs, sautéed mushrooms, any roasted vegetable really, any cooked protein for that matter, Swiss cheese, dressed salad greens. But I'll go crazy with any savory leftover (saag paneer, pad thai, and beef and broccoli will rock your world, too!).

In my overall estimation, there is NO limit to what a crepe filling can be.

CREPES

Makes 8

Though I have never been big on the brunch thing, I do love to man (woman?) the kitchen for a morning meal with friends and family. Whether it's after an epic sleepover or on a sleepy Sunday with Frankie and Sonny, I get my crepe batter ready, heat up my pan, pull out a buffet of sweet and/or savory fillings from the fridge and pantry, and let the diners pick their own fillings. Bonus points if you pull out a beret as your headgear, or at minimum draw a curly mustache on your upper lip.

- -

⇨ Going for specifically savory crepes? Reduce the sugar to 1 teaspoon and remove the vanilla outright.

- -

2 eggs
1 cup milk
$1/3$ cup sugar
$1/2$ teaspoon vanilla

1 cup flour (all-purpose, whole-wheat, buckwheat will all work)
1 teaspoon kosher salt

Unsalted butter, super soft, for the pan

1. In a blender, on low speed with the lid on, combine the eggs, milk, sugar, and vanilla until the mixture is smooth, about 15 seconds. Measure in the flour and salt, and blend on low speed with the lid on until everything is smooth, another 15 seconds. Transfer the batter to a medium bowl, and set it aside to hydrate and rest for 20 minutes. Meanwhile, get your act together and pull out crepe fillings, plates, silver, napkins, make a fresh batch of coffee, etc.

2. Heat a heavy-bottomed medium-sized nonstick pan over medium-high heat, then add a tiny pat of butter. The pan should be hot enough that the butter melts and sizzles immediately. If this doesn't happen, keep heating the pan and try again.

3. Ladle about $1/4$ cup crepe batter into the buttered pan, and flick your wrist to swirl the batter, evenly coating the bottom. This is a learned technique, and it may take you one or two crepes to get the hang of it. Consider them your snack. Cook the crepe until it bubbles and the edges are dry and golden brown, 1–2 minutes. Flip it, and let the other side of the crepe kiss the pan and caramelize, about 30 seconds. Transfer the crepe to a plate (I use my fingertips for this—I have never found a tool that works for crepes!). Repeat with the remaining crepe batter.

4. To fill each crepe, arrange your fixings across the center, then roll or fold the crepe up, and serve! If you have any leftover crepes, adorn them with fixings that will freeze well, roll or fold them up, wrap them individually in plastic or store them in individual baggies, and freeze them fully assembled. They make a pretty solid breakfast on the go if you microwave them in 30-second bursts until they're warm, right before you plan to crush them.

OLD-FASHIONED DONUTS

Makes 4

If you ask me, donuts are just about the best creation—fluffy and sweet, and an acceptable way to basically have cake for breakfast. There's a donut for every mood: classic glazed for when you are feeling minimal; sprinkle-covered for when life needs some excitement; frosting-filled (my teenage self's Dunkin' Donuts go-to for race day); apple-cinnamon flavored for those crisp fall days. Donuts make the world go round.

⇨ Swap the vegetable oil out for shortening to achieve maximum exterior donut texture. It's a move, trust me.

4 cups vegetable oil

¹/₃ cup sugar
2 tablespoons vegetable oil
1 egg

¹/₄ cup milk
2 tablespoons heavy cream
2 teaspoons apple cider
   vinegar
1 teaspoon vanilla extract

1¹/₄ cups flour + more for
   dusting
³/₄ teaspoon baking powder
¹/₂ teaspoon kosher salt
¹/₂ teaspoon cinnamon
¹/₈ teaspoon baking soda

Confectioners' sugar
   and/or cinnamon sugar
   (page 106) and a paper
   bag, for dusting/coating

1. In a heavy-bottomed medium-sized pot, bring 4 cups of the oil to 325°F over medium heat. This will take about 10 minutes.

2. In the meantime, in a medium bowl, whisk together the sugar, remaining 2 tablespoons of oil, and the egg until combined, about 30 seconds. Whisk in the milk, heavy cream, vinegar, and vanilla until everything is combined.

3. Measure the flour, baking powder, salt, cinnamon, and baking soda into the mixing bowl. Toss together only the dry ingredients on top with the whisk first, before truly stirring them into the wet ingredients below—you can ditch the whisk for a sturdy spatula. Mix until everything is just combined, but still sticky.

4. Plop the dough out onto a lightly floured work surface. Flour your hands and bring the dough together, patting the surface and sides with the palms of your hands to press the dough into roughly a 4-inch square, about ³/₄ inch thick.

5. Using cutters or larger- and smaller-sized cups, cut out donut rounds with 3¹/₂-inch diameters and a ³/₄-inch diameter center. You should have four donuts and four donut holes. (If you have extra dough left after cutting out, stick it all together, press it out, and repeat the process until you have used up all of the dough.)

6. Gently drop one donut hole into the hot oil to do a temperature check. It should sizzle immediately, float, and become golden brown within 1–2 minutes. If it sinks, or doesn't sizzle at all, the oil is not hot enough, so wait a few more minutes or turn up the heat a bit. If the donut hole fries too quickly and browns immediately (leaving the batter raw inside), pour some room-temperature oil into the pot to cool the overall temperature down, and turn down the heat. Fry another donut hole until you reach the sizzle/float/golden-brown sweet-spot target, in 1–2 minutes. (Remove all these donut holes from the oil, obvi.) Then fry a full donut round, gently placing the donut into the oil facing away from you, so as not to splash up on you. It

- DO YOU -
BAKE CLUB

Add pumpkin spice to the sugar in your brown paper bag for pumpkin-spice donuts.

Heck, tap into the Glaze (page 34) and make a lemon-glaze donut, a strawberry-glaze donut—you get it, keep going!

should sink, then float within 10 "Mississippi"s, and sizzle and become golden brown within 3 minutes. Flip it, and fry the other side until it's golden brown, 2–3 minutes.

7. Gently remove the donut from the oil, transfer it to a paper-towel-lined baking tray, sprinkle both sides immediately with confectioners' sugar, or toss it in a brown paper bag with cinnamon sugar, and eat. Don't you dare try to save a donut for later. Eat it! Now!

CINNAMON BUNS
with BROWN SUGAR GOO

Makes 12

If you know anything about me, you know I bake cinnamon buns twice a year: the morning of Thanksgiving and the morning of Christmas. See, I grew up taking in the marvelous smell that is a warm cinnamon bun only at the local mall or airport terminal. So, as an adult, I became obsessed with figuring out how to make the greatest cinnamon bun from scratch. But only for special occasions, because if I made them all the time, I'd neither leave the house nor get anything done. Consider yourself forewarned.

- -

⇨ Read more on yeast, gluten development, and the wonder that is yeast-risen baked goods on page 119.

⇨ If I am being honest, there's no way I'm waking up at 5:00 a.m. to start baking, unless it's because I'm on the opening shift at Milk Bar. I make this recipe through Step 8 the night before I want to serve it, then wrap the dough-filled baking dish in plastic and refrigerate it overnight to slow the growth of the yeast in the rising process. I wake up and pull the buns out to come to room temperature as I make my cup of coffee, and continue rising for 2–3 hours, then proceed with Step 9.

⇨ Ditch the spatula and by-hand approach and use a stand mixer fitted with the dough-hook attachment if you like.

⇨ If your brown-sugar goo is too loose, pop it into the fridge or freezer. The butter will firm up in a cooler environment, making it easier to spread without running. Alternatively, if it is too firm, pop it into the microwave for 10-second bursts until it loosens up to a spreadable state.

- -

Bun Dough

1 packet (2¼ teaspoons)
   active dry yeast
1 cup milk, warmed
1 tablespoon warm water

4½ cups flour + more for
   dusting
½ cup sugar
1 teaspoon kosher salt

1 egg
1 egg yolk
1 stick (8 tablespoons)
   unsalted butter, melted

Vegetable oil, for greasing

Brown Sugar Goo

1 cup light brown sugar
6 tablespoons butter,
   melted
2½ tablespoons cinnamon
½ teaspoon kosher salt

Cream Cheese Frosting

3 ounces cream cheese,
   softened
½ stick (4 tablespoons)
   unsalted butter, softened
½ teaspoon vanilla extract

1½ cups confectioners'
   sugar
⅛ teaspoon kosher salt

- DO YOU -
BAKE CLUB

Anna McGorman, VP of Culinary at Milk Bar, swaps the brown-sugar goo for sweetened condensed milk, coconut flakes, and chocolate chips, and ignores the cream cheese frosting altogether for an almost German-chocolate swirl effect. Pretty brilliant, if you ask me.

1. **Start by making the buns:** In a large bowl, whisk together the yeast, warm milk, and warm water until the yeast is dissolved and foamy, about 1 minute. Let it sit as is for another 5 minutes to continue foaming and growing, until it's ready to do its work.

2. Ditch the whisk and grab a sturdy spatula. Measure the flour, sugar, and salt into the bowl. Toss together only the dry ingredients on top with the spatula first, before truly stirring them into the wet ingredients below. This will result in a dry, shaggy mixture. Add the egg, egg yolk, and melted butter, and mix until the dough comes together as a thick, almost sticky mass. This should take 2–3 minutes.

3. Ditch the spatula this time, after scraping any doughy remains into the bowl, and roll up your sleeves to start kneading. Kneading dough is simple: push it away from you with the heel of your hand, then use your fingers to fold it over itself and pull it back. Either in the bowl or on a clean kitchen counter, knead the dough for 5–6 minutes to fully develop the gluten; your dough will become a smooth, round mass.

4. Grease a fresh large bowl, toss the dough in that fat, and leave it seam side down. Cover it with a dry towel, and place the bowl in a draft-free spot (I like the microwave or a turned-off oven) to rise for an hour, until it's doubled in size.

5. **While the dough is rising, make the brown-sugar goo:** In a small mixing bowl, with a sturdy spatula, stir together the brown sugar, butter, cinnamon, and salt until they are fully combined, about 1 minute. Cover the mixture with plastic or a dry towel and set it aside, at room temp.

6. Grab the proofed dough, punch it down, and knock it out onto a clean, floured counter. Using a rolling pin, roll it into a 16-inch square, flouring the surface of the dough and the rolling pin as and if needed.

7. Spread the cinnamon goo evenly over the surface of the dough square, being more sparse on the edges to the right, left, and farthest from you, since the goo will spread a little. Roll the dough away from you and up into a big, tight tube.

8. Using a sharp knife, slice the tube into twelve rounds, each about 1⅓ inches thick. Arrange the rounds, swirl side up, in a greased 9-by-13-inch baking dish, leaving 1 inch between them. Cover the dish, and place it back in that same secret spot, letting the buns rise for another 1–2 hours, until they've doubled in size.

9. Heat the oven to 375°F, and bake the buns for 20 minutes, or until they are just starting to brown on the edges.

10. **Meanwhile, make the cream cheese frosting:** In a large bowl, with a sturdy spatula, mix together the cream cheese, butter, and vanilla until they are smooth and fully combined, about 2 minutes. The cream cheese will clump if it's too cold or you rush this first step, so be purposeful and patient! Add the confectioners' sugar and salt, and mix, flexing your muscles for 2–3 minutes, until the frosting is a smooth, pale white and incredibly fluffy. Set it aside.

11. Remove the buns from the oven, and let them cool for 10 minutes in the pan. While they are still warm (but not piping hot), spread the frosting generously over them. Serve them immediately. If for some reason there are any left over, the buns will keep fresh in an airtight container in the fridge for 1 week. I highly recommend reheating individual buns, either in the microwave in 30-second spurts or in a 300°F oven for 5–10 minutes, before serving anew.

Wake Up, Yeast!

Active dry yeast must be "woken up" in order to do its work in any recipe. We do this with a foolproof approach, by whisking it together with warm water, milk, or both to foam and dissolve completely. A bit like Goldilocks: if the water isn't tepid enough, it won't wake up the yeast, and if it's too hot, it will kill it. Because I don't have a thermometer for my home kitchen, I'm betting you don't, either. I liken the ideal temperature to what you'd use to bathe a newborn baby—warm enough to sense by touch, but not so much that it's unbearable.

Once yeast is awake, it needs to be fed. Which is why we mix it with flour and other ingredients, pretty shortly thereafter.

Once yeast is fed, it needs to be worked or kneaded for a total of 7 minutes to fully achieve its worth—GLUTEN—the bouncy, stringy, chewy best part of bread.

Troubleshooting: Every kitchen has a different humidity level. As such, if your dough is too wet and sticky, add 2 tablespoons of flour and continue kneading. Repeat as needed. If your dough is too dry and dense, add 2 tablespoons of water. Repeat as needed.

Once fully woken up, fed, and kneaded, it needs an hour to relax, grow, and develop its structure and flavor. This happens in a dark, warm place. Once it's formed into the mold or shape intended, we let the dough relax, grow, and develop one last time before baking.

Deep golden brown is always the ideal visual cue for baking bread, but when baking loaves, you should be able to knock on the toasty exterior and hear a hollow center. If you're ever uncertain, much the same as with cake, a toothpick or skewer inserted into the center should come out clean; that cues she's baked all the way through.

And after all of that, make sure to cool your baked good all the way through before enjoying it. Slicing and eating a loaf before it's fully cooled will lead to a sad and gummy experience that you can't recover from.

Essentially, patience and care are key when you're going to bread town.

QUICHE

Makes 1

It's hard to put into words what makes a quiche so, so tasty, and fun to put together. It really should be a superstar item, yet it's so highly underrated and underproduced! Did I mention the plethora of options?! Quiche can hold its own with anything you bring to it. Add some mushrooms, maybe some sausage (breakfast, or sweet or spicy). Or spinach! Maybe even Ricotta (page 56) if you're feeling it.

⇨ You can absolutely make the pie crust by hand in a large mixing bowl, or even in a stand mixer. It's really a "different strokes for different folks" kind of thing. I find that, if it's your first quiche, the food processor, though kind of a pain to pull out, actually sets you up for greatest ease and guarantees a nice, tender crust without overmixing.

For the Pie Crust

1½ cups flour + more for
   dusting
2 tablespoons sugar
¾ teaspoon kosher salt

1 stick (8 tablespoons)
   unsalted butter, cold, cut
   into ¼-inch cubes

1½ tablespoons cold water

For the Quiche Filling

6 eggs
½ cup whole milk
¼ cup sour cream
2 teaspoons kosher salt
½ teaspoon black pepper

1. **Make the pie crust:** In a food processor with the blade attachment, pulse the flour, sugar, and salt together to combine them. Add all of the cold, cubed butter, and pulse until the mixture is consistently sandy in texture and color, approximately fifteen pulses. Add in the cold water, and pulse for five blitzes or so, just until the dough comes together, yet is still a tad sandy in areas.

2. Knock the sandy dough bits out onto a sheet of plastic wrap, and seal the edges to enclose it. Use the palm of your hand to tap the sandy dough pieces together. The plastic wrap keeps your hands and the counter from getting dirty and keeps the dough in one place! It also ensures that you don't overmix the dough as it comes together. Continue tapping until you have one dense, consistent, pale yellow mass. Tap the dough down and out as far and wide as you can, to allow it to chill quickly and evenly and minimize how much work you have to do with a rolling pin when the time comes. Refrigerate the dough for 30 minutes.

3. Heat the oven to 375°F, and pan-spray a 10-inch pie dish.

4. **Make the filling:** In a large bowl, whisk together the eggs, milk, sour cream, salt, and pepper, and continue stirring until the egg yolks and whites have both broken down and all the ingredients are well combined, about 2 minutes. Stir in any other items you please (cheeses! veggies! meats!) and set the filling aside.

(···)

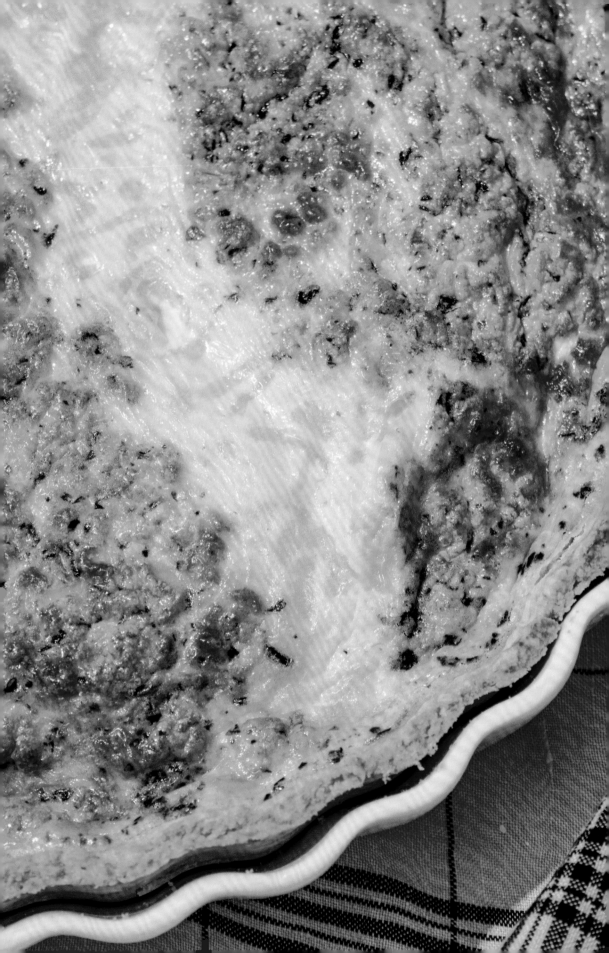

5. Unwrap the pie dough on a floured surface, lightly flour the top, and begin rolling the dough out to make a 12-inch circle (about 2 inches bigger around than the face of your pie dish), $\frac{1}{2}$ inch thick. Turn the dough clockwise after every roll to ensure it does not stick to the countertop. Continue dusting it lightly with flour as needed if at any point the dough begins to stick. Work quickly—you want to keep your dough as cold as possible.

6. Fold the round in half, drape it into the greased pie dish, and unfold it, allowing the edges to hang over the side. Use the palm of your hand and fingertips to ensure that the dough is flush with the inner contours of the dish. With a clean pair of scissors or a sharp paring knife, trim any dough along the pie dish that drapes just below the outer edge (this should be minimal). Crimp the edges of the pie crust with your thumb and forefinger.

7. Pour the filling into the crust, and bake at 375°F for 30–45 minutes, until the edges of the pie crust have become a confident golden brown, the quiche top has begun to puff and caramelize, and the bull's-eye eggy center is just set. Keep a close watch! For a more caramelized top, broil your quiche for a minute or two at the very end of this baking process. Cool for 5–10 minutes before slicing and serving. In an airtight container in the fridge, the quiche will keep fresh for 5 days. I highly recommend reheating individual slices in a 300°F oven for 5–10 minutes before serving anew.

#bakeclub

- DO YOU -
BAKE CLUB

I love to make a little something I call "kitchen sink quiche" when I know I'll have a crowd to feed and I need to clean out my fridge. No two kitchen sink quiches are the same, and really anything will do, but my go-to is:

- $\frac{1}{2}$ pound sliced sandwich meat, griddled
- 1 cup shredded cheese
- $\frac{1}{2}$ cup whatever veggies you have in the fridge (caramelized onions! mushrooms . . . !)

The more filling you add, the taller your quiche will be. The less filling, the shorter.

BISCUITS

Makes 4

Yes, biscuits are incredible on the side of a plate of good barbecue or next to your Thanksgiving turkey. But don't undersell their ability to be the star attraction: sliced and loaded up with eggs and veggies as a breakfast icon, or slathered with gravy for a brunch heavy hitter, or dolloped on a pan of chicken for a pot-pie-style dinner. Biscuits have serious main-character energy, are incredibly easy to whip up, and don't require yeast, so they are a shortcut to getting some breakfast bread into your life if you are short on time.

- -

⇨ You can make your biscuits the way you would pie dough in the food processor (page 120), but I find I always end up overmixing my biscuits, leaving them tasty but a tad less tender. You do YOU.

- -

1½ cups flour + extra for
   dusting
1½ teaspoons baking
   powder
½ teaspoon baking soda
½ teaspoon kosher salt

6 tablespoons unsalted
   butter, cold, cut into
   ¼-inch cubes

⅔ cup heavy cream

1. Heat the oven to 425°F, and pan-spray a half sheet pan.

2. In a large mixing bowl, whisk together the flour, baking powder, baking soda, and salt to combine them.

3. Add the butter to the dry ingredients, and pinch the mixture together with your fingers, working until you no longer see chunks of butter, about 2 minutes. Add the cream in two additions. Mix the dough gently with your hands to start. Once the cream is incorporated, start pressing and squeezing with your hands, just to bind the dough together, being careful not to overmix or overwork (which will give you a more dense and bready, less tender and flaky outcome).

4. Dust a clean, dry section of your countertop with flour. Form your dough into a 4-by-4-inch square, about ½ inch thick. Use a butter knife to cut out four 2-inch squares.

5. Place the biscuits on the sheet pan, and transfer it to the refrigerator to chill for 30 minutes.

6. Bake at 425°F for 15 minutes, until the biscuits are golden brown on the top crust and at the edges. These are absolutely best served fresh and warm out of the oven, but in an airtight container on the counter, they will keep fresh for 3 days.

- DO YOU -
BAKE CLUB

Rock a cheddar-chive biscuit by adding in ¼ cup shredded cheddar cheese and 1 tablespoon finely chopped fresh chives or green onions at Step 3.

BAGELS

Makes 6

Ever had a freshly boiled and baked bagel? I definitely hadn't until I moved to Brooklyn. Eeeeaaaayyyyh. Seriously, though, this idea of boiling and then baking something—pretty brilliant tactically. A fresh bagel is one of the most swoon-worthy items that my industry produces, and I love that we've really carved out a breakfast-bagel schmear moment, a lunch bagel sammy excuse, and the, always on in my house, dinner-bagel pizza move.

⇨ Read more on yeast, gluten development, and the wonder that is yeast-risen baked goods on page 119.

⇨ Ditch the spatula and by-hand approach and use a stand mixer fitted with the dough-hook attachment if you like.

⇨ If you're out of molasses, sub in light or dark brown sugar in its place.

⇨ You can make this recipe through Step 4, then wrap the bagel rounds on a fresh greased sheet pan in plastic and refrigerate overnight to slow the growth of the yeast in the rising process. I wake up, pull out the bagels, and let them come to room temperature and continue rising for 2–3 hours, then proceed with Step 5 on. It doesn't make a better or worse bagel, IMHO, just a time-management thing if you choose.

For the Dough

1 packet (2¼ teaspoons)
 active dry yeast
1 cup warm water
1 tablespoon molasses

2⅔ cups all-purpose flour
 + more for dusting
2 teaspoons kosher salt

Vegetable oil, for greasing

For the Cooking Water

4 quarts water
¼ cup sugar
1 tablespoon baking soda

For the Topping

Your ideal seasonings (salt!
 poppy seeds! everything!)

1. **Make the dough:** In a large bowl, whisk together the yeast, warm water, and molasses until the yeast is dissolved and foamy, about 1 minute. Let it sit as is for another 5 minutes to continue foaming and growing, until it's ready to do its work.

2. Ditch the whisk and grab a sturdy spatula. Measure the flour and salt into the bowl. Toss together only the dry ingredients on top with the spatula first, before truly stirring them into the wet ingredients below. This will result in a dry, shaggy mixture at first, but as you knead—pushing the dough away from you with the heel of your hand, folding it over itself with your fingers, and pulling it back—the dough will form a nice smooth ball. Knead this ball for a total of 7 minutes, to ensure you develop the chewy strands of gluten we know and love so well.

3. Grease a fresh large bowl, toss the dough in the fat, and leave it seam side down. Cover the bowl with a dry towel and place it in a draft-free spot (I like the microwave or a turned-off oven) to rise for an hour, until it's doubled in size.

(...)

4. Grab the proofed dough, knock it out onto a clean, floured counter, and divide it into six equal pieces. Roll each into a long rope 8–10 inches long, then bring the ends together to form a bagel shape—rolling the dough so there is no visible seam. Cover the bagel rounds with the same dry towel on the countertop, and let them rest for 30 minutes.

5. **Heat the oven to 450°F, and make the cooking water:** In a heavy-bottomed large pot, bring the 4 quarts of water, sugar, and baking soda to a boil. Gently drop the bagels into the water (I do mine one at a time), and boil for 20 seconds on each side, using a slotted spoon or large fork to flip them. Remove each boiled bagel round from the water, and transfer them to a baking rack sitting on top of a half sheet pan. Fill the bottom of the sheet pan with about 1/2 inch of water.

6. **Make the topping:** Top the boiled bagel rounds with the seasonings of your choice. My advice is to be recklessly generous; they always taste better that way.

7. Bake for at 450°F for 10 minutes to get a mondo crust and great caramelized toast on the seasonings and outer bagel shell, then lower the oven temperature to 350°F and bake for another 15 minutes, to bake out any gumminess inside.

8. Cool the bagels on the same racked sheet pan for 15 minutes before digging in! In an airtight container on the counter, the bagels will keep fresh for 5 days, and will freeze marvelously, stored the same way, for up to a month.

- DO YOU -
BAKE CLUB

@missjihaebakes riffs with a jalapeño-cheddar topping, a black-sesame topping, and an oatmeal topping; @azcookielove gets down with pepperoni and mozzarella or Asiago and Parmesan as toppings; @lsctrojan rocks a za'atar-and-shallot topping, a black truffle salt topping, and a fennel, shallot, and dill topping. Y'all are crushing.

@azcookielove

ENGLISH MUFFINS

Makes 12

1 packet (2¼ teaspoons)
active dry yeast
⅔ cup milk, warmed
2 tablespoons warm water

1 teaspoon apple cider
vinegar

2 cups flour + more for
dusting
2 tablespoons sugar
2 teaspoons kosher salt

3 tablespoons unsalted
butter, super soft

Vegetable oil, for greasing
Cornmeal, for dusting

Though I grew up toasting English muffins from the package, my relationship with their nooks and crannies really escalated during my time working under Chef Wylie Dufresne at the revolutionary restaurant wd~50. Wylie was a master of many things, paving the way for modern molecular gastronomy, and I was lucky enough to have him as my sounding board for recipe development. He loved to eat burgers on English muffins, and I desperately wanted to prove to him I could master this seemingly tricky baked good. He would taste batch after batch and ask questions to push me forward. Ultimately, I landed on this recipe—and a lifelong partner in deliciousness with Wylie.

⇨ Read more on yeast, gluten development, and the wonder that is yeast-risen baked goods on page 119.

⇨ I make this recipe through Step 4, then wrap the dough-filled baking dish in plastic and refrigerate it overnight to slow the growth of the yeast in the rising process. The muffins get more tunnel-y and fragrant if you choose this adventure, and get even better after being refrigerated for 2 days. In the morning, pull the muffins out and let them come to room temperature and rise for 2–3 hours, then proceed with Step 5.

⇨ Ditch the spatula and by-hand approach and use a stand mixer fitted with the dough hook attachment if you like.

1. In a large bowl, whisk together the yeast, warm milk, and warm water until the yeast is dissolved and foamy, about 1 minute. Let it sit as is for another 5 minutes to continue foaming and growing, until it's ready to do its work.

2. Ditch the whisk and grab a sturdy spatula. Stir in the vinegar, and mix to combine it. Then measure the flour, sugar, and salt into the bowl. Toss together only the dry ingredients on top with the spatula first, before truly stirring them into the wet ingredients below. This will result in a dry, shaggy mixture. Stir in the butter with the spatula until you can form the dough into a ball shape.

3. Ditch the spatula, and roll up your sleeves to start kneading by hand in the mixing bowl. Kneading dough is simple: push it away from you with the heel of your hand, then use your fingers to fold it over itself and pull it back. Knead the dough for 7 minutes to fully develop the gluten; your dough will become a smooth, round mass.

4. Grease a fresh large bowl, and transfer the dough ball to it. Toss the dough in the fat, and leave it seam side down. Cover the bowl with a dry towel and place it in a draft-free spot (I like

the microwave or a turned-off oven) to rise for an hour, until it's doubled in size. Transfer the bowl, still covered, to the fridge, and chill for 30 minutes (this makes the dough easier to handle). While you're waiting, line an ungreased half sheet pan with a thin layer of cornmeal.

5. Grab the proofed, chilled dough, knock it out onto a clean, floured counter, and separate the dough into twelve even pieces. With lightly floured hands, shape the dough pieces into rounds, seam down. As you shape them, transfer the balls to the cornmeal-lined baking sheet, ensuring that the bottoms of the dough balls pick up some of the cornmeal; then flip them, to ensure that the tops pick up some cornmeal, too, but leave the center ring of dough without cornmeal. Cover the dough balls with a towel, and let them rest for 30 minutes.

6. Heat the oven to 250°F. Warm a cast-iron skillet or griddle over the lowest heat possible for 3 minutes. Scatter the pan with a thin, even layer of cornmeal.

7. Grab the proofed, cornmealed muffins one by one, and transfer them to the warm pan, working in batches. Slowly. You almost can't take enough time searing the bottom of the muffins in this stage. After about 4 minutes, the tops of the muffins will begin to puff and dome and the bottoms will turn a slight golden brown: that's your cue to flip them. After 4 or 5 minutes on the second side, repeat until all muffins are seared and transferred back to the half sheet pan, and bake at 250°F for 10 minutes, to bake out the gummy interior and finish the set of those marvelous nooks and crannies. Cool the muffins completely before forking them open—the sign of a real English muffin pro! In an airtight container on the counter, the muffins will keep fresh for 5 days.

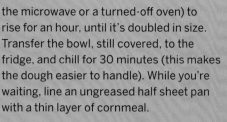

CROISSANTS

Makes 12

If I am being completely honest, when I close my eyes and picture my ideal breakfast, a croissant is my singular vision. My love of the golden (I'm talking color *and* status) pastry stems from my time in Italy, when I got very well acquainted with the croissant's foreign cousin, the cornetto. Back on American soil, the croissant was much more readily available, and I fell deeper in love, so much so I knew I had to master the folds and lamination as best I could in my home kitchen, harnessing the power to turn any rainy morning into a "close your eyes and sip your cappuccino in peace" kind of day.

⇨ Read more on yeast, gluten development, and the wonder that is yeast-risen baked goods on page 119.

⇨ Ditch the spatula and by-hand approach and use a stand mixer fitted with the dough-hook attachment if you like.

⇨ If you're not going to serve the croissants the same day, I recommend stopping once you complete Step 10. Either proceed with Step 11 up until the point when you turn on the oven, and refrigerate overnight, or, in an airtight container, side by side, freeze the croissants until you're ready to bake them. I have a friend who pulls one a day to bake for themself—talk about self-care.

For the Dough

1 packet (2¼ teaspoons) active dry yeast
½ cup milk, warmed
½ cup warm water

3 cups flour + more for dusting
¼ cup sugar
2 teaspoons kosher salt

3 tablespoons unsalted butter, melted

For the Butter Packet

2 sticks + 4 tablespoons (20 tablespoons) unsalted butter

For the Egg Wash

1 egg
1 teaspoon water

- DO YOU -
BAKE CLUB

For the plain butter, sub any flavor butter you dream up (page 16), and/or as you go to roll the triangles into a crescent shape, sneak some sweet or savory surprise into the middle, such as:

- stuffed with strawberries and cream cheese
- stuffed with blueberries and white chocolate chips
- pistachio butter, topped with toasted pistachios
- cinnamon-sugar butter, stuffed with plumped raisins
- mustard butter, stuffed with ham and cheese

@whitneyjweiss

1. **Make the dough:** In a large bowl, whisk together the yeast, warm milk, and warm water until the yeast is dissolved and foamy, about 1 minute. Let it sit as is for another 5 minutes to continue foaming and growing, until it's ready to do its work.

2. Ditch the whisk and grab a sturdy spatula. Measure the flour, sugar, and salt into the bowl. Toss together only the dry ingredients on top with the spatula first, before truly stirring them into the wet ingredients below. This will result in a dry, shaggy mixture at first. Add the melted butter, and continue kneading, pushing the dough away from you with the heel of your hand, folding it over itself with your fingers, and pulling it back; the dough will form a nice smooth ball. Knead this ball for a total of 3 minutes. (You're not focused on fully developing gluten here; that will happen during the rolling-and-folding process!)

3. Flatten the dough ball into a rectangle, wrap it in plastic, and refrigerate it for 30 minutes.

4. **Prep the butter packet:** In the meantime, put the butter between two sheets of plastic wrap or parchment, and use a rolling pin to roll it into a rectangle a little smaller than 6 by 12 inches.

5. On a floured surface, roll the rectangle of dough out to 6 by 24 inches, twice the length of the rolled-out butter. Remove the butter from the plastic wrap or parchment paper, and place it in the middle of the dough. Then fold the dough in half, completely covering the butter.

6. Turn this dough packet 90 degrees, then roll it out to the original size of the rectangle (double its current length), dusting the surface and rolling pin as needed.

7. Visually divide the rectangle into quarters, then literally fold the half of the right half into the right center, then half of the left half into the left center. Then fold the dough at that center line. This is called a double book fold.

8. Wrap the dough in plastic, and refrigerate it for 30 minutes.

9. Repeat this rolling-and-folding procedure two more times, rolling the dough out to 6 by 24 inches and then making a double book fold, rotating the right edges of the dough 90 degrees each time. Refrigerate the dough for 30 minutes between the repetitions.

10. After the third go and 30-minute refrigeration, on a floured surface, roll out the dough one last time, to 6 by 40 inches. Cut it into twelve back-to-back triangles; then roll each triangle up tight into a crescent, starting with the widest edge.

11. Place the croissants on two pan-sprayed half sheet pans, about 4 inches apart, and cover them loosely in plastic to proof for 60 minutes. At 45 minutes, heat the oven to 375°F.

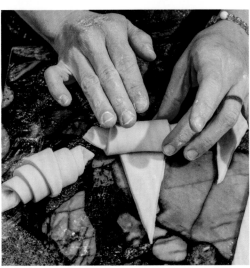

12. **Make the egg wash:** In a small bowl, whisk together the egg and water, making what we in the business call an egg wash— essentially the thing that makes any shiny pastry's top shiny. Just before putting your croissants in the oven, using a brush or your fingers, gently coat the tops in the egg wash.

13. Bake the croissants at 375°F for 18–20 minutes, until they are a deep golden brown all around. Cool them on the baking sheet for 2–3 minutes before digging in while they're warm, or wait until they cool to room temperature. Use a serrated knife to saw down the middle and marvel at the insane layers you labored over! In an airtight container at room temperature, the puffs will stay fresh for 3 days, but I highly recommend taking a page out of the French's book and slicing day-old croissants on the bias, stuffing them with almond paste, topping that with sliced almonds, and baking anew. No croissant should ever really be eaten on Day 2, unless you're making it into something else (*cough* v. fancy grilled cheese *cough*).

DAILY BREAD

Easy, Can't Mess It Up Bread   140

Buns   145

Brioche   147

Flour Tortillas   151

Flaky Bread   152

Pita   154

Pizza   156

Soft Pretzels   161

Cheese Fondue   165

Popovers   166

Ham and Cheese Puffs   169

Stuffing Croissants   170

@mburke421

@cpg1203

#bakeclu

@tartetatin

Looking beautiful and puffy!

@prestons.kitchen

@samsfoodventu

@jessmakesfoods

@mburke421

#bakeclu

They say an apple a day keeps the doctor away. But if you ask any pastry person, they TOTALLY got it wrong: it's a bread a day keeps all bad away. There is a reason why the diets of so many cultures around the world have revolved around bread for thousands of years: it's delicious. I mean, yes, technically, there are agricultural reasons, but this simple creation wouldn't have stood the test of time had it been less fluffy, less versatile, less all-around comforting. From the simple sliceable loaf, to flaky rounds, to twisted pretzels, bread comes in all shapes and sizes, and typically only requires a few ingredients and a couple easy steps to master.

Despite its relative simplicity, many folks are timid about donning the apron and throwing flour onto their counters to create their own bread at home, which is what led me to create this chapter. BAKING BREAD IS EASY! I know I am betraying the many fine carb-based institutions and my comrades in the baked-good business when I tell you all this, but you can make a restaurant-quality loaf/pita/bun in your home kitchen. I don't know where the apprehension to work with yeast or get your gluten on comes from, but I am here to put an end to it. You are just a few recipes away from being a dough pro, looking for any and every excuse to get breading (and the best part is, you don't need to look hard!). These recipes can be the bedrock of your weekly meal planning; they can solve the dreaded question of "What's for dinner?" once and for all. Once you've got some killer bread moves in your pocket, you're the master of your own destiny. So I say, bring me your weary, your gluten, your marvelously chewy inner, gloriously caramelized crust . . . Let's go.

Note: Read up on flour (page 4), your trusty friend all through this chapter! Better yet, if you have a bag of bread flour in your cupboard, substitute it in full or part (I recommend 50:50) for any flour anywhere in this chapter! Ditto for alternative flours—whole-wheat! rye! corn! You get the gist. Power to the Flour!

@ _kathleen.kelly_

EASY, CAN'T MESS IT UP BREAD

Makes 1 loaf

The name does the heavy lifting here! The reality is, we all need a back-pocket recipe for an awesome loaf—whether it's for a holiday gathering, a family vacation when the nearest grocery store is too far away, or when you just feel like treating yourself to two fresh slices for your PB&J. Somewhere between Wonder Bread and potato bread in look and taste, it's great as soft rolls, if that's your vibe.

⇨ Read more on yeast, gluten development, and the wonder that is yeast-risen baked goods on page 119.

⇨ Ditch the spatula and by-hand approach and use a stand mixer fitted with the dough-hook attachment if you like.

1 packet (2¼ teaspoons)
  active dry yeast
1½ cups warm water

3¼ cups flour + more as
  needed
⅓ cup sugar
⅓ cup vegetable oil + more
  for greasing the bowl and
  brushing the top
1¼ teaspoons kosher salt

1. In a large bowl, whisk together the yeast and warm water until the yeast is dissolved and foamy, about 1 minute. Let it sit as is another 5 minutes to continue foaming and growing, until it's ready to do its work.

2. Ditch the whisk and grab a sturdy spatula. Stir in the flour, sugar, oil, and salt, and mix to combine, about 1 minute, until you have a dough ball that's neither sticky nor stiff, but glossy and soft. (Everyone's kitchen humidity level is different. If your dough is way too sticky, add more flour, 2 tablespoons at a time, up to ½ cup. Err on the side of slightly sticky rather than slightly dry and tough.)

3. Ditch the spatula now, and with your hands knead the dough ball in the bowl, pushing the dough away from you with the heel of your hand and folding it over itself with your fingers, then pulling it back. Do this for 7 minutes total to fully develop the chewy, stretchy tunnels of gluten.

4. Grease a fresh large bowl with a thin coat of vegetable oil, and transfer the dough ball to it. Toss the dough in the fat, and leave it seam side down. Cover the bowl with a dry towel and place it in a draft-free spot (I like the microwave or a turned-off oven) to rise for an hour, until it's doubled in size.

5. Heat the oven to 350°F, and pan-spray a 1-pound (8.5-by-4.5-inch) loaf pan.

(⋯)

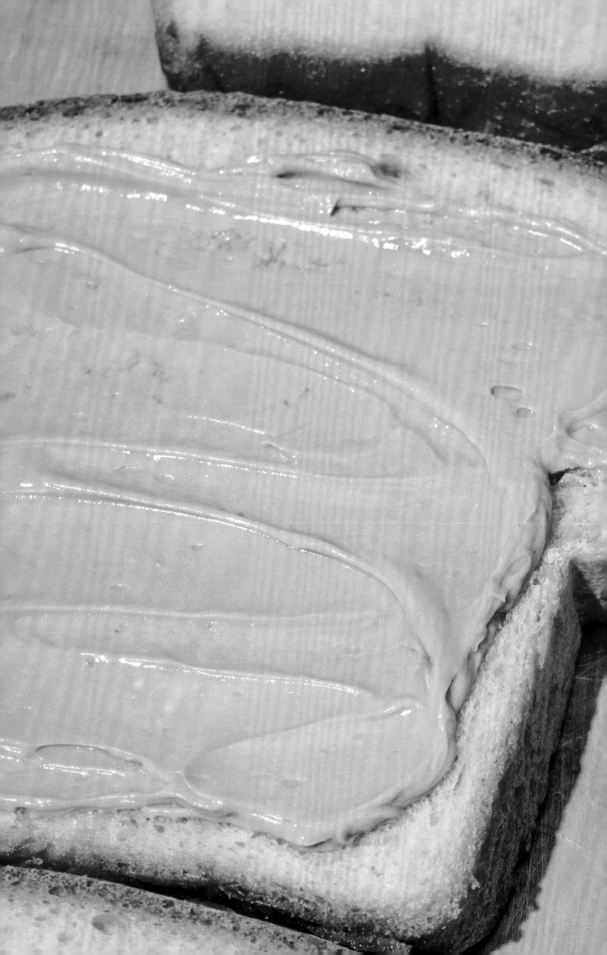

6. Knock the dough out of the bowl onto a clean work surface to deflate it, then stretch and tuck the dough until it's vaguely rectangular. Place it into the pan seam side down, cover it with the same towel, and return it to the warm, dark place to sit for 30 minutes, until the dough has risen 1 inch above the pan's brim.

7. Brush the surface of the dough's top with a light coating of vegetable oil (I do this with my hands, but you can use a brush if you prefer), then bake at 350°F for 40 minutes, until the loaf is glossy, golden brown on top, and beginning to pull back from the sides of the pan. The bread should sound hollow when knocked on. If you're unsure, you can always insert a toothpick—the bread's done when it comes out clean—but this also means you'll have a hole in your loaf.

8. Let the bread cool in the pan for 5 minutes before coating its top anew with vegetable oil. Carefully, remove the loaf from the pan to finish cooling (you can cool it on a wire rack, on the clean grate of your oven, or on a clean sheet pan). Let it cool entirely for 45 minutes before you slice and serve it. In an airtight container at room temperature, the bread will stay fresh for 7 days.

BUNS

Makes 6

In the summer, is there anything you love more than bringing friends and fam together for an al fresco meal?! These hang sessions can happen relatively spontaneously, with you tossing together whatever is in the freezer or growing in the garden. But you know what pulls it all together? Some freshly baked buns! Burgers! Pulled-pork sliders! Loaded hot dogs! Sausage buns! Egg salad sammies! Fresh buns are a breeze to make, which means you are never more than an hour and a few cups of flour away from making some open-air memories with your crew.

- -

⇨ Read more on yeast, gluten development, and the wonder that is yeast-risen baked goods on page 119.

⇨ Ditch the spatula and by-hand approach and use a stand mixer fitted with the dough-hook attachment if you like.

⇨ Milk powder gives this recipe a luscious depth of flavor, omit if you don't have any.

- -

For the Dough

1 teaspoon (½ packet) active dry yeast

1 cup warm water

2 teaspoons sugar

2 cups flour + more for dusting

¼ cup milk powder

1 teaspoon kosher salt

2 tablespoons unsalted butter, melted

For the Egg Wash

1 egg

2 teaspoons water

2 tablespoons sesame seeds

- DO YOU -
BAKE CLUB

Make these buns any size and shape you want—the dough makes an awesome hoagie, or miniature dinner rolls, respectively.

Swap the sesame seeds for any other fun topping, or omit them altogether if you please.

1. **Make the dough:** In a large bowl, whisk together the yeast, warm water, and sugar until the yeast is dissolved and foamy, about 1 minute. Let it sit as is another 5 minutes to continue foaming and growing, until it's ready to do its work.

2. Ditch the whisk and grab a sturdy spatula. Stir in the flour, milk powder, salt, and butter, and mix to combine everything, about 1 minute, until you have a dough ball that's neither sticky nor stiff.

3. Ditch the spatula this time and, with your hands, knead the dough ball in the bowl for 7 minutes total to fully develop the chewy, stretchy tunnels of gluten: pushing the dough away from you with the heel of your hand, folding it over itself with your fingers, and pulling it back.

4. Grease a fresh large bowl with a thin coat of vegetable oil, and transfer the dough ball to it. Toss the dough in the fat, and leave it seam side down. Cover the bowl with a dry towel, and place it in a draft-free spot (I like the microwave or a turned-off oven) to rise for an hour, until it's doubled in size.

5. Knock the dough out onto a clean, dry countertop and divide it into six equal pieces. Round each piece into its own smaller ball. Pan-spray a half sheet pan and place the balls 2 inches apart with the seam side down. Cover the pan with the same towel, and let the dough rest and rise another hour, until each ball has doubled in size.

(···)

6. Gently flatten each ball partially with the palm of your hand to mimic the size of a hamburger bun. Cover the balls with the same towel, and let them proof about 30 minutes more, until the dough relaxes and starts to grow anew.

7. **In the meantime, heat the oven to 350°F and make the egg wash:** In a small bowl, whisk together the egg and a splash of water, making what we call in the business an egg wash— essentially, the thing that makes any shiny pastry's top shiny (it also acts as glue for seeds). Just before putting your buns into the oven, use a brush or your fingers to gently coat the tops in the egg wash. Sprinkle the tops generously with sesame seeds.

8. Bake the buns for 20–25 minutes, until they're a confident and glossy golden brown on top. Cool them completely before slicing them in half (otherwise the insides will be gummy!). In an airtight container on the counter, the buns will keep fresh for 5 days.

BRIOCHE

Makes 1 loaf

Brioche is a real testament to one of life's greatest truths: most things are made better with some (okay, a lot) of butter. Brioche is technically an "enriched bread"—the pastry world's fancy way of saying the same thing—and though a classic loaf of Easy, Can't Mess It Up Bread (page 140) is great and all, when it's time to go all in, I go brioche. Butter's creamy fattiness brings roundness and depth to this recipe (as do the sugar and eggs, my other two BFFs), to create a loaf that has a place at every mealtime.

- -

⇨ Read more on yeast, gluten development, and the wonder that is yeast-risen baked goods on page 119.

⇨ A stand mixer is a MUST in this recipe—the heat of your hands will melt all the butter otherwise!

- -

For the Dough
1 packet (2¼ teaspoons) active dry yeast

⅓ cup + 1 tablespoon warm water

1 tablespoon sugar

4 eggs, out of the fridge

3 cups flour (half bread flour if you have it!) + more for the counter

3 tablespoons sugar

2 teaspoons kosher salt

1½ sticks (12 tablespoons) unsalted butter, cold, cut into ¼-inch cubes

For the Egg Wash
1 egg

Splash water

1. **Make the dough:** In the bowl of a stand mixer, whisk together the yeast, warm water, and 1 tablespoon sugar until the yeast is dissolved and foamy, about 1 minute. Let it sit as is another 5 minutes to continue foaming and growing, until it's ready to do its work.

2. Whisk in the eggs until they're combined. Then ditch the whisk and add the flour, the remaining 3 tablespoons of sugar, and the salt. With the dough hook in hand, bring the mixture together to a shaggy state. Lock the bowl onto the mixer's stand, engage the dough-hook attachment, and mix on low speed until the mixture comes together into a clean mass of dough, about 2 minutes.

3. Set a timer for 5 minutes, and allow the dough to continue kneading on low speed for the entire time, to maximize gluten development.

4. When the timer goes off, begin adding the butter pieces into the mixer (set the butter paper aside), still on low speed, a few at a time, being sure the pieces are incorporated before adding more. This takes 10–15 minutes. The dough will begin crawling up the hook and/or stick to the sides of the bowl. In either case, turn off the mixer and scrape down the sides before continuing. I usually have to stop and scrape down five to seven times. Once all of the butter is fully incorporated, the dough will be consistently a rich yellow-orange color, glossy from the eggs and butter, and also a bit "sticky" to the eye and touch.

(⋯)

5. Very lightly grease a medium bowl with the butter paper and knock the brioche dough out into it. Cover the bowl with plastic, and refrigerate it for 12 hours for flavor development and easy handling. I call this "overnight," but feel free to split over an a.m./p.m. baking sesh.

6. On Day 2, pan-spray a 1-pound (8.5-by-4.5-inch) loaf pan. Knock the dough out onto a clean and lightly floured surface. With a rolling pin, roll the dough out into an 8.5-by-5.5-inch rectangle (long side facing you), then roll the dough up (think cinnamon-bun technique!) into a perfectly eggy, buttery log.

7. Tuck the tails (about 1/2 inch on each side) of the log, and place the dough into the prepped pan, seam down. Cover the pan with a towel or plastic wrap, and put it in a draft-free spot (I like the microwave or a turned-off oven) to rise for 2 hours, until the dough has grown in size and risen above the pan (but not doubled in size, like traditional bread dough, because there are so many rich ingredients in it).

8. Heat the oven to 375°F (one of this bread's calling cards is a very toasty brown ring round its edge) and make sure you have a single rack ready that's not too close to the bottom or top heat source of your oven.

9. **Make the egg wash:** In a small bowl, whisk together the egg and a splash of water, making what we call in the business an egg wash—essentially, the thing that makes any shiny pastry's top shiny. Just before putting your brioche in the oven, use a brush or your fingers to gently coat the top in the egg wash.

10. Bake the loaf for 60 minutes. Fifty minutes in, when the bread is close to finished, I like to remove it carefully from the pan and knock on it—listening for a hollow sound, like when you're choosing a cantaloupe—then put it back in the oven, without the pan, right on the oven rack, for the last 10 minutes.

11. Let the loaf cool completely, out of the pan, 6 hours or so, before slicing. If you cut in too soon, the steam still trapped inside will make the bread gummy; wrap it too soon and the steam will make the outer crust soggy. In an airtight container at room temperature, the bread will stay fresh for 7 days.

> - DO YOU -
> # BAKE CLUB
>
> There are tons of ways to mold and bake brioche—in small fluted molds (à tête), with 90-degree angles (a Pullman loaf)—to name a couple. If you're making your brioche to eat, not look at, any 1-pound (8.5-by-4.5-inch) loaf pan will do, but brioche translates to bigger and smaller forms, too. Your call.

FLOUR TORTILLAS

Makes 8

In my book, taco night has always been the superior dinner night. When I was growing up, it was all about the hard-shell tacos from the grocery store kit. Now that I am the one in charge of the taco making, I do things a little differently, swapping them out for these fresh, classic, could-not-be-easier tortillas. I like to stuff the raw dough with my taco fillings, then shallow-fry them for a flauta moment, but they are equally delicious rolled out and griddled, then assembled. (And don't snooze on the power move of a breakfast burrito now that you have a tortilla recipe in your pocket!)

⇨ Crisco (or any other vegetable or animal shortening) makes the most tender tortillas, but feel free to sub in vegetable oil in a pinch.

2 cups flour + more for dusting
1 teaspoon kosher salt

3 tablespoons vegetable shortening, melted
1/2 cup warm water + more if needed

1. In a large bowl, with a sturdy spatula, mix together the flour and salt, stirring to combine, about 15 seconds. Stir in the melted fat and warm water, and stir from the bottom up until the dry ingredients are incorporated and the dough begins to come together to form a shaggy ball, about 30 seconds.

2. Turn the dough out onto a clean counter surface, and knead it with the heel of your hand ten to twelve times, pushing the dough away from you with the heel of your palm, folding it over itself with your fingers, and pulling it back—adding a little flour or water if needed to achieve a soft, smooth dough. This will be a less elastic experience than with a yeast-risen dough.

3. Form the dough into a ball, and cut it into eight equal wedges. Use your hands to shape the wedges of dough into round balls, and place them on the counter seam side down.

4. Sprinkle your countertop with a bit of flour, and use a rolling pin to flatten your dough into even thin 8-inch rounds (about 1/4 inch thick), using your hands to help create a rounded shape as needed. Do not stack the dough rounds on top of each other.

5. Heat a heavy-bottomed medium-sized skillet or cast-iron pan over medium heat. Transfer one tortilla at a time to the warm surface, and cook it for 1 minute, or until the bottom surface of the tortilla has a few brown spots on it. If it's taking longer, increase the heat a tad. Flip the tortilla, and cook the other side for 20 seconds, to get the same brown spots. Remove the tortillas from the pan carefully and stack them on a plate; cover them with a towel to keep the heat in. Repeat until all the dough rounds are cooked. Dinner is served (unless they get layered and stacked with cheese and other fun things for quesadillas).

- DO YOU -
BAKE CLUB

Stuff and roll any leftover, cooked tortillas, as burritos and store them in an airtight container in the fridge for up to 5 days or in the freezer for up to a month. It's an awesome dinner in a jiffy move.

Take fully cooked tortillas, cut them into smaller triangles, and fry them to make . . . tortilla chips! Season them with salt when they're hot out of the fryer, please!

FLAKY BREAD

Makes 6

1½ cups flour + more for
  dusting
½ teaspoon kosher salt

4 tablespoons unsalted
  butter, melted
⅓ cup warm water

4 tablespoons vegetable oil
  + more for greasing the
  bowl

4 tablespoons unsalted
  butter, softened

2 tablespoons unsalted
  butter, softened
½ teaspoon kosher salt

There is a reason why so many cultures have a shiny, flaky, load-up-able bread: it makes eating more fun. Seemingly random ingredients like onions and chickpeas, peppers and sausage, beans and potatoes feel like a hearty meal when served on a round of flaky bread. Soups feel like a main event; a dip spread goes up to 11 with freshly toasted slices. Curling up the dough in pinwheel patterns is pretty fun, too.

⇨ If you have a brush—silicone or otherwise—use it! If not, a spoon or small offset spatula will do, for painting your dough with butter.

1. In a large bowl, with a sturdy spatula, mix together the flour and salt, stirring to combine, about 15 seconds. Stir in 4 tablespoons melted butter and the warm water, and stir from the bottom up, until the dough becomes a soft, velvet ball, about 1 minute.

2. Grease a fresh large bowl with a thin coat of vegetable oil, and transfer the dough ball to it. Cover the bowl with a dry towel, and place it in a draft-free spot (I like the microwave or a turned-off oven) to rest and relax for 4 hours.

3. Knock the dough out onto a clean, dry counter and divide it into six equal pieces. Round each piece into a ball, then, one by one, with a rolling pin, flatten and roll out each dough ball into a very thin 7-inch round.

4. With a brush, paint the surfaces of the rolled dough pieces with 4 tablespoons of the softened butter, divided equally among the pieces. Roll the dough pieces up lengthwise, like fruit roll-ups, and coil them tight into pinwheels or snail shells. Set them aside.

5. Roll each pinwheel out, as thin as you can, 6 to 7 inches (a tad thicker than ¼ inch or your standard tortilla).

6. Heat a heavy-bottomed, medium-sized skillet or cast-iron pan over medium heat, and brush it with a thin layer of vegetable oil. Transfer one flattened dough disc at a time to the warm surface, and cook it for 2 minutes, or until the bottom of the bread has a few brown spots on it and it starts to puff a little and become slightly translucent. If it's taking longer, increase the heat a tad. Flip the disc, paint the pan anew with oil, and cook the bread on the other side for 30–60 seconds to get the same brown spots.

7. Remove the bread from the pan, brush both sides with the final 2 tablespoons of softened butter, sprinkle from above with some of the ½ teaspoon of salt, and set it on a plate, covered with a towel. Repeat until all the flaky breads are cooked, buttered, and salted. DIG IN! In an airtight container at room temperature, the breads will keep for 5 days. Regriddle this flaky royalty to warm, soften, and crisp it up before serving.

- DO YOU -

BAKE CLUB

For scallion pancakes, use sesame oil instead of vegetable oil, and slice some scallions to add during Step 4, just after you paint the butter across the dough but before you roll it up and coil it.

For cheesy or garlicky flaky bread, add 1 cup shredded cheddar or Parmesan or 2 garlic cloves, minced, during Step 4 just after you paint the butter across the dough but before you roll it up and coil it.

PITA

Makes 6

1 teaspoon (1/2 packet)
active dry yeast
1 cup warm water

2 2/3 cups flour + more for
dusting
2 tablespoons olive oil +
more for greasing
1 teaspoon sugar
1 teaspoon kosher salt

Over a little sibling reunion for my dad's birthday, my older sis, Ang—an AMAZING home cook and meal-planning visionary who gets very little credit for many of the incredible things she is—suggested we make something Mediterranean. I quickly combined what I love about eating pita with a few of my Daily Bread go-to recipes to make what is now my family's mainstay. It's grill time at least once a week in summertime thanks to this delicious bready pocket, and a friendly collection of pickles, tahini, and herbs. It's a grill-on, lights-out kind of meal.

⇨ Read more on yeast, gluten development, and the wonder that is yeast-risen baked goods on page 119.

⇨ Ditch the spatula and by-hand approach and use a stand mixer fitted with the dough-hook attachment if you like.

⇨ I get the best results from cooking my pita on a very hot grill (even in the winter—it's Will's job!), but a 475°F oven with a cast-iron pan preheated in it will come close, too, if the grill is not your thing. Work one by one rather than making the entire batch at once, but follow the same timing and visual cues listed in Step 7.

1. In a large bowl, whisk together the yeast and warm water until the yeast is dissolved and foamy, about 1 minute. Let it sit as is another 5 minutes to continue foaming and growing, until it's ready to do its work.

2. Ditch the whisk and grab a sturdy spatula. Stir in the flour, oil, sugar, and salt, and mix to combine everything, about 1 minute, until you have a dough ball that's neither sticky nor stiff.

3. Ditch the spatula now and, with your hands, knead the dough ball in the bowl, pushing the dough away from you with the heel of your hand and folding it over itself with your fingers, then pulling it back. Do this for 7 minutes total, to fully develop the chewy, stretchy tunnels of gluten.

4. Grease a fresh large bowl with a thin coat of oil, and transfer the dough ball to it. Toss the dough in the fat, and leave it seam side down. Cover the bowl with a dry towel, and place it in a draft-free spot (I like the microwave or a turned-off oven) to rise for an hour, until it's doubled in size.

5. Knock the dough out onto a clean, dry countertop, and divide it into six equal pieces. Round each piece into its own smaller ball. Place the balls 2 inches apart, cover them with the same towel, and let them rest and rise another hour, until each has doubled in size.

6. With a rolling pin, flatten and roll each dough ball out to a 6-inch round (about ½ inch thick, twice the thickness of a tortilla). Do not to stack the dough rounds but, rather, spread them, rolled out, on the countertop, side by side.

7. Heat the grill to 400°F (face scorchingly hot). Open the lid, and quickly transfer all the rolled pita discs onto the clean, dry grates. Close the lid, and keep it closed for 2 minutes, while your pitas start to take on the smallest amount of color and pouf up like a pillow or pocket. Open the lid and, with tongs, gently flip the pita, close the lid, and cook it another 1 minute. (If you're worried your grill is not at the right temperature, try one pita at a time until you get maximum puff. If the pita does not puff at all, the grill is not hot enough—turn it up. If the pita takes on a ton of color, the grill is too hot—keep the lid open, and if there's a dial, turn it down.)

8. Transfer the pita onto a plate covered with a towel and speed-walk it to the table— it's time to load that pita up and eat! In an airtight container at room temperature, the pitas will stay fresh for 5 days, but I recommend freezing them for up to 1 month, then defrosting them at room temperature and griddling them on the stovetop just before serving.

PIZZA

Makes 6

1 teaspoon (¹⁄₂ packet)
  active dry yeast
1 cup warm water

2¹⁄₂ cups flour
2 teaspoons kosher salt
1 teaspoon olive oil + more
  for greasing

Cornmeal, for dusting

Pizza fixings galore—
  you're the chef
Simple Pizza Sauce
  (recipe follows, page 160)
Shredded mozzarella
  cheese

Even before I trial-and-errored my way to a great homemade version, Friday nights were reserved in my heart—and the Tosi home—as pizza night. A good movie, paper towel napkins, a triangle of cheese-and-sauce-covered bread—what more could one need to close out the week? And with this could-not-be-easier dough recipe, you're just steps away from having pizza night whenever the mood hits. A little cornmeal dusting helps give your dough the crispy edge you long for. I pull out everything from my fridge and pantry that could possibly be a pizza topping or saucy spread, and encourage you to do the same. My POV these days is that, as long as pizza's on the menu, any night can feel like Friday night.

- -

⇨ Read more on yeast, gluten development, and the wonder that is yeast-risen baked goods on page 119.

⇨ Ditch the spatula and by-hand approach and use a stand mixer fitted with the dough-hook attachment if you like.

- -

1. In a large bowl, whisk together the yeast and warm water until the yeast is dissolved and foamy, about 1 minute. Let it sit as is another 5 minutes to continue foaming and growing, until it's ready to do its work.

2. Ditch the whisk and grab a sturdy spatula. Stir in the flour, salt, and oil, and mix to combine everything, about 1 minute, until you have a dough ball that's neither sticky nor stiff.

3. Ditch the spatula now and, with your hands, knead the dough ball in the bowl, pushing the dough away from you with the heel of your hand and folding it over itself with your fingers, then pulling it back. Do this for 7 minutes, total, to fully develop the chewy, stretchy tunnels of gluten.

4. Grease a fresh large bowl with a thin coat of oil, and transfer the dough ball to it. Toss the dough in the fat, and leave it seam side down. Cover the bowl with a dry towel, and place it in a draft-free spot (I like the microwave or a turned-off oven) to rise for an hour, until it's doubled in size.

5. Knock the dough out onto a clean, dry countertop, and divide it into six equal pieces. Round each piece into a smaller ball. Place the balls 2 inches apart, cover them with the same towel, and let them rest and rise another hour, until each has doubled in size.

6. In the meantime, position an oven rack close to your oven's heating element. Heat the oven to its highest temperature, 500° or 550°F. Sprinkle two half sheet pans liberally with cornmeal.

7. Like a pizzaiolo/a, punch each dough ball down, stretch it, and throw it into a 6-inch round—or, alternatively, using a rolling pin, flatten and roll each dough ball out to the same size, shooting for a thinner center ($\frac{1}{4}$ to $\frac{1}{2}$ inch) and slightly thicker edges ($\frac{1}{2}$ to $\frac{3}{4}$ inch) to represent the crust.

8. **Make a pizza bar:** Grab anything and everything that could make awesome pizza toppings, and lay them out on the counter for folks to don their individual pizzas as they like.

9. When the oven is as hot as can be, throw the pizza (either raw on cornmeal-lined pans or par-cooked) into the oven. Bake until the cheese begins to bubble and the crust is golden brown, 7 to 8 minutes from raw, 2–3 minutes for par-cooked. Have a cutting board and sharp knife or pizza roller ready so that, as the pizzas come out of the oven, you can slice and serve them hot. I don't think you need me to tell you how to store leftover pizza—everyone does their own thing. We wrap ours in plastic in the fridge overnight, because Frankie really likes pizza for breakfast the next day. I don't encourage you to keep it for more than 2 days. Eat it cold, or reheat it in the oven to attempt to bring a little texture back, though nothing is like the fresh-out-of-the-oven thing.

@ __kathleen.kelly__

- DO YOU -
BAKE CLUB

This dough is game for whatever cooking method you are rocking. I'm a BIG fan of grilling the dough rounds bare, dressing the pizza, then melting the toppings in the oven on summer nights, and an even BIGGER fan of frying the dough rounds bare, dressing the pizza, then melting the toppings all winter long. After Step 7, either grill the dough rounds or fry them (using the oil from frying Old-Fashioned Donuts, page 114, or Potato Chips, page 215), then top and finish the pizza in your home oven.

The toppings are really where your vision takes off—leftover Indian food, cold cuts, traditional and nontraditional cheeses, spreads, and condiments, freshly minced garlic, and more. Take your flavor stories and run with them!

Stromboli! Calzone! This dough also works for any pizza-adjacent vision you have!

2 teaspoons olive oil

2 tablespoons diced yellow
   onion (¹/₈ of a small
   onion)
1¹/₂ tablespoons diced
   garlic (4 or 5 cloves)

One 14.5-ounce can
   crushed or diced
   tomatoes
1 stalk (about 5 leaves)
   fresh basil, chopped
¹/₂ teaspoon balsamic
   vinegar
¹/₂ teaspoon kosher salt

Simple Pizza Sauce

Makes about 1 ¹/₂ cups

1. In a heavy-bottomed medium-sized saucepan, over medium
   heat, warm the olive oil for about 30 seconds, then sweat
   the diced onions and garlic in the pan until they're soft and
   translucent, about 2 minutes, stirring intermittently with a
   sturdy heat-safe spatula.

2. Still over medium heat, add the crushed tomatoes, basil,
   balsamic vinegar, and salt, stir to combine everything, and
   reduce the mixture by half, stirring intermittently, about
   7 minutes.

3. Take the pan off the heat, transfer the sauce to a blender, and
   purée it to the consistency of a pizza sauce. Cool it completely
   before using it. In an airtight container the sauce will keep
   fresh in the fridge for a week.

#bakeclub

SOFT PRETZELS

Makes 6

From street stands and baseball stadiums to fresh from your own microwave, a warm, salt-covered, malty soft pretzel is downright transformative. When you get down to it, a pretzel is a combination of pretty common ingredients, just prepared in a way most folks aren't used to replicating at home. The baking soda bath gives these braided babes their undeniably delicious scent and beautiful brown shell—best served with a sidecar of mustard (or Cheese Fondue, page 165), honey mustard, cheese, marinara, cinnamon sugar.

⇨ Read more on yeast, gluten development, and the wonder that is yeast-risen baked goods on page 119.

⇨ Ditch the spatula and by-hand approach and use a stand mixer fitted with the dough-hook attachment if you like.

For the Dough
1 teaspoon (½ packet)
  active dry yeast
½ cup milk, warmed
⅓ cup warm water

2 cups flour
2 teaspoons light brown
  sugar
1 teaspoon kosher salt

2 tablespoons unsalted
  butter, melted

For the Cooking Water
3 cups water
¼ cup baking soda

Make the Coating
3 tablespoons unsalted
  butter, melted
½ teaspoon salt

1. **Make the dough:** In a large bowl, whisk together the yeast, warm milk, and ⅓ cup warm water until the yeast is dissolved and foamy, about 1 minute. Let it sit as is another 5 minutes to continue foaming and growing, until it's ready to do its work.

2. Ditch the whisk and grab a sturdy spatula. Measure the flour, sugar, and salt into the bowl. Toss together only the dry ingredients on top with the spatula first, before truly stirring them into the wet ingredients below. This will result in a dry, shaggy mixture at first. Stir in the melted butter to help bring the shaggy mass further together. Ditch the spatula now, and with your hands begin to knead: push the dough away from you with the heel of your hand, fold it over itself with your fingers, and pull it back. The dough will form a nice smooth ball. Knead this ball for a total of 7 minutes, to ensure that you develop the chewy strands of gluten we know and love so well.

3. Grease a fresh large bowl with vegetable oil, toss the dough in the fat, and leave it seam side down. Cover the bowl with a dry towel, and place it in a draft-free spot (I like the microwave or a turned-off oven) to rise for an hour, until it's doubled in size.

4. Heat the oven to 450°F, pan-spray a half sheet pan, and make the **cooking water.** In a heavy-bottomed medium-sized shallow pot, bring the water and baking soda to a boil over medium heat.

5. Grab the proofed dough, knock it out onto a clean, floured counter, and divide it into six equal pieces. Roll each into a very long rope, 20 inches long, then twist and bring the ends together to form a pretzel shape (find a video on the internet if you need help!). Cover the pretzels on the countertop with a towel, and let them rest for 15 minutes.

(...)

- DO YOU -
BAKE CLUB

Make them into knots and dust them with cinnamon sugar, or chai-spice them up like @prestons.kitchen or take a page from @elainedarer and take them on a savory Parmesean-garlic ride.

6. Once the water begins to boil, gently drop one of the pretzels into the water, face-down. Boil it for 20 seconds per side, 40 seconds total, using a slotted spoon or large fork to flip it.

7. Remove the boiled pretzel from the water and transfer to the prepped baking sheet. Repeat until you have boiled all the pretzels, placing them 2 inches apart from one another on the baking sheet.

8. **Make the coating:** Using a brush or your fingers, gently coat the tops in melted butter (giving your pretzels even more flavor and shine). Sprinkle the surface of each with salt.

9. Bake for 10–12 minutes at 450°F, until they're a deep, hearty brown. Remember: color equals flavor. Remove them from the oven and paint them once more with melted butter.

10. Serve them warm, solo or with your favorite dipping sauce as a sidecar. In an airtight container at room temperature, the pretzels will stay fresh for 5 days, though nothing is as great as them fresh!

CHEESE FONDUE

Makes about 3 cups

1 teaspoon lemon juice

1 cup white wine

1 tablespoon + 1 teaspoon
cornstarch

1 pound cheese (I like
Gruyère/Swiss, but any
single type or combo will
do!), cubed or shredded

1½ teaspoons liqueur or
beer, to give an edge, if
you're into it!

Black pepper, to season
very lightly

Nutmeg, to season very
lightly

Pretzels, crusty bread,
veggies (raw or roasted),
bite-sized pieces of meat
for serving—you're the
boss

To my minimalist husband's chagrin, I live for the hunt of junk-shop treasures.
A perfectly worn leather bag. A broken-in pair of Levi's. A hilarious piece
of handmade art. The resale shop is an embodiment of one human's trash
being another's treasure. One day, while scouring the aisles of my local
Goodwill, I laid eyes on a real beauty: a yellow enamel fondue set complete
with wonderfully tiny metal forks. I tossed it into my cart and raced home
to develop this recipe, and now I can't imagine life without either. Turns out,
a minimalist can be persuaded of pretty much anything over a soft pretzel
dipped in cheese.

1. In a heavy-bottomed medium-sized pot, off heat, whisk the
   lemon juice and a splash of white wine into the cornstarch until
   the mixture is smooth and dissolved. Whisk in the remaining
   white wine.

2. Fire up the stove and, over medium heat, bring the cornstarch
   mixture to a boil, whisking intermittently, about 2 minutes.

3. Lower the heat to a simmer, and slowly add in a handful of
   cheese, whisking to melt it gently. Still over low heat, when
   your first round of cheese has melted, add another handful,
   whisking to melt that gently. Continue this process over low
   heat, adding cheese by the handful and gently bringing your
   fondue together. Too much heat will burn and/or break your
   mixture. Be patient! When all the cheese has melted, season
   your fondue with liqueur or beer, pepper, and nutmeg.

4. Serve over very, very low heat in the same pot or in a
   preheated fondue pot.

5. Dunk pretzel pieces, or other fork foods (boiled pearl onions!
   cornichons! boiled potatoes! tortilla chips [page 151]!), into
   your cheese masterpiece, twisting and turning the cheese
   mixture over the pot with each dunk to ensure that any cheese
   left behind goes back into the pot of glory.

6. Leftover fondue does not like to be reheated. You've made it
   this far, so keep dipping. Do like the Swiss and let the bottom
   of the pot caramelize so you have crispy cheese as your final
   course. If you must, refrigerate any unconsumed fondue in an
   airtight container, then slice it thin and use it in place of store-
   bought cheese for your next grilled cheese.

POPOVERS

Makes 12

3 eggs
2 egg whites
1³/₄ cups milk
1³/₄ cups flour
2 teaspoons sugar
2 teaspoons kosher salt
¹/₈ teaspoon black pepper

¹/₄ pound cheddar cheese,
  shredded

I'm warning you, do NOT open the oven door! Just don't do it.

Okay, now that I've got that on the record, here's my love letter to these little pillows of warm goodness, crispy on the outside, gooey on the inside; a steakhouse-style delight that also makes a magical brunch or breakfast star. They are SO simple to make . . . and, honestly, it feels like magic when the oven timer dings! The popover PR campaign has begun, because, if popovers are making an appearance on your table, you know the meal (or snack time) is going to be a good one.

1. Heat the oven to 425°F, and very, very, very lightly pan-spray a 12-cup muffin pan. (If your popover doesn't pop, it's because you greased your pan too much!)

2. In a blender, on low speed with the lid on, combine the eggs and egg whites, milk, flour, sugar, salt, and pepper until the mixture is smooth and well combined, about 30 seconds. The batter will be pretty thin—don't panic.

3. Pour ¹/₃ cup batter into each greased muffin hole. (Some people swear by preheating the muffin pan, but it's up to you. If it's too early in the morning, I never do.) Each cup should be a little more than half full. Scatter the shredded cheese equally over the centers of the filled cups.

4. Bake at 425°F for 30–40 minutes, until the popovers have tripled in size, are hollow in the center, and a healthy golden-brown color and crispy-cheese vis on top. You can stalk this process from the window of your oven, but DO NOT OPEN THE DARN DOOR until they're done. This is an extremely delicate process. Opening the oven will prevent your batter from popping up and over (hence the name).

5. While they're still very hot from the oven, carefully but quickly pop the popovers out of the pan, and serve them immediately. (Some people bring them to the table in a basket with a towel to help insulate the heat and keep the popovers as fluffy as possible.) Devour them all, or peer-pressure your friends and family into joining you—popovers lose their crunchy magic if you attempt to save them after they cool.

- DO YOU -
BAKE CLUB

Swap in any shredded cheese you please—Parmesan! Swiss!—the stronger the better (mellow cheeses like mozzarella don't do much here).

- DO YOU -
BAKE CLUB

If you like a little spice, add ⅛ teaspoon cayenne pepper in with the flour and salt in Step 2.

Substitute any shredded cheese you please, the sharper the better. @samsfoodadventure made a cacio e pepe puff, which is very inspired!

Substitute any meat product you please, the saltier and bigger in flavor the better! Bacon! Chorizo! Sausage! That said, the ham addition is my American twist on the French classic, so feel free to omit meat altogether if you please.

HAM AND CHEESE PUFFS

Makes 24

One of my favorite categories of baked goods is *things that seem fancy but are actually super simple to make*. Call them Gougères instead, and all of a sudden these hamy, eggy breads are turning heads. These meat-and-cheesy puffs don't require any wild ingredients and can be on the table in under an hour, which makes them a perfect last-minute party pleaser or dinner-table side—*oh là là*—just be prepared to have folks hella impressed.

- -

For the Dough

6 tablespoons unsalted
    butter
1 cup milk

1¼ cups flour
1 teaspoon kosher salt

4 eggs

1½ cups shredded Gruyère
    cheese
¼ cup diced ham

For the Egg Wash

1 egg
Splash of water

1. Heat the oven to 375°F. Pan-spray a half sheet pan, or line it with parchment paper.

2. **Make the dough:** In a heavy-bottomed medium-sized saucepan, bring the butter and milk to a boil over medium heat, stirring intermittently with a sturdy heat-safe spatula or wooden spoon (classic French style!).

3. Off the heat, measure the flour and salt into the saucepan. Toss together only the dry ingredients on top with the spatula first, before truly stirring them into the wet ingredients below to combine, about 30 seconds.

4. Bring the saucepan back to medium heat, and stir the mixture vigorously for 2–3 minutes, until it pulls away from the sides of the pan and forms a ball, and a dry film develops on the bottom and sides of the pan.

5. Transfer the dough ball to the bowl of a stand mixer fitted with the paddle attachment. On high speed, paddle the dough for 1–2 minutes, until all the steam subsides.

6. On medium speed, add the eggs, one at a time, ensuring that each egg incorporates fully before adding the next, about 30 seconds per egg. Scrape down the sides of the mixing bowl, and paddle in the cheese and meat on low speed until everything is combined, about 15 seconds.

7. Scoop or pipe small balls, the size of heaping tablespoons, onto the prepared pan, about 2 inches apart.

8. **Make the egg wash:** In a small bowl, whisk together the egg and a splash of water. Just before putting your puffs in the oven, use a brush or your fingers and gently coat the tops and sides in the egg wash. (This treatment also acts as a smoothing agent if you have any jagged edges or tails from scooping or piping!)

9. Bake the puffs for 20 minutes at 375°F until they have, well, puffed, and are golden brown on the outside.

10. Eat them warm or cold—it's your party. In an airtight container in the fridge, the puffs will stay fresh for 5 days. I strongly recommend reheating them in the oven or a toaster oven.

STUFFING CROISSANTS

Makes 12

Once you've mastered the croissant game in "Baking for Breakfast" (page 133) and Fancy Butter (page 16) is a flex you're showing off with on the regular, you're ready to take it to the stuffing-croissant level. Even better, if you have holiday leftovers, fold them into the crescent as you roll it up, to make Thanksgiving croissants or Christmas croissants or Easter croissants. The idea of flavoring the butter you fold into your croissant is one I've been obsessed with for nearly two decades—I love a great croissant, and there's so much room to amp it up beyond chocolate or almond (although I'm also a member of their fan clubs), especially in the savory department, and especially when there are leftovers that need a home.

For the Dough
See page 133

For the Stuffing Butter Packet
2 sticks + 4 tablespoons butter, softened
1 tablespoon + 2 teaspoons onion powder
1½ teaspoons sugar
1½ teaspoons black pepper
1½ teaspoons ground dried thyme
1½ teaspoons celery salt
1¼ teaspoons ground dried sage

For the Filling (Optional)
Shredded turkey, gravy, cranberry sauce (portioned and frozen into 12 small mounds)

For the Egg Wash
1 egg
1 teaspoon water

1. Follow Steps 1–3 of the recipe for Croissants (page 133).

2. **Make the stuffing butter packet:** In the meantime, in a medium bowl, with a sturdy spatula, mix the butter with all of the other ingredients for the butter packet, mixing until everything is fully combined and evenly speckled throughout, about 2 minutes. Put the stuffing butter between two sheets of plastic wrap or parchment, and use a rolling pin or the heel of your hand to shape it into a rectangle a little smaller than 6 by 12 inches.

3. Follow Steps 5–10 of the croissant recipe, stopping to nestle some turkey, gravy, and cranberry sauce into the widest parts of the triangles if using before rolling them up into a crescent shape.

4. Follow Steps 11–13 of the croissant recipe to proof, egg-wash, bake, and eat (though you probably won't need much instruction there!).

CAKE
EVERY
WHICH
WAY

- -

Carrot Cake Marshmallow Rolls   176

Lemon Honey Ginger Babycakes   179

Black Bottom Cupcakes   183

Chocolate Mayo Cake   184

Blueberry Muffin Bundt Cake   186

Brownie Cake   188

Lemon Loaf   191

Maple Sheet Cake   195

Ice Cream Loaf Cake   196

Skillet Veggie Cake   199

Sprite Cake   200

Peaches and Cream
Upside Down Cake   203

@alicekollinzas

@ sweetsbyglory

@rachies.bak

@cookingbysamm

#bakeclub

#bakeclub

@mburke421

@jessmakesfoods

@handsomeca

Cake is a pretty powerful thing. Birthdays, weddings, going-aways, and welcomes—it always seems to show up when we're in need. No pressure, though: that's actually NOT cake's only reason for being, which took me a second to learn as I forged my relationship with it in my early days as a baker.

I used to spend hours studying technique, making sponges, scrutinizing every frosted angle, perfecting the décor, until I realized that neither I nor the cake was here for all that pressure. It's my belief that cakes are meant to be carefree, with a come-as-you-are spirit. And, as with so much in life, it's actually what is on the inside that matters most. Cakes, above all else, arrive for these moments because they're meant to be eaten—in the company of one or many. As such, I believe these superstars of the pastry world are actually better off casual. Why would we limit something with so much potential for flavor and excitement to just the few days on the calendar that are considered "special"? Cake just wants to show up and bring you joy, bond you together, give you something to smile about during the rest of those calendar moments.

Big cakes! Small cakes! Hot cakes! Right side up! Upside down! Flat! Rolled up! Fluffy! Dense! My friends, the wild, wonderful world of cakes that I love to bake at home is here, ready for you. Just promise me you won't save this chapter for the highlight reel of your life, but use it to create more celebrations in the day-to-day. No fear. Let's cannonball into cake!

#bakeclub

@carpedolce

CARROT CAKE MARSHMALLOW ROLLS

Makes 8

I've got no beef with a cream cheese frosting coated vegetal babe, a year-round delight that gets extra love at Easter, but it has always felt a little ho-hum to me. These roll-ups give a nod to the classic version, with a carrot-loaded sponge, but it's rolled with a slathering of marshmallow creme for bounce and vanilla flavor. The format also harks back to another nostalgic baked-good creation—a Little Debbie Swiss Roll—but that's a story for another time.

⇨ Transform this into a tabletop treat by making one giant roulade and spreading all of the marshmallow over the surface, rather than cutting the cake into smaller segments in Steps 5–6.

⇨ Feel free to make your own Marshmallow (page 47) to spread while it's still warm, though I'm just as happy with store-bought fluff or creme!

3 tablespoons unsalted
  butter, melted
1 tablespoon vegetable oil
1/3 cup light brown sugar
1/4 cup sugar

2 eggs

1/2 cup + 3 tablespoons
  flour
1/2 teaspoon baking powder
1/2 teaspoon kosher salt
1/4 teaspoon cinnamon
1/8 teaspoon baking soda

11/4 cups carrots finely
  shredded with a
  Microplane or the
  finest tooth of a grater
  (1 medium-sized carrot)

3/4 cup marshmallow creme
  or fluff
Confectioners' sugar, for
  dusting (optional)

1. Heat the oven to 350°F. Pan-spray a half sheet pan, line it with parchment paper, and spray anew.

2. In a large bowl, using a whisk, mix together the butter, oil, and sugars, flexing your muscles for about 2 minutes, until everything is fully combined. Whisk in the eggs, and mix vigorously for another 2 minutes to yield a fluffier mixture.

3. Measure the flour, baking powder, salt, cinnamon, and baking soda into the mixing bowl. Ditch the whisk and, with a sturdy spatula, toss together only the dry ingredients on top first, before truly stirring them into the wet ingredients below. Mix until everything is just combined. Stir in the shredded carrot, and mix to combine.

4. Spread the carrot cake batter evenly over the prepared baking sheet, and bake at 350°F for 10 minutes. The cake will pouf in height and start to pull back from the sides of the pan. Remove the cake from the oven, and immediately flip the hot pan upside down onto a new piece of parchment paper or a clean, dry towel. Carefully but quickly, peel off the bottom layer of parchment that the cake baked on, then roll the warm cake up into a tight log. Let it cool completely at room temperature in this log shape for 10 minutes.

(···)

- DO YOU -
BAKE CLUB

Amp the spice up or mellow it out, adjusting the amount of
cinnamon (my fave) or adding in any other spices you like
(ginger, pumpkin-pie spice, etc.) . . .

Swap the marshmallow with any spreadable filling—Cream
Cheese Frosting (page 117), Caramel (page 21), etc.—that
connects to your flavor story.

5. Gently unroll the cooled cake, and cut it in half by width and by length so you have four equal rectangles of cake that want to roll back up on their own.

6. Scoop 2–4 tablespoons of marshmallow fluff onto the surface of each rectangle, and use an offset spatula or a butter knife to spread it evenly almost to the edge of each, then roll each cake back up, and place the outer seam down to keep the roll intact. Slice each of these rolls in half lengthwise.

7. Dust the top with confectioners' sugar if you please, before eating or sharing! In an airtight container at room temperature, the rolls will keep fresh for 1 week. They're also pretty awesome out of the freezer for up to 1 month.

All I Do Is Cake, Cake, Cake, Cake, Cake

Any cake recipe in this book can be scaled up or down, will happily shape-shift into any size pan you like (or have). The general rule of thumb for cake doneness is:

- **Cupcakes:** 15 minutes, 350°F
- **9-inch cakes:** 20–25 minutes, 350°F
- **Half sheet cake or 9-by-13-inch cakes:** 15–20 minutes, 350°F
- **8.5-by-4.5-inch loaf pan (filled three-quarters full):** 45–50 minutes, 350°F
- **Bundt pan (filled three-quarters full):** 60 minutes, 350°F
- **. . . never underestimate the power of a mug cake (filled with 1/2 cup batter):** microwave 2 minutes, let sit 30 seconds before digging in

Toothpick-clean is the name of the game if you're ever uncertain with any cake. If a toothpick inserted into the center comes back with cake batter on it, add 3–5 minutes more.

As with bread, you always want the cake to cool completely before slicing, to eliminate any possibility of gumminess.

For any cakes that you're worried about releasing from the pan, pan-spray the pan, cut parchment the size of the pan—square, rectangle, circle—and place the parchment down, then spray anew. Cake will very quickly become your best friend, as opposed to your biggest fear.

LEMON HONEY GINGER BABYCAKES

Makes 4

One of the most underused levers of cake is its uncanny ability to carry flavor. Yes, you can add extracts and spices straight into the batter, but soak a baked cake with flavored liquid and you've not only made it deliciously moist but also cranked up the flavor. These tiny cakes were born out of my love for lemon-ginger tea. When you're a pro eater like I am, a nice cup of something gingery helps settle the stomach. Soaking these small loaves in a honey-lemon-ginger liquid delivers big comfort and makes them a great "get well" treat—or teatime sidekick.

⇨ Bake this cake in a 1-pound (8.5-by-4.5-inch) loaf pan for 60 minutes, or smaller loaves for 20 minutes, if you prefer other shapes and sizes.

⇨ If you've got cake flour and it's looking for a home, this recipe is an awesome use for it in place of all-purpose flour.

⇨ You can make this recipe without a stand mixer; your cakes will just be a bit more dense and chewy, which isn't necessarily a bad thing.

For the Cake

1 stick (8 tablespoons) unsalted butter, softened
1/4 cup sugar

2 eggs

1/4 cup vegetable oil
1/4 cup honey
Grated zest and juice (1/3 cup) of 3 lemons

1 cup flour
1 teaspoon baking powder
1 teaspoon ground ginger
1/2 teaspoon kosher salt

For the Soak

3 tablespoons honey
2 tablespoons lemon juice
1/2 teaspoon ground ginger

1. Heat the oven to 350°F, and pan-spray four 4-inch mini–cake pans.

2. **Make the cake batter:** In the bowl of a stand mixer fitted with the paddle attachment, cream the butter and sugar on high speed for 1–2 minutes, until the mixture is light and fluffy, scraping down the sides of the mixing bowl with a spatula as needed as you go. Mix in the eggs on medium-high speed until everything is combined and fluffy, 1–2 minutes. Mix in the oil, honey, lemon zest, and lemon juice, and mix on medium-high speed until it's well combined, another 1–2 minutes, still scraping down the sides of the mixing bowl as needed.

3. Measure the flour, baking powder, ginger, and salt into the bowl, and use your spatula to toss together only the dry ingredients on top. Engage the paddle anew and, on medium-low speed now, mix until everything is just combined, about 30 seconds.

4. Using a cookie scoop or a large spoon, divide the batter equally among the prepared molds, and bake them for 15 minutes, until they're golden brown on the edges and a toothpick comes out clean when inserted into the center.

(···)

5. **While the cakes are baking, make the soak:** In a small heavy-bottomed saucepan, over low heat, stir together the honey, lemon juice, and ground ginger until the ginger dissolves and the mixture comes to a boil, about 5 minutes.

6. When the baby cakes are out of the oven, while they're still warm, pour 1 tablespoon of the soak over the surface of each cake, letting it sponge up and fall down into each tin. Bake the soaked cakes at 350°F for 5 minutes. Out of the oven, leave the cakes in their vessels for 10 minutes, then invert them onto a plate while they're still warm, but cool enough to handle with your hands. Serve them warm or at room temperature. In an airtight container at room temperature, the cakes will keep fresh for 1 week. I love to split, toast, and butter them for breakfast in the winter, with a layer of Raspberry Jam (page 27), or pop them into the microwave and serve them warm, anew; wearing PJs def make these baby cakes taste even better.

> - DO YOU -
> # BAKE CLUB
>
> Swap the lemon for any other citrus you like—grapefruit and orange work best, and bring their own personality!
>
> Swap the honey in this cake for molasses to yield a deeper, more moody look and flavor.
>
> Remove the ginger altogether if the soothing heat is not your thing.

- DO YOU -
BAKE CLUB

Like a PB cheesecake?
Add some peanut-
butter chips in
alongside the
chocolate chips. Like a
strawberry-cheesecake
moment? Add a
spoonful of Strawberry
Jam (page 27) in with
the cheesecake filling.

BLACK BOTTOM CUPCAKES

Makes 6

Some recipes are classics for a reason, like these chocolate cupcakes with a cheesecake core. I can guarantee you, no one will get mad at that. The cheesecake weighs some of the cake batter down, keeping it dense and fudgy. THAT is a black-bottom cupcake, my friends. Mic drop.

⇨ Swap the milk and vinegar for ¼ cup buttermilk or the runoff liquid from your latest batch of Ricotta (page 56).

For the Cake Batter
4 tablespoons unsalted
  butter, softened
⅓ cup sugar
2 tablespoons light brown
  sugar

1 egg

¼ cup vegetable oil
¼ cup milk
1 teaspoon vanilla extract
¼ teaspoon apple cider
  vinegar

¾ cup flour
⅓ cup cocoa powder
1½ teaspoons baking
  powder
½ teaspoon kosher salt

For the Cheesecake Filling
2 ounces cream cheese,
  at room temperature
¼ cup confectioners' sugar
⅛ teaspoon vanilla extract
Pinch of salt
¼ cup chocolate chips

1. Preheat the oven to 350°F, and line a cupcake pan with papers.

2. **Make the cake batter:** In a large bowl, using a whisk, mix together the butter and sugars, flexing your muscles for about 2 minutes, until the mixture is light, fluffy, and fully combined. Whisk in the egg, stirring to aerate and combine it, about 1 minute. Whisk in the oil, milk, vanilla, and vinegar, and mix vigorously for another 2 minutes, to yield a looser, smoother mixture.

3. Measure the flour, cocoa powder, baking powder, and salt into the mixing bowl. Ditch the whisk and, with a sturdy spatula, toss together only the dry ingredients on top first, before truly stirring them into the wet ingredients below. Mix until everything is just combined.

4. **Make the cheesecake filling:** In a small bowl, with a cereal spoon or a small but sturdy spatula, mix the cream cheese, sugar, vanilla, and salt together, and stir until the mixture is smooth and luscious, about 1 minute.

5. Divide the cake batter evenly among the cupcake cavities, filling each two-thirds full. Divide the cheesecake filling equally across the tops of the cake batter with a spoon, then press the cheesecake filling deeper down into the batter, nearly hitting the bottom, but stopping short. The cupcake cavity will be three-quarters full in total. Sprinkle chocolate chips evenly atop the cupcakes.

6. Bake at 350°F for 16–18 minutes, until the chocolate batter poufs up around the cheesecake portion, which will set in the center. Cool the cupcakes completely in the pan before checking out those chocolatey bottoms! In an airtight container in the fridge, the cakes will keep fresh for 1 week.

CHOCOLATE MAYO CAKE

Makes 1 cake

Yep, you read that right. Don't make a face: mayonnaise makes an INCREDIBLE cake. I mean, think about it. It has all the elements you need—oil, eggs, sugar, salt, acid. So why not harness it as a secret weapon for moisture and sponge?! But maybe wait until people have a bite to let them in on the secret, just in case there are any mayo haters in the crowd.

- -

⇨ Line the bottom of the baking pan with parchment paper if you've got it, for an even easier release.

⇨ If you can get your hands on the extra-dark version of your average grocery store cocoa powder, it works wonders here, in both color and depth of flavor.

⇨ If you've got cake flour and it's looking for a home, this recipe is an awesome use for it in place of all-purpose flour.

- -

2 eggs
1¼ cups sugar
¼ cup light brown sugar

⅔ cup mayonnaise
½ cup milk
2 teaspoons vanilla extract

1 cup flour
½ cup + 1 tablespoon
   cocoa powder
1½ teaspoons baking
   powder
1½ teaspoons kosher salt

1. Heat the oven to 350°F, and pan-spray a 9-inch cake pan.

2. In a large bowl, using a whisk, mix together the eggs and sugars, flexing your muscles for about 2 minutes, until they are light, fluffy, and fully combined. Whisk in the mayonnaise, milk, and vanilla, and mix vigorously for another 2 minutes, to yield a looser, smoother mixture.

3. Measure the flour, cocoa powder, baking powder, and salt into the mixing bowl. With the whisk toss together only the dry ingredients on top first, before truly stirring them into the wet ingredients below. Then whisk until everything is just combined and smooth.

4. Spread the cake batter evenly over the prepared baking pan, and bake at 350°F for 30–35 minutes. The cake will pouf in height and begin to pull back from the edge of the cake pan, and a toothpick should come out clean when inserted into the center.

5. Cool the cake completely in the pan before inverting and serving it. In an airtight container at room temperature, the cake will keep fresh for 2 weeks.

- DO YOU -
BAKE CLUB

10/10 you can bake and dust this cake as a single layer for a very classy, understated, knockout of a chocolate-cake experience.

Divide the cake batter over two greased 9-inch cake pans, bake them for 20 minutes (thinner layers of batter bake more quickly), and layer Frosting (page 269), Fudge Sauce (page 22), Caramel (page 21), or otherwise, to make it a birthday cake mainstay.

Take this show into Tabletop Desserts land and get your Mirror Glaze on (page 281).

BLUEBERRY MUFFIN BUNDT CAKE

Makes 1 cake

1 cup sugar + more for
   dusting

3 eggs

1 cup milk

Grated zest and juice of
   2 lemons

1 teaspoon kosher salt

12–14 day-old blueberry
   muffins (about 2 pounds
   total)

I don't know about you, but I always have muffins lying around—you make a batch or bring some home from a bakery, but at some point, the fam starts to look at you all side-eye—like, "Stop trying to pawn your muffin leftovers on us." Until, that is, I took a page out of my mother's waste-not, want-not rule book and started repurposing muffins for . . . muffin cake! Bread-pudding-like in its construction, yet fresh and bright on account of the blueberries, here the muffins do a presto chango to magically become dessert. When you serve this with a scoop of vanilla ice cream, your fam will be all, "Woah. Where did this come from?!"

⇨ Only have one or two leftover muffins? This recipe scales down in a cinch, occupying cupcake molds or a pan much smaller than a large-format Bundt. Adjust the bake time accordingly.

1. Heat the oven to 350°F, pan-spray a 12-cup Bundt pan, and lightly dust it with sugar to coat the crevices.

2. In a large bowl, using a whisk, mix together the sugar, eggs, milk, lemon zest and juice, and salt until everything is fully combined, about 1 minute.

3. Ditch the whisk for a sturdy spatula, and break up the muffins into bite-sized pieces (think the size of a donut hole—not much smaller or they will disintegrate, not much bigger or they will be too big and rocky and will not take on much liquid), and stir them into the bowl, tossing to coat and soak them in the wet mixture.

4. Pour the mixture into the Bundt pan and bake at 350°F for 50 minutes. Your cake will only puff slightly, but it will have a caramel-colored top and a rich caramelized flavor.

5. Out of the oven, let the cake cool in the pan for 30 minutes, then run a small butter knife or offset spatula between the edge of the cake and the pan to help release it. Invert the pan onto a plate to fully release the cake, and let it cool completely, about 2 hours. Serve it upside down for a caramelized mountainous muffin vis, or right side up. Slice and serve it. In an airtight container at room temperature, the cake will keep fresh for 1 week, though I like to freeze the individual pieces for a dessert moment any night I'm in need.

- DO YOU -
BAKE CLUB

Swap in Brown Butter Chocolate Chip Muffins (page 110) and remove the lemon zest and juice.

BROWNIE CAKE

Makes 1 cake

1 stick (8 tablespoons)
unsalted butter

½ cup chocolate chips

1 cup sugar

3 eggs, whites and yolks
separated

1½ teaspoons vanilla extract

⅓ cup flour
¼ cup cocoa powder
½ teaspoon kosher salt

You know when someone offers you a perfectly fine light, fluffy chocolate cake, but you find yourself secretly wishing it was a dense, fudgy brownie? This is a real and totally normal feeling—and one that I experience time and time again. Chocolate cake is a totally worthy dessert, but brownies bring with them so much more flavor and depth and lusciousness, it's really not even a fair comparison. So I set out to make a bit of a hybrid. Now you can have your cake and eat your brownie, too.

⇨ Don't hate me: You need both a bowl/spatula/whisk setup and a stand-mixer/bowl/whisk attachment. A few extra dirty dishes in pursuit of this glory won't kill you, I promise. We're trying to combine the dense and fudgy with the light and cakey—defying gravity takes some extra techniques and tools!

1. Heat the oven to 325°F, and pan-spray an 8-by-8-inch baking pan.

2. In the microwave, in a large heatproof bowl, melt the butter and chocolate chips together, working in 30-second spurts, stirring with a sturdy heat-safe spatula in between blasts, until the mixture is smooth, about 2 minutes.

3. Switch mixing tools: Whisk in the sugar and mix until it's combined, about 30 seconds. Whisk in the egg yolks and vanilla, and stir until the mixture is smooth and glossy, about 30 seconds.

4. Measure the flour, cocoa powder, and salt into the mixing bowl. Switch back to the spatula, and toss together only the dry ingredients on top first, before truly stirring them into the wet ingredients below. Mix until everything is just combined.

5. In a stand mixer fitted with the whisk attachment, whip the egg whites on high speed until they are light and fluffy, 3–4 minutes.

6. Take a heaping spatula-full (about ½ cup) of egg whites and mix it into the chocolate mixture until it disappears and the chocolate is lighter. Then spatula in the remainder of the egg whites, and carefully mix the two together, folding the egg in— or tracing the spatula through the center of the bowl, pulling the mixture toward you, then tracing the sides of the bowl to scoop any unmixed chocolate mixture on top of the egg whites, repeating until the egg whites are fully incorporated, any white streaks having disappeared in full, and only a lighter chocolate mixture remains.

(···)

7. Pour the batter into the greased pan, and spread it evenly across the surface. Bake at 325°F for 30 minutes. Much as with Brownies (page 74), you will have a thin layer of flint, but a taller-still gooey-in-the-center mixture.

8. Cool the cake completely at room temperature before slicing and serving it. In an airtight container at room temperature, it will keep fresh for 1 week.

- DO YOU -
BAKE CLUB

If you're feeling extra, go for it and bring in a Snickers-inspired moment. Add a layer of Caramel (page 21), then a layer of Peanut Butter Nougat (page 228).

Spruce this gal up by swapping in a 9-inch cake pan.

LEMON LOAF

Makes 1 loaf

I fell in love with the lemon tea cake a team of bakers would be just pulling out of the oven around 6:00 a.m., when I showed up for my shift at my first professional pastry job. If I was lucky, at the end of my night, I would get a slice. WOWEEE! It wasn't until years later, when I reverse-engineered my memory of this cake, that I realized that the only way to get it incredibly moist and insanely gorgeous was to use a multi-step process of baking, soaking, and then glazing. All this time, I thought the overnight bakers just saved it as the last item on their prep list, but really they did it this way because it's such a multi-step labor of love (but well worth it!).

⇨ Substitute sour cream for the yogurt for an awesome riff. I'd also happily take a flavored yogurt, for a little back note in your cake, if that's all you've got.

⇨ If you don't have access to lemons, swap the lemon zest for 1 tablespoon lemon extract, and lemon juice for milk in the soak and glaze. You will still be very happy.

⇨ If you've got cake flour and it's looking for a home, this recipe is an awesome use for it in place of all-purpose flour.

⇨ You can make this recipe without a stand mixer; your cake will just be a bit more dense and chewy, which isn't necessarily a bad thing.

For the Cake

3 eggs
1 cup sugar
1 cup (8 ounces) plain
   Greek yogurt
Grated zest of 4 lemons
1/2 cup vegetable oil

1 1/2 cups flour
2 teaspoons baking powder
1/2 teaspoon kosher salt

For the Soak

1 cup confectioners' sugar
6 tablespoons lemon juice

For the Glaze

1 cup confectioners' sugar
2 tablespoons lemon juice

1. Heat the oven to 350°F, and pan-spray a 1-pound (8.5-by-4.5-inch) loaf pan.

2. **Make the cake batter:** In the bowl of a stand mixer fitted with the whisk attachment, mix the eggs, sugar, yogurt, lemon zest, and oil on medium-high speed until the mixture is fluffy and well combined, 1–2 minutes, scraping down the sides of the mixing bowl as needed as you go.

3. Measure the flour, baking powder, and salt into the bowl, and use your spatula to toss together only the dry ingredients on top. Engage the whisk attachment anew and, on medium-low speed now, mix until everything is just combined, about 30 seconds.

4. Pour the batter into the prepared pan, and bake at 350°F for 55–60 minutes, or until the cake is golden brown, the corners of the cake begin to pull from the sides of the pan, and a toothpick comes out clean when inserted into the center.

(···)

5. **While the cake is baking, make the soak:** In a small bowl, whisk together the 1 cup confectioners' sugar and 6 tablespoons lemon juice, stirring until the mixture is smooth and nearly translucent, about 2 minutes. Set this aside, uncovered, and **make the glaze:** In another small bowl, whisk together the 1 cup confectioners' sugar and 2 tablespoons lemon juice, stirring until smooth and both thicker and whiter than the soak, about 2 minutes. Cover this with a piece of plastic wrap, and set it aside.

6. Pull the cake out of the oven, and cool it for 10 minutes in the pan to allow it to sturdy a bit. While it's still warm, lift up the cake to confirm that you'll be able to release it easily, then secure the cake back in the pan. Drizzle the soak over the warm cake, and watch it sponge up the flavor and moisture, about 10 minutes for all the soak to be sopped up. Gently lift the cake up once more to confirm its easy release.

7. Once the cake is cooled, after about 1 hour, remove it from its pan and transfer it to a plate. Drizzle the glaze back and forth over the top, allowing some to drip down the edges— my favorite part! Allow the glaze to set, another hour, before slicing and serving the cake. In an airtight container at room temperature, it will keep fresh for 2 weeks. This cake becomes deeper in flavor and moisture with age, so don't be ashamed to bake it a day or two or three in advance!

- DO YOU -
BAKE CLUB

If you have a bevy of other citrus, swap the lemons for any single fruit—or a combo! Limes! Tangerines! Yuzu!

Add in 2 teaspoons of clear vanilla extract for a creamsicle or any kind of citrus-cicle moment!

MAPLE SHEET CAKE

Makes 1 cake

An excuse to bake with that maple syrup that's been in the door of your fridge forever, this cake is also a cozy fall dessert power move. This beaut kinda tastes like a pancake in all the right ways; it's an amazing starting place for a breakfast moment, something to ritz up with flavored Whipped Cream (page 24) and fresh berries, or to just lob a knob of ice cream on top for a *Fast & Furious* movie marathon.

⇨ This cake batter translates into other cake forms—bake it in a 6-cup Bundt cake form, a 9-inch cake round; line a twelve-cavity cupcake pan with cupcake papers—whatever size or shape you please. Just adjust the baking time up or down depending.

⇨ Primo maple syrup means primo maple flavor and color. Don't skimp here.

⇨ If you've got cake flour and it's looking for a home, this recipe is an awesome use for it in place of all-purpose flour.

4 tablespoons unsalted butter, softened + more for serving

1¾ cups maple syrup + more for serving

2 eggs

½ cup vegetable oil
½ teaspoon vanilla extract
¼ teaspoon apple cider vinegar

1¾ cups flour
2 teaspoons baking powder
½ teaspoon kosher salt

1. Heat the oven to 350°F, and pan-spray a half sheet pan.

2. In a large bowl, using a whisk, mix together the butter and syrup, flexing your muscles for about 2 minutes, until the mixture is light, fluffy, and fully combined. Whisk in the eggs, stirring to aerate and combine them, about 1 minute. Whisk in the oil, vanilla, and vinegar, and mix vigorously for another 2 minutes, to yield a looser, smoother mixture.

3. Measure the flour, baking powder, and salt into the mixing bowl, and with the whisk toss together only the dry ingredients on top first, before truly stirring them into the wet ingredients below. Mix until everything is just combined.

4. Spread the batter evenly across the prepared baking pan, and bake at 350°F for 25–30 minutes, until it's golden brown and a toothpick comes out clean when inserted into the center.

5. This cake is my ultimate favorite served slightly warm out of the oven with a pat of butter on top and maple syrup drizzled over it, dripping down. That said, it will keep fresh wonderfully in an airtight container at room temperature for 1 week.

- DO YOU -
BAKE CLUB

Think of this cake as a jumping-off point, like you would a good stack of pancakes. Me? I rock a banana-caramel topping (page 21) and some chocolate chips to finish. But maybe you're more a cinnamon-sugar or strawberries-and-cream!

ICE CREAM LOAF CAKE

Makes 1 cake

Think about ice cream—it's eggs, milk, sugar, salt, acid, fat . . . all the things we always pull out and measure individually when we go to make a cake. Self-rising flour is a kick start—a three-for-one of all-purpose flour, baking powder, and salt. So why not give all the squats, reaches, lids-on, lids-off, measuring-cup madness a break?

⇨ Line the baking pan with parchment paper if you've got it, for an even easier release.

⇨ If you don't have self-rising flour, mix together 1 cup flour, 1½ teaspoons baking powder, and ¼ teaspoon salt.

2 cups (1 pint) ice cream, softened, nearly melted

1 egg

1 cup self-rising flour

3 tablespoons fun stuff (sprinkles! chocolate chips! dried cherries! cut-up candy bars!) (optional)

1. Preheat the oven to 350°F, and pan-spray a 1-pound (8.5-by-4.5-inch) loaf pan.

2. In a large bowl, using a sturdy spatula, mix together the ice cream, egg, and flour, stirring just until they're combined, about 30 seconds. Stir in any fun stuff that helps tell your flavor story, being careful not to overmix.

3. Spread the batter evenly across the prepared pan, and bake at 350°F for 40–45 minutes, until the cake has risen and turned golden brown on the edges, and a toothpick comes out clean when inserted into the center.

4. Out of the oven, let the cake cool in the pan for 30 minutes, then run a small butter knife or offset spatula between the edge of the cake and the pan, to help release it. Invert the pan onto a plate to fully release the cake, and let it cool completely, about 2 hours. In an airtight container at room temperature, the cake will keep fresh for 1 week.

- DO YOU -
BAKE CLUB

I opt for the Milk Bar Birthday Cake ice cream, which I make on the fly for anyone who's a "not too sweet" kind of person in need of celebrating their birth or anything else—but of course you bring your own ice cream energy to this party. Chocolate peanut-butter loaf cake? Yes, please. Mint-chip loaf cake? Always on repeat.

- DO YOU -
BAKE CLUB

ANY veggie that shreds will do here—parsnips, butternut squash, beets, sweet potato—heck—zucchini! (Though if your veggie is wet once it's shredded, wring out the water before adding it to the cake batter.)

SKILLET VEGGIE CAKE

Makes 1 cake, serving 8–10

There's vegetables in my cake! Carrot cake is normal, but why stop there? I've found that an awesome, not too sweet, very lightly spiced cinnamon-cake batter—baked in a skillet to caramelize the bottom and sides—brings out the flavor of any delicious vegetables shredded and snuck in. A little cream cheese frosting on top keeps the line of sweet and savory in my ideal balance. I say, have your cake and eat your veggies, too.

⇨ Any size skillet will work here; just adjust the bake time up or down.

8 tablespoons (1 stick)
  unsalted butter, softened
1/2 cup light brown sugar
1/2 cup sugar

2 eggs

1/4 cup vegetable oil

11/4 cups flour
11/4 teaspoons kosher salt
1 teaspoon baking powder
3/4 teaspoon cinnamon
1/4 teaspoon baking soda

21/2 cups peeled and
  shredded veggies

Cream Cheese Frosting
  (page 117)

1. Heat the oven to 350°F, and pan-spray an 8-inch cast-iron skillet.

2. In a large bowl, using a whisk, mix together the butter and sugars, flexing your muscles for about 2 minutes, until they're fully combined. Whisk in the eggs, and mix vigorously, another 2 minutes, to yield a fluffier mixture. Whisk in the oil, and mix until it's smooth and glossy, about 1 minute.

3. Measure the flour, salt, baking powder, cinnamon, and baking soda into the mixing bowl. Ditch the whisk, and with a sturdy spatula toss together only the dry ingredients on top first, before truly stirring them into the wet ingredients below. Mix until everything is just combined. Stir in the shredded veggies, and mix to combine it.

4. Spread the cake batter evenly in the skillet, and bake at 350°F for 25–30 minutes. The cake will rise and puff, caramelizing in color on top and starting to pull from the sides of the skillet. At 25 minutes, gently poke the edge of the cake with your finger: it should bounce back slightly, and the center should no longer be jiggly. Leave the cake in the oven for an extra 3–5 minutes if it doesn't pass these tests.

5. Make the cream cheese frosting as the cake bakes, cover it with a towel, and set it aside.

6. Remove the cake from the oven, and cool it in the skillet on a wire rack or, in a pinch, in the fridge or freezer (don't worry, that's not cheating). Frost the cooled cake by spreading or piping across the surface of the cake just to the edge. Store your skillet cake in the skillet in the fridge or at room temperature, wrapped in plastic wrap, for up to 5 days.

SPRITE CAKE

Makes 1 cake, serving 12

It was as a kid spending summers on my grandma's farm in Ohio—where everyone called soda POP—that I first saw a 7 Up cake in the grocery store. My mind was BLOWN. No way Grams was going to let us buy it, but you better believe we went home that day, popped open her old-school meat-cooler fridge, and got to recipe-testing. Including soda here isn't just a killer marketing ploy—it's a cheat code for giving flavor and moisture to the cake, and a real testament to the ingenuity of the Midwest.

➪ You can make this recipe without a stand mixer; your cake will just be a bit more dense and chewy, which isn't necessarily a bad thing.

➪ Zesting is a labor of love for this cake—stick with it!

➪ If you've got cake flour and it's looking for a home, this recipe is an awesome use for it in place of all-purpose flour.

2 sticks (16 tablespoons)
   unsalted butter, softened
3 cups sugar
Grated zest of 5 lemons
Grated zest of 3 limes

4 eggs

$1/2$ cup vegetable oil
Juice of 5 lemons and
   3 limes (about $2/3$ cup)

3 cups flour + more for
   dusting
2 teaspoons baking powder
2 teaspoons salt
$13/4$ cups Sprite

1 Recipe Sprite Glaze
   (recipe follows)

1. Heat the oven to 350°F, and pan-spray and flour a 12-cup Bundt pan.

2. Make the cake batter: In the bowl of a stand mixer fitted with the paddle attachment, mix the butter, sugar, and citrus zests on medium-high speed until the mixture is fluffy, fragrant, and well combined, 1–2 minutes, scraping down the sides of the mixing bowl as needed as you go. Mix in the eggs on medium-high speed until everything is combined and fluffy, 1–2 minutes. Mix in the oil and citrus juices, and mix on medium-high speed until they're well combined, another 1–2 minutes, still scraping down the sides of the mixing bowl as needed.

3. Measure the flour, baking powder, and salt into the bowl, and use your spatula to toss together only the dry ingredients on top. Engage the paddle anew, and on medium-low speed, mix for 3 "Mississippi"s. Turn off the mixer, and pour in half of the $13/4$ cups Sprite. Turn the mixer back on at medium-low speed, and let it mix for 6 "Mississippi"s. Turn off the mixer, and pour in the remaining Sprite. Turn the mixer back on at medium-low speed, and finish mixing until everything is just combined, about 6 "Mississippi"s more.

4. Pour the batter into the Bundt pan, and bake at 350°F for 60–70 minutes, until the cake rises, puffs, and caramelizes and a toothpick comes out clean when inserted into the center.

(...)

- DO YOU -
BAKE CLUB

I'm a lemon-lime girl myself, but if you're a Coca-Cola or Dr Pepper person, omit the lemons and limes and the Sprite, sub in your favorite soda, and give it a little context—maybe a little cocoa powder for Coca-Cola, a little molasses for Dr Pepper; heck, swap orange for the lemon and get that Sunkist energy going in full swing!

5. While the cake is baking, make the glaze.

6. Out of the oven, let the cake cool in the pan for 30 minutes, then run a small butter knife or offset spatula between the edge of the cake and the pan to help release it. Invert the pan onto a plate to fully release the cake, and let it cool completely, about 2 hours. Once the cake is cooled completely, drizzle the glaze over its surface, allowing some to drip down the edges—my favorite part! Add a little extra zest for freshness and a pop of yellow and green color, if you please. Allow the glaze (and zest) to set, about 10 minutes, before slicing and serving the cake. In an airtight container at room temperature, it will keep fresh for 2 weeks. This cake becomes deeper in flavor and moisture with age, so don't be ashamed to bake it a day or two or three in advance!

Sprite Glaze

2¼ cups confectioners' sugar
2 tablespoons Sprite
1 teaspoon lemon juice
Pinch of salt

Grated zest of additional 1 lemon and 1 lime (optional), for top

In a small bowl, whisk together the confectioners' sugar, 2 tablespoons Sprite, lemon juice, and salt, stirring until the mixture is smooth and nearly translucent, about 2 minutes. Cover the bowl with plastic and set it aside.

PEACHES AND CREAM UPSIDE DOWN CAKE

Makes 1 cake

My family was never much into pineapple, so it was years before I ever tried my hand at a pineapple upside-down cake. But when I finally did, it was a light-switch moment: a sneaky way to infuse flavor and texture and a POV into an otherwise tasty (albeit a little boring) cake. For this recipe, I've opened up my aperture to include peaches, which play famously with the deep sugar and nutty butter flavors and hold their shape and texture during baking. This gal is a favorite with Mom (aka Greta aka GG), who swears it's like a fine wine or a great human, only getting better with age.

⇨ You can make this recipe without a stand mixer; your cakes will just be a bit more dense and chewy, which isn't necessarily a bad thing.

⇨ Swap the milk and vinegar in the batter for 1/2 cup buttermilk or the runoff liquid from your latest batch of Ricotta (page 56).

⇨ If you've got cake flour and it's looking for a home, this recipe is an awesome use for it in place of all-purpose flour.

For the Top/Bottom
30 peach slices (3 or 4 whole, ripe fresh peaches sliced about 1/2 inch thick, or frozen slices)

For the Caramel
1/2 cup sugar

2 tablespoons milk
1 teaspoon vanilla extract

For the Cake Batter
1 stick (8 tablespoons) unsalted butter, softened
3/4 cup sugar
1/4 cup light brown sugar

3 eggs

1/2 cup milk
1/3 cup vegetable oil
2 teaspoons vanilla extract
1/2 teaspoon apple cider vinegar

11/2 cups flour
1 teaspoon baking powder
1 teaspoon kosher salt
3/4 cup white chocolate chips

1. Heat the oven to 350°F, and pan-spray a 9-inch cake pan. Arrange the top (which will start out on the bottom) by arranging the peach slices artistically to cover the bottom of the greased pan (this will be the mosaic for all to see when your cake is fully baked).

2. **Make the caramel:** In a heavy-bottomed medium-sized saucepan over medium-high heat, cook the 1/2 cup sugar. As soon as the sugar starts to melt into a translucent phase, use a sturdy heat-safe spatula to move it constantly around the pan—you want it to melt and caramelize evenly. Cook and stir, cook and stir, until the caramel is amber-colored, about 3 minutes from when the sugar starts to melt, being careful to never let it burn.

3. Once the caramel has reached the target color, remove the saucepan from the heat. Very slowly and very carefully, pour in the 2 tablespoons milk and 1 teaspoon vanilla extract. The caramel will bubble up and steam; stand away until the steam dissipates. Put the pan back over medium heat if there are clumps or lumps, cooking until the sugar mixture is completely smooth. Use the heat-safe spatula to stir the mixture together, then drizzle this hot mixture evenly over the peach mosaic in the cake pan.

(...)

4. **Make the cake batter:** In the bowl of a stand mixer fitted with the paddle attachment, mix the butter and sugars on medium-high speed until everything is fluffy and well combined, 1–2 minutes, scraping down the sides of the mixing bowl as needed as you go. Mix in the eggs on medium-high speed until they're combined and the mixture is fluffy, 1–2 minutes. Mix in the milk, oil, vanilla, and vinegar, and mix on medium-high speed until the mixture is well combined but much looser, another 1–2 minutes, still scraping down the sides of the mixing bowl as needed.

5. Measure the flour, baking powder, and salt into the bowl, and use your spatula to toss together only the dry ingredients on top. Engage the paddle anew, and on medium-low speed, mix until everything is just combined, about 30 seconds. Mix in the white chocolate chips until they're just combined.

6. Pour the cake batter over the caramel-covered peaches and bake at 350°F for 30–35 minutes, until the cake rises and poufs, is golden brown around the edges, and begins to pull back from the sides of the cake pan, and a toothpick comes out clean when inserted into the center.

7. Out of the oven, cool the cake in the pan for 5 minutes, then carefully invert the hot cake pan onto a plate or cake dish so the bottom peach brilliance becomes the top. (If any peaches became stubborn and stayed in the pan, just remove them gently and transfer them over to the top of the cake, where they belong. There will be indentations, so it will be easy to find their places!) Cool the cake fully for another hour before slicing and serving it. In an airtight container at room temperature, the cake will keep fresh for 2 weeks. This cake becomes deeper in flavor and moisture with age, so don't be ashamed to bake it a day or two or three in advance!

- DO YOU -
BAKE CLUB

Swap peaches for any other fruit that will make magic with caramel and hold its shape during baking: Apples! Pears! Plums! Nectarines! Cherries! (Pineapple, obvi!)

Instead of white chocolate chips, use any other chip that tells the flavor story—I'm not mad at an apple-butterscotch or a cherry–chocolate chip upside-down cake, for the record.

SNACK
AISLE

Marshmallow Treats 211

Potato Chips 215

Chewy Granola Bars 216

Pop Rocks 218

PB Cups 221

Popcorn 225

Peanut Butter Nougat 228

Gummy Bears 233

Fudge 234

Graham Cracker Toffee 239

Lemon Ice 240

PB-Pretzel Freezer Cookies 243

Peppermint Patties 244

Caramel Apples 246

Puppy Chow 248

Turtles 253

@elainedarer

#bakeclub

@jerseykellya

@joyosity

#bakeclub

@Leighelswilde

@timross41

#bakeclub

@carpedolce

If you know ANYTHING about me, it's that my love of food was found and defined in the aisles of the grocery store—yes, the cereal aisle; and the baking aisle, of course; but most especially the SNACK AISLE. Though technically I'm a highly trained pastry chef, I swore long ago to never stop loving or seeking inspiration from my favorite childhood and adolescent bites—candy bar flavor combos, boxes of crunchy, salty things, bags of sweet, gummy things, and every naughty and nice thing in between. I believe grocery stores are where so many of our most informative flavor moments are first forged, and those tasty tidbits are some of the most powerful and important ones to tap into—regardless of whether there's a white tablecloth or it's melting in your hand at the campsite.

These grocery store bites remind us of our past, and help us remember who we are into the future. They're also moments that we share in parallel with one another. You think you're the only one who got down with mixing melted chocolate and peanut butter with cereal in a Ziploc bag dusted with powdered sugar in your PJs during an epic sleepover? Or who got caramel blissfully stuck in your teeth as you bit into a fall apple with the crunch of leaves under your feet? You think you're the only one who poured soda into your mouth, already loaded with Pop Rocks, to watch your hair tickle all the way down your spine? No way. Doesn't make it any less special, just shows you the power of the snack aisle.

The recipes in this chapter are DIY versions of snack aisle favorites and are meant to really ignite your imagination and engage your sense of "what if." What if *you* were in charge of deciding exactly what flavors and sizes and shapes of snacks were in the snack aisle? Every recipe starts with making the basic snack from scratch, but if you ask me, the sky is truly the limit—me and a few of my long-standing Bake Clubbers will even show you some moves.

You can practically open a minimart with the recipes that follow. Always wished your favorite fudge tasted like a malted marshmallow milkshake? Or your marshmallow treats had pretzels and caramel in them? Pistachios and dark chocolate in place of pecans in a turtle? Cinnamon sugar or cheddar cheese or both (try it before you hate on it) dusted on your potato chips? The snack aisle is officially open for business!

@ausome86

MARSHMALLOW TREATS

Makes 9

All through my tenth-grade year in school, I'd make a batch of marshmallow treats each night, changing up the cereals—sometimes single flavors, sometimes a combination—and mix-ins (chips, nuts, flakes, bits), cut them into eight, and bring them to school for my friends. Everyone would meet after second period to sample the treat of the day, and everyone had their favorite. That is the best part of this recipe: it's always joyful, each batch is its own excuse to clear a moment for an epic snack.

- -

⇨ Swap the butter for oil to make it vegan! (Make sure those marshmallows are vegan themselves—there are a lot of great ones on the market.)

⇨ There are a lot of great coincidentally gluten-free and vegan cereals out there, too, if you have any special requests!

⇨ A great marshmallow treat is all about the ratio of butter to marshmallows to cereal and salt. I'm a fan of more butter, less cereal, so when you bite in it really means it :) But if you want a more considered approach (read: less buttery and sweet), feel free to take out 1–2 tablespoons butter and add a cup or two of cereal.

⇨ I'm a super fan of the taller Rice Krispie treat, but if you like a shorter square, use a 9-by-13-inch pan instead of the 8-by-8-inch pan.

- -

5 tablespoons unsalted butter (save the paper it's wrapped in!)
One 10-ounce bag marshmallows

6 cups Rice Krispies
¼ teaspoon kosher salt

1. Pan-spray an 8-by-8-inch baking pan.

2. In a very large heatproof bowl, gently melt the butter and marshmallows together in the microwave for 2 minutes. Remove the bowl from the microwave, and stir the mixture with a sturdy heat-safe spatula to combine the two ingredients, then microwave for 1 more minute to ensure a completely melted butter-marshmallow mixture.

3. Add the cereal and salt to the bowl, and coat the cereal fully and quickly—as the marshmallow mixture cools, it gets harder and harder to work with.

4. Transfer the mixture to the prepared pan and, with your heat-safe spatula, spread it evenly across the surface and into every corner. I like to use a used butter wrapper to do this—Grandma's trick!

5. Let the mixture cool and set for 10 minutes before cutting it into squares. At room temperature, covered with a lid or a sheet of foil or plastic, the treats will stay fresh for up to a week.

- DO YOU -
BAKE CLUB

You can use a baking sheet and cookie cutters to bring some pizzazz to the form of these treats. That said, you can also free-form them into different sizes and shapes.

Over the holidays, I sub in cornflakes and add a little green food coloring to my marshmallow goo, to make cereal-treat wreaths, which I adorn with red dot candies.

Current Favorite Marshmallow Treats Moves

Up the butter quantity to 8 tablespoons and brown it first (page 111), to give an unreasonably delicious nutty note.

Add ½ cup nut butter or paste (like Biscoff or dulce de leche) or melted chocolate chips to the mixture at the end of Step 2. It's important that this add-in not be too "wet," or it will add sog to your cereal (so jam, fudge sauce, caramel sauce, etc., are off the table).

Add in ½ teaspoon of any extract (vanilla, lemon, banana, coconut, etc.) at the end of Step 2, to up the flavor profile of your treat.

Heck, swap the Rice Krispies for any cereal you choose! Smaller cereals, with pieces the size of Rice Krispies, are a great one-for-one swap, but if you're using bigger pieces, like Golden Grahams or Cinnamon Toast Crunch or cornflakes, you'll likely need 1–2 cups more cereal to occupy the buttery marshmallow mixture. Never be afraid to combine big and little size cereals, or two flavors, regardless of size, that you just love!

Feel free to amp up your flavor story by adding or entirely replacing cereal with popcorn, rice cakes broken into smaller pieces, mini-pretzels, or other salty cracker pieces. Sweet replacements, like cookie crumbs, also work here.

Sprinkle in from 1 tablespoon up to ½ cup of other fun mix-ins—toasted nuts, sprinkles, raisins, shredded coconut—to amp up the surprise flavor moments and vis.

GAZILLIONAIRE ENERGY
7 cups Cocoa Krispies + 1 cup pretzels + ½ cup dulce de leche

BLUEBERRY PIE
4 cups Rice Krispies + 1 cup pie crust pieces (page 120) + ¼ cup dried blueberries

FLUFFERNUTTER
7 cups Golden Grahams + ½ cup peanut butter + ½ cup mini-marshmallows folded in at the end

CHERRY PIE
6 cups Cheerios + 1 cup dried cherries

CINNAMON APPLE
7 cups Cinnamon Toast Crunch + 1 cup freeze-dried apple pieces

STRAWBERRY CORN
7 cups Cap'n Crunch + 1 cup freeze-dried strawberries

STRAWBERRY SHORTCAKE
7 cups Kix + 1 cup freeze-dried strawberries

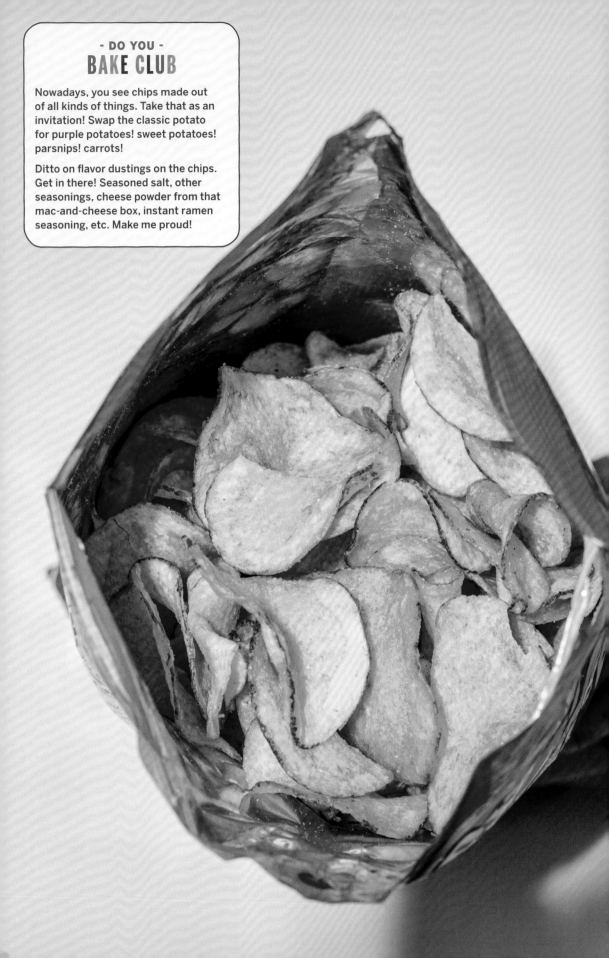

- DO YOU -

BAKE CLUB

Nowadays, you see chips made out of all kinds of things. Take that as an invitation! Swap the classic potato for purple potatoes! sweet potatoes! parsnips! carrots!

Ditto on flavor dustings on the chips. Get in there! Seasoned salt, other seasonings, cheese powder from that mac-and-cheese box, instant ramen seasoning, etc. Make me proud!

POTATO CHIPS

Makes 4 cups, 1 bowlful

Lest you think I am a sweets-only snacker, we need a serious pit stop in savory-ville. On the side of a sandwich. With your fave dips. On their own, by the handful, while you're standing in the pantry. Potato chips are snack aisle royalty, and yet folks rarely DIY 'em. Do you not dream of having freshly made potato chips at arm's reach whenever the craving strikes?

- -

⇨ Sub in apple-cider, rice-wine, or any other vinegar you have in place of white vinegar. However, steer clear of sherry or balsamic vinegar, because they impart too much color and flavor.

⇨ Reuse your oil from Old-Fashioned Donuts (page 114) or from your Pizza (page 156).

- -

1 russet potato (about 1 pound), washed and dried, skin on

1 tablespoon white vinegar

4 cups canola oil + more as needed

Kosher salt, to taste

1. With a Mandoline or a sharp knife and cutting board, slice your potato as thin as you consistently can, about 1/8 inch thick. Transfer your potato slices to a bowl of cold water and rinse; replace the cold water as many times as needed until the water remains clear, probably three or four times. Add the vinegar to the clear water, and let the potato slices sit in the acidulated water for 30 minutes.

2. In the meantime, heat a heavy-bottomed medium-sized pot filled with 4 cups oil to 300°F over medium heat. This will take about 8 minutes.

3. As the oil heats up, pour the liquid out of the bowl of sliced potatoes and, with paper towels, pat each slice of potato dry (oil and water don't like each other!).

4. Test the oil temp by gently lowering one dried slice of potato into the oil, using a slotted spoon. It should fizz immediately and curl slightly, taking on color 2–3 minutes in (flip it as needed). If the chip sinks or it doesn't take on color as quickly, let the oil heat for another few minutes, then try again. Alternatively, if your chip takes on color almost immediately, turn the heat off, or add 1/2 cup of unheated canola oil to cool it down, then try again. Gently remove the chip with the slotted spoon, and transfer it to a plate lined with a few paper towels to soak up the residual oil. Season it with a pinch of salt.

5. Once you've confirmed that your oil is at the target temp, fry a handful of slices at a time, using the same technique—gently lowering the potato slices into the oil on a slotted spoon, frying them to the target color, flipping them as needed, then removing them from the oil with the slotted spoon and seasoning with salt immediately. You're crazy if you don't crush/share these right away, but if for some reason you don't, they'll keep in an airtight container for up to 24 hours.

CHEWY GRANOLA BARS

Makes 12

2½ cups old-fashioned
    oats
2 cups sweetened coconut
    flakes

½ cup honey
6 tablespoons unsalted
    butter
¼ cup light brown sugar
1 tablespoon milk powder
1 teaspoon vanilla extract
½ teaspoon kosher salt

In regular lunch-box rotation, always there when you need a pick-me-up on the go, I think a great granola bar is one of the unsung heroes of our snacking existence. Yet too many folks have put too many "labels" on this simple delight: Is it *super healthy* from all the oats? Or *super sugary* from the honey and sugar? Can't we just let it live its life?! This recipe will make sure you are never far from the comforting embrace of a granola bar, your trusted companion in chasing down life.

⇨ Triple-check that you've got rolled or old-fashioned oats at the ready (NO instant oats allowed anywhere near this recipe!).

⇨ Toasting the oats and coconut deepens the flavor of the granola without your having to bake the bars in the oven.

⇨ If you have a coconut allergy or just aren't a fan, substitute more rolled oats for the coconut flakes.

⇨ If you don't have milk powder, you can make the recipe without it—it just won't be quite as chewy or deep in flavor.

1. Heat the oven to 350°F. Pull out an ungreased half sheet pan, and set it aside. Pan-spray the bottom and sides (for easy release) of an 8-by-8-inch baking pan, or line it with parchment paper and then pan-spray the parchment paper.

2. Spread the oats and coconut flakes evenly across the ungreased baking sheet. Bake at 350°F for 8 minutes, until they're lightly toasted. Transfer them to a large bowl.

3. In a small heavy-bottomed saucepan, over medium heat, bring the honey, butter, light brown sugar, milk powder, vanilla, and salt to a full boil, stirring occasionally with a sturdy heat-safe spatula, until the butter has melted and the sugar has fully dissolved.

4. Pour the saucepan mixture over the bowl of toasted oats and coconut flakes, and mix to combine everything with the spatula.

5. Pour the mixture into the prepared 8-by-8-inch pan, and use the spatula to tamp it down evenly across the surface and into each corner. Cover the pan, and refrigerate it for 1 hour before removing the mixture from the pan. Cut it into twelve bars—two rows by six columns. In an airtight container at room temperature, granola bars will keep fresh for up to 2 weeks.

- DO YOU -
BAKE CLUB

Add up to ¼ cup mini–chocolate chips, raisins, or any other flavorful flair you're feeling, after Step 4. If you're adding something meltable (like chocolate chips), let the mixture cool for 10 minutes first before stirring it in.

If you're looking for a punchier (read: caffeinated) granola bar for pick-me-up moments, add ½–1 teaspoon ground coffee or ground tea after Step 4.

POP ROCKS

Makes 1 cup

1/4 cup water
1 cup sugar
1/4 light corn syrup

1 1/2 teaspoons baking soda
1 tablespoon citric acid
1 1/2 teaspoons powdered
  drink mix (lemonade,
  Kool-Aid, iced tea, etc.)

If your household is anything like mine, when the mood strikes for Pop Rocks, it's a grocery scavenger hunt until you track them down. Usually with my nieces, and usually when they're in their braces stage of life, in which certain candy is off limits, Pop Rocks are one of the great wonders of the snack aisle. Fun to eat (they're like sugary fireworks in your mouth) and a hilariously good time to make on your own, now they'll never go out of stock in your home.

⇨ Substitute honey for the corn syrup if needed.

⇨ Read up on soft ball stage sugar (page 220) so that you know what it is and what it looks like when you cook just beyond it to hard-crack stage.

⇨ If you can't get your hands on citric acid, sub in 1 tablespoon plus 1 1/2 teaspoons (about 2 packs) of Emergen-C (it's a drink mix that has citric acid in it!).

⇨ Any drink mix works here! Kool-Aid, Country Time Lemonade, Jell-O powder packs, etc.

1. Lightly pan-spray a half sheet pan, and set it aside.

2. In a heavy-bottomed, medium-sized saucepan, combine a splash of water, sugar, and corn syrup. Over medium heat, without stirring whatsoever, heat the mixture to soft ball stage (technically 235°F), or when your bubbles are approximately the same size across your mixture and when you dip a spoonful of it into ice water you get a . . . soft ball of sugar. Though never mixing, you can swirl the saucepan around with the flick of your wrist if the mixture seems like it is uneven in temperature. We need to take this mixture to the next stage— hard crack (technically 300°F). Your bubbles will continue growing and popping quickly, turning the slightest-lightest yellow-orange tint without actually changing color (that would make it caramel), and, when you dip a spoonful of it into ice water, you get a . . . piece of sugar that can firmly crack in half, aka hard crack.

- DO YOU -
BAKE CLUB

Flavored extracts and food coloring are also welcome here in place of the 1 1/2 teaspoons powdered drink mix.

@hotmessbakingmama77 rocks lemon-lime Kool-Aid Pop Rocks.

(···)

3. Off the heat, with a sturdy heat-safe spatula, immediately stir in the baking soda, citric acid, and powdered drink mix. The mixture will react a little like a science project—swelling and bubbling up. Don't worry! Keep stirring until all the ingredients are incorporated, and immediately pour the mixture onto the prepared pan. Cool it completely at room temperature for 2 hours before breaking it up into smaller pieces. In an airtight container at room temperature, your candy will stay fresh for up to a month.

Soft Ball Sugar

Soft ball sugar is one of my favorite stages of sugar because so many cool things happen at this stage—nougat, pop rocks, marshmallows, and beyond. Technically 235°F, soft ball stage is the temperature that your sugar and water mixture gets to when the bubbles are all growing and popping in the same size and the same time, a slightly grayish color just before turning to hard crack and then caramel. It's called soft ball because when it's at this target temperature, you can spoon a small amount into ice-cold water and it will turn into a soft, gooey ball. (Hard crack turns into a hard, crackable state, etc.) Finding this temperature is a learned skill, there's plenty of how-to online from me (and others), and I find knowing and understanding it is much more valuable than trying to find, and then read a candy thermometer, which can be super frustrating and not at all foolproof. Once you've got a handle on reaching the soft ball sugar stage on your own, it's super simple/second nature.

GO FOR IT:

In a heavy-bottomed, medium-sized saucepan, combine a splash of water and sugar, and, gently, with a clean finger, stir the ingredients around to ensure they are incorporated, with minimal agitation. Over medium heat, without stirring whatsoever from here on out, heat the mixture. Once it is at a boil, the bubbles in the pan will change size and speed. The mixture will also gray a tad in color, but never take on any more color than that. You are looking for a very special state of sugar syrup—soft ball (technically 235°F), or when your bubbles are approximately the same size across your mixture and when you dip a spoonful of it into ice water you get a . . . soft ball of sugar. Though never mixing, you can swirl the saucepan around with the flick of your wrist if the mixture seems like it is uneven in temperature.

If you ever take your sugar too far, just fill the pan with water, bring it to a boil to clean the sugar off, and start anew. Sugar and water are very easy ingredients to replace!

PB CUPS

Makes 6

At least 30 percent of my body is made up of chocolate and peanut butter, largely fueled by my intake of peanut-butter cups. I once commissioned someone to make a PB cup slicer, and we've had PB cup tasting panels over Thanksgiving meals. For a person who is kin to me, it's kind of mandatory to love this killer flavor combination and its format. So, obviously, I'm going to figure out how to make them at home, and then turn my brain on to all the different riffs, layers, identities, and flavor stories a cup can hold. Party on, family.

⇨ Fancy chocolate is totally allowed here! Sub it in for chocolate chips if you have it and, va va voom, the classy factor will really be showstopping.

For the Chocolate Cups
²/₃ cup chocolate chips
1 teaspoon vegetable oil

For the PB Filling
¹/₂ cup peanut butter
4 tablespoons unsalted butter, melted

²/₃ cup confectioners' sugar
1 teaspoon vanilla extract
¹/₄ teaspoon kosher salt

1. **Make the chocolate cups:** Line six cupcake molds with paper liners.

2. In a small heatproof bowl, gently melt the chocolate chips and oil in the microwave. Work in 30-second spurts, stirring with a sturdy heat-safe spatula in between blasts, until the mixture is smooth, 1–2 minutes.

3. Load a Ziploc bag with two-thirds of the chocolate, and cut a small hole in the corner.

4. Gently squeeze the chocolate into the bottom and halfway up the sides of each of the lined cupcake molds. Pop the molds into the fridge and chill for 10 minutes, to set the chocolate walls and base.

5. **In the meantime, make the PB filling:** In a medium bowl, with a sturdy spatula, stir together the peanut butter and butter until they're smooth, about 30 seconds. Stir in the confectioners' sugar, vanilla, and salt, and mix until the combination is smooth, about 30 seconds.

6. Load a second Ziploc bag with all of the PB filling, and cut a medium-sized hole (it's a relatively thick filling) in the corner.

7. Pull the chocolate cups out of the fridge. Gently and evenly, squeeze the PB filling into the six shells, their walls and floors. Tap the cups on the counter to remove any air bubbles and flatten the surface of the filling. The PB filling should fill the cups three-quarters up the sides of the chocolate walls.

(···)

8. Load a last Ziploc bag with the remaining melted chocolate (feel free to gently heat the chocolate in the microwave for 15–30 seconds if it has begun to set), and cut a small hole in the corner. Gently and evenly, pipe the chocolate over the surface of the PB filling, covering it completely. Tap the cups on the counter again, if needed, to smooth the top layer.

9. Pop your PB cups into the fridge and chill them for 10 minutes, to set the tops completely, before crushing or, okay/fine, sharing! In an airtight container at room temperature, your cups will stay fresh for up to a week, or in the fridge or freezer for up to 1 month.

- DO YOU -
BAKE CLUB

Replace standard chocolate chips with any other meltable chip out there (dark, milk, white, peanut butter, butterscotch, etc.).

Swap the peanut butter with any other nut butter, spread, or filling (lemon jam, fudge sauce, caramel!) you like. Or think broader—this is where the fun really, really comes in—frostings, curds, nougat . . . cookie dough! As long as you can get it in, it can be a cup!

@mburke421 folds crushed, toasted peanuts into her filling (brill!).

@elainedarer adds a layer of caramel, a layer of PB filling, and a layer of pretzels in some, and folds Rice Krispies into the chocolate lids of others.

@aleshia.k swaps in dark chocolate, almond butter, and sea salt.

POPCORN

Makes 5 cups

I was a full-on grown-up before I learned the amazing flex of making fresh popcorn, which opened my brain to a higher level of snacking execution! If fresh popcorn is my first love, kettle corn is my second—the brilliant reality that salty and sweet can crash together to make magic, a lever I've been pulling at home and on the job as a pastry chef ever since. Of all the salty snacks, it is the most fresh, flavorful, and fun to make and play with (my favorite boxes to check).

⇨ If you have microwave popcorn, pop away! One bag of plain microwave popcorn produces the same quantity as ¼ cup kernels. But once you go with fresh popcorn, I promise you'll never go back!

1 tablespoon vegetable oil (if cooking on the stovetop only)
¼ cup popcorn kernels

Any combo of fat and flavor (page 226)

STOVETOP METHOD

1. In a large heavy-bottomed pot with a lid, over medium heat, warm the oil and popcorn kernels. Cover the pot, and wait for the kernels to start popping, which will take 3–4 minutes. As the kernels begin to pop, with the lid still on, feel free to swirl around the contents of the pot with a flick of your wrist. The popcorn will start popping more rapidly, then slow down again. Remove the popcorn from the heat shortly thereafter, so as not to burn it.

2. Remove the lid, and dump the popcorn into one or more serving or mixing bowls, depending on how many different popcorns you want to dream up and serve up!

MICROWAVE METHOD

1. Put the corn kernels in a large paper bag, and microwave them for 3–4 minutes. Listen, as you would to a store-bought microwave popcorn, for the kernels to start popping, then pop nearly in unison, then slow down; stop the microwave and remove the popcorn shortly thereafter so it does not burn.

2. Dump popcorn into one or more serving or mixing bowls depending on how many different popcorns you want to dream and serve up!

- DO YOU -
BAKE CLUB

Once your popcorn is popped, think of the infinite possibilities! The basic formula:

Delicious Liquid Fat + Flavorful Seasoning(s). The makings for some of my favorite moments are given on the next page.

Cheddar–Old Bay Popcorn

1 batch popcorn
4 tablespoons unsalted
   butter, melted

1 pack of seasoning from a
   box of mac-and-cheese
2 teaspoons Old Bay
   Seasoning
1 teaspoon sugar
Pinch of kosher salt

Cinnamon Sugar Kettle Corn

1 batch popcorn
4 tablespoons unsalted
   butter, melted

2 tablespoons sugar
1 teaspoon cinnamon
Pinch of kosher salt

Lemon–Olive Oil Popcorn

1 batch popcorn
3 tablespoons olive oil

Grated zest of 3 lemons
1 tablespoon sugar
Pinch of kosher salt

1. Toss the popped popcorn with up to 4 tablespoons of delicious liquid fat (melted butter! olive oil! pumpkin-seed oil! etc.).

2. Toss the coated popcorn with up to 1/4 cup flavorful seasonings. The liquid fat will act as glue, so the popcorn will hold the flavor and color of whatever you dream up.

Salted Dark Chocolate–Almond Popcorn

1 batch popcorn

1/2 cup dark-chocolate
   chips
1 teaspoon vegetable oil

1/4 cup slivered almonds,
   toasted
1/4 teaspoon kosher salt

As you are making your popcorn, melt the chocolate and oil together gently in the microwave, working in 15-second blasts. Drizzle the melted chocolate mixture atop the popcorn, then sprinkle in the almonds and salt. Let the popcorn set until the chocolate hardens (you can speed this up by popping it into the fridge or freezer for a few minutes).

Caramel Popcorn

1 stick unsalted butter
1/2 cup light brown sugar
1 teaspoon vanilla extract
1/4 teaspoon baking soda
Pinch of kosher salt

1 batch popcorn

In a heavy-bottomed medium-sized saucepan, over medium heat, heat the butter and light brown sugar, stirring constantly until the mixture comes to a boil. Reduce the temperature to medium-low, and cook for an additional 2 minutes without stirring. Add the vanilla, stir to mix it in, and, once the mixture has returned to a simmer, turn the heat off, sprinkle in the baking soda and salt, and stir. The mixture will expand and change color slightly. Carefully pour it over the bowl of popcorn, using a spatula to gently mix until all kernels are covered.

PEANUT BUTTER NOUGAT

Makes 2 cups

2 egg whites

³/₄ cup water
1 cup sugar

¹/₂ cup peanut butter
1 teaspoon kosher salt

Snickers! Milky Way! Baby Ruth! These are the candy bars that cracked the door for my nougat imagination, leading to: peanut-butter nougat! I find the texture of nougat so incredibly alluring because of its polar opposites: light but rich, fluffy but dense, tender but chewy, it's both complex in its eatability and simple in its execution. Plus, the possibilities for nougat flavor stories and applications seem to go on and on. Take some egg whites and give them a whip around with soft ball sugar and tell me I'm wrong!

⇨ This recipe is a stand-mixer affair. Do not attempt it by hand!

⇨ Nougat also acts as an awesome layer or top to any cake (page 173), a filling for Crepes (page 113), to crumble over an ice cream sundae with Fudge Sauce (page 22), and more.

⇨ Read up on soft ball stage sugar on page 220.

1. Lightly pan-spray a 1-pound (8.5-by-4.5-inch) loaf pan, and set it aside.

2. To the clean, dry bowl of a stand mixer fitted with the whisk attachment, add the egg whites. Engage the hook, and whisk on medium-high speed to get medium-stiff peaks, 2–3 minutes. Turn off the mixer, but leave the whisk in the mixture. When Step 3 is complete, you've gotta move quickly, and you want to be ready!

3. In a heavy-bottomed, medium-sized saucepan, combine a splash of water and sugar. Over medium heat, without stirring whatsoever, heat the mixture to soft ball stage (technically 235°F), or when your bubbles are approximately the same size across your mixture and when you dip a spoonful of it into ice water you get a . . . soft ball of sugar. Though never mixing, you can swirl the saucepan around with the flick of your wrist if the mixture seems like it is uneven in temperature.

4. Turn the mixer back on to medium-high speed, and carefully but quickly stream the sugar syrup in, down the side of the bowl. Once all the syrup is added, increase the speed to high, and whip for 6–7 minutes, to temper the egg whites, cool the mixture down, and ultimately transform the contents into a glossy, fluffy, marshmallow mixture.

5. Remove the bowl from the mixer, scrape the whisk attachment clean with a sturdy spatula, and fold in the peanut butter and salt.

(···)

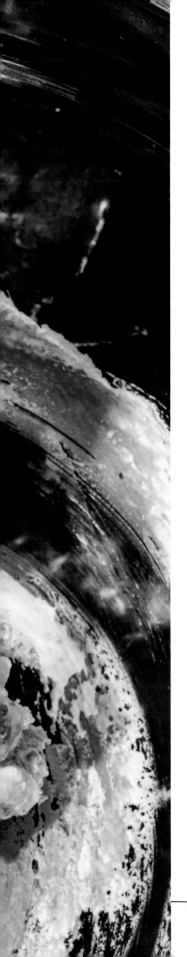

6. With the spatula, transfer the nougat into the prepared pan, and spread it evenly across the surface and into the corners; cut it into pieces, or crumble and store it. In an airtight container, nougat will keep fresh in the fridge for up to 1 week.

Nut (or Seed) Butter

In a blender or food processor, blitz ¾ cup nuts (or seeds) that have been warmed in the microwave or oven until warm to the touch with 2 tablespoons vegetable oil.

- DO YOU -
BAKE CLUB

Add an "I see you" wink of texture with 1 cup of whole nuts (toasted or raw). Dried fruit pieces work well here, too.

Swap the peanut butter for any other nut (or seed) paste (see above): Tahini! Pecan! Pistachio! Pumpkin seed!

Alternatively, remove the peanut butter altogether, and swap in melted chocolate or chocolate chips.

Add up to 2 tablespoons of powdered flavor (cocoa powder! corn powder! tea!) in with or in place of the peanut butter.

Add ½ teaspoon of any extract (almond, maple, vanilla) in with the peanut butter to give your flavor combo a little something more.

- DO YOU -
BAKE CLUB

Any freshly squeezed citrus juice or fresh fruit purée works: lemon, lime, grapefruit. Just no bottled juices (they have additives that combat the gelatin's setting agent)!

No extract needed if you don't have it—it's a flavor amplifier! Any extract works here or remove the extract altogether if you don't have a corresponding flavor that makes sense!

If you want to turn the flavor up to LOUD, mix ½ cup water with any Kool-Aid, Country Time Lemonade, or other killer-flavor drink mix you like. You're the boss re the mix-to-water ratio. More mix = more flavorful gummy bears. Remove ¼ cup sugar if your drink mix is already pre-sweetened.

GUMMY BEARS

Makes 1 snacking session's worth, or about 36 bears

This recipe will really put you in legend territory. Most who walk the aisles of the grocery store cannot even fathom a guess at what sorcery goes into gummy candy. But you know me, I can't help reverse-engineering the things I love. The shape is irrelevant; if anything, "gummy objects" is probably the more apt name for this recipe, but "bears" is what really hooked you, so I'm going to start there.

⇨ Substitute the corn syrup with honey if you don't have corn syrup in the pantry.

⇨ Read up on Blooming Gelatin on page 48.

½ cup orange juice, freshly squeezed

3¾ teaspoons (1½ packets) unflavored gelatin

¼ cup sugar

1 tablespoon corn syrup

½ teaspoon orange extract

1. Pan-spray a silicone mold (bears! donuts! Legos! an ice-cube tray!) or pan of your choice.

2. To a heavy-bottomed medium-sized saucepan, off heat, add the freshly squeezed OJ, sprinkle the gelatin evenly over it, and let the mxture sit for 5 minutes, to allow the gelatin to bloom, becoming bouncy and translucent.

3. With a sturdy heat-safe spatula, slowly mix in the sugar, corn syrup, and extract, and heat over medium-low heat, to dissolve all ingredients together into an even liquid state, warm but not boiling, about 2 minutes.

4. Carefully fill each mold, and let them sit for 5 minutes at room temperature before carefully transferring them to the fridge to chill for 30 minutes and set completely.

5. Once they're cool and set, knock the gummy objects out onto a clean plate or pan, cut them down to size if you're looking for objects smaller than your mold(s), and leave them out at room temperature, uncovered, for 6–24 hours, to allow a thin skin to form around the outside. Your gummies will shrink up to 25 percent (this won't be obvious to the eye, don't worry), and the longer you can resist and let them sit out, the chewier they become. Patience is a virtue here!

6. Store your gummy bears lightly covered (or uncovered) at room temperature for up to 1 month.

- DO YOU -
BAKE CLUB

If you're into a sugared or Sour Patch Kids effect, after Step 5, roll the gummy objects in a bowl of sugar or sugar and citric acid, for a little extra texture and personality.

@mburke421 makes pineapple-flavored-and-shaped gummies. @janehemm makes gummies without molds, cutting her gummy mass into thin strips to make worms. @annettejosephstyle sneaks Aperol into hers!

FUDGE

Makes 24 pieces

One 12-ounce bag
  chocolate chips
One 14-ounce can
  sweetened condensed
  milk
1½ teaspoons vanilla
  extract
1 teaspoon kosher salt

No one can agree on exactly where fudge was invented, but it really blew up in the nineteenth century on women's college campuses because, duh, a smart woman knows a great dessert when she mixes it. Whoever introduced it into the world gets a great deal of gratitude from me, because fudge is something I turn to time and time again, when desperation is high and supplies are low. It's a few steps up from munching on chocolate chips straight from the bag—so thanks, mystery fudge-ster!

⇨ Besides pan-spraying it, I also like to line the pan with parchment or plastic across the bottom and up the sides for easy release; opt in if you like.

⇨ Fancy chocolate is totally allowed here! Sub it in for chocolate chips if you have it and, va va voom, the classiness factor will be off the charts.

1. Pan-spray an 8-by-8-inch baking pan, and set it aside.

2. In the microwave, in a large heatproof bowl, gently melt the chocolate chips in the sweetened condensed milk. Work in 30-second spurts, stirring with a sturdy heat-safe spatula in between blasts until the mixture is smooth, 1–2 minutes.

3. Stir in the vanilla and salt, and mix until they're fully incorporated, about 30 seconds.

4. Transfer the mixture to the prepared pan, and use the spatula to spread and tamp it across the surface and into the corners, to yield a nice, even, dense, and fudgy mass.

5. Refrigerate the fudge for 1–2 hours to set it completely before slicing. In an airtight container at room temperature or in the fridge, the fudge will keep for up to a month.

- DO YOU -
BAKE CLUB

@cornflakecrunchers fudges it up with cornflake crunch, mini-marshmallows, and mini-chips folded in at the end, in addition to cookie pieces (brilliant); @b.joybakes makes a Caramel-Popcorn (page 226) fudge—the most inspired combo of two snack aisle moments at once.

Fudge it up!

Swap the standard chocolate chips for any other meltable chip out there (dark, milk, white, peanut butter, butterscotch, etc.)

Swap the vanilla for any extract you like (orange, mint, etc.).

During Step 3, stir in 2 tablespoons of any sugar syrup that tells a great fudge flavor story—honey, maple syrup, molasses, Caramel Sauce (page 21).

Add in up to 2 cups of shelf-stable fun stuff between Steps 3 and 4 to help bring your flavor story to life (nuts! mini-marshmallows! corn chips! Cracker Jacks! banana chips! licorice [did I take it too far?]).

MALTED MARSHMALLOW CHOCOLATE FUDGE
(fun fact: molasses + chocolate make the chocolate taste malted!)
2 tablespoons molasses + 2 cups mini-marshmallows

ROCKY ROAD FUDGE
1 cup slivered almonds + walnuts, toasted, + 1 cup mini-marshmallows

BREAKFAST FUDGE
1 cup butterscotch chips + 2 tablespoons maple syrup + 2 cups Cheerios + $\frac{1}{2}$ teaspoon cinnamon

TRAIL MIX FUDGE
2 tablespoons honey + 1 cup peanuts + $\frac{1}{2}$ cup oats + $\frac{1}{4}$ cup raisins + $\frac{1}{4}$ cup M&M's Minis

MINT COOKIES AND CREAM FUDGE
$\frac{1}{2}$ cup chocolate chips, $\frac{1}{2}$ cup white chocolate chips + mint extract + clear vanilla extract + 2 cups crushed Chocolate Wafers (page 33) + 2 tablespoons light-green sprinkles

INSIDE OUT PB CUP FUDGE
$\frac{1}{2}$ cup peanut-butter chips + $1\frac{1}{2}$ cups Chocolate Wafers (page 33) + $\frac{1}{2}$ cup mini–chocolate chips

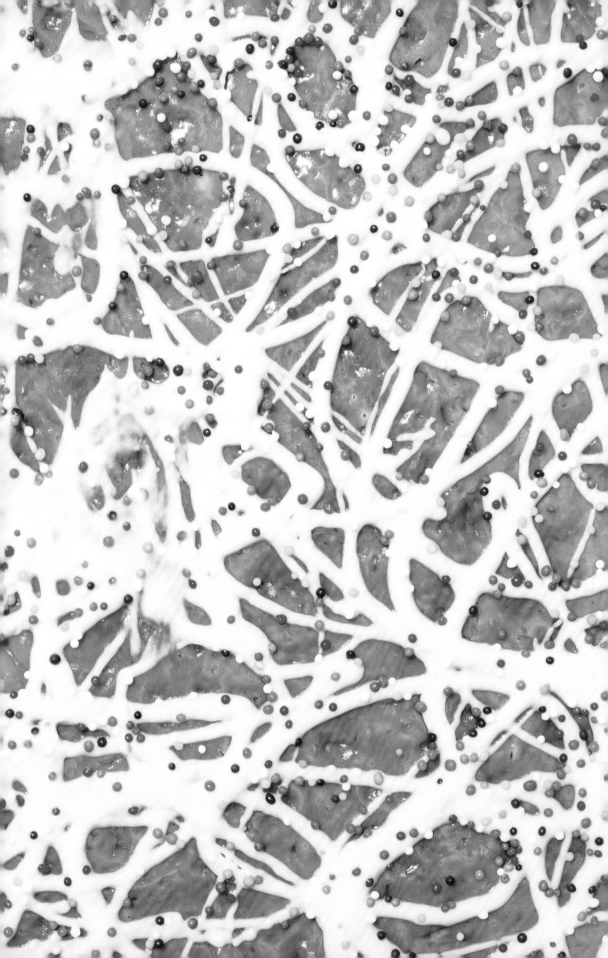

GRAHAM CRACKER TOFFEE

Makes 24 pieces

This is a bit of a plus-up to the snack aisle staple, putting a caramel, candy-coated spin on the standard graham cracker. Consider this my reminder that many of our favorite snacks are simple evolutions of what the grocery store offers.

⇨ Make your own Graham Crackers for a full-on flex (page 37).

1 full sleeve graham
   crackers (8 pieces)

12 tablespoons (1½ sticks)
   unsalted butter

One 14-ounce can
   sweetened condensed
   milk

½ cup sugar

1 tablespoon vanilla extract

1 teaspoon kosher salt

1. Heat the oven to 350°F, and pan-spray a 9-by-13-inch baking pan.

2. Line the prepared baking pan with crackers, then line again, double stacking the crackers, breaking them as necessary to fill the entire dish's surface.

3. In a heavy-bottomed, medium-sized saucepan, over medium heat, combine the butter, sweetened condensed milk, sugar, vanilla, and salt, whisking everything together to bring the mixture to a boil, about 1 minute. Turn the heat down to a low simmer, and continue cooking until the mixture slowly takes on a soft caramel color, about 2 minutes more.

4. Pour the warm caramel mixture evenly over the cracker layer, and bake at 350°F for 15–20 minutes; it will bubble and deepen in flavor and texture, transforming into a toffee state.

5. Cool the toffee completely at room temperature for 2 hours before removing it from the dish and breaking into about twenty-four pieces. In an airtight container at room temperature, the graham cracker toffee will keep fresh for up to 2 weeks.

- DO YOU -
BAKE CLUB

If you're feeling more of a salty-sweet edge, swap the graham crackers with one full sleeve of salty crackers, like Saltines or Ritz.

Tell a fancier vis-and-flavor story by melting and drizzling or piping white chocolate chips and colored sprinkles over the toffee once it's cooled completely in Step 5. This adds a frosted sugar-cookie effect, too.

Take things in a chocolate-covered graham-cracker toffee direction by alternatively drizzling a little or spreading a lot of melted milk, semisweet, or dark chocolate over the surface once it's cooled completely in Step 5. Heck, top it with some toasted nutty pieces for a real showstopper.

@mamas.salsa swaps graham crackers for animal crackers, and @oh_my_ganache_bakery rocks flaky salt on her toffee bop and hides butterscotch chips between the graham crackers.

@sweetsbyglory swaps in saltines alongside white chocolate, peanut butter, chocolate chips, and pistachios; @jerseykellyad swaps in Ritz crackers, then hides bananas and Oreos in the middle!

LEMON ICE

Makes 3 cups, serving 2–4 people

To me, a snack is something that satisfies you outside of mealtime, and I can think of few things more satisfying than a cool lemon ice on a warm summer's day. Gloriously simple, the way most of life's real gifts are, lemon ice is a stroke of pure "turning lemons into lemonade" brilliance. A few ingredients, a little bit of thinking ahead, some arm muscle, and you're in business.

➩ Take those lemon rinds and make lemon jam (page 28).

1¹/₃ cups sugar
1 cup water

³/₄ cup fresh lemon juice
   (from 5 or 6 medium-
   sized lemons)
¹/₄ teaspoon kosher salt

1. In a heavy-bottomed medium-sized saucepan, over medium heat, bring the sugar and water to a boil, whisking intermittently, to dissolve the sugar fully. Remove the pan from the heat, and whisk in the fresh lemon juice and salt to combine them.

2. Pour the mixture into a medium bowl, and clear out a place for it in the freezer where it can hang out for a while without being disturbed. Freeze the mixture for 30 minutes, then give it a healthy whisk. Freeze it again for 30 minutes, then whisk it up. Continue with this cadence until the mixture is frozen into a stretchy, almost sorbetlike state, 3–4 hours.

3. Scoop the lemon ice into small cups and refresh yourself! In an airtight container in the freezer, lemon ice will keep fresh for up to 3 months.

- DO YOU -
BAKE CLUB

Swap out lemon for any tangy flavor you please—grapefruit, lime, orange. If tang is not your thing, this recipe also works for any fruit juice—strawberry, mango, raspberry, pineapple.

PB-PRETZEL FREEZER COOKIES

Makes 12

This recipe was born of the desire to normalize what we all want in life: to eat cookie dough. My theory is, there is something about the temperature of the dough that plays into its irresistible nature; something cool and unbaked just feels craveable. So here's a log of dough, sliced and ready to serve, a cookie that's still in dough form—no raw eggs, no raw flour, no worries whatsoever.

⇨ Make this babe gluten-free by using gluten-free pretzels, or subbing the pretzels for another crunchy gluten-free moment (Rice Krispies? crushed peanuts?), or removing this element altogether.

⇨ Toast the pretzels at 300°F for 10 minutes to deepen their flavor before adding them to the mix if you want a more pretzel-forward moment.

¾ cup peanut butter
2 teaspoons vanilla extract

¾ cup confectioners' sugar
⅓ cup light brown sugar
1 tablespoon +
   1½ teaspoons milk powder
⅛ teaspoon kosher salt

⅓ cup pretzels

1. In a medium bowl, with a sturdy spatula, mix together the peanut butter and vanilla until the combination is smooth, about 30 seconds. Mix in the sugars, milk powder, and salt, and stir until they're combined, about 30 seconds. Mix in the pretzels, using the spatula to break them down into bite-sized pieces as you mix, about 1 minute.

2. Place a sheet of plastic wrap 12 inches long on the counter. Transfer the dough to the center of the plastic wrap, and form it into a wide log, about 2½ inches in diameter and 5 inches long. Roll the plastic wrap up around the log, twisting at the ends to form a taut, even cylinder of dough.

3. Freeze the dough for a minimum of 1 hour before slicing and eating it! In an airtight container, the cookies will keep fresh in the freezer for up to 1 month.

- DO YOU -
BAKE CLUB

Swap the peanut butter for other nut butters, the light brown sugar for some other sugar energy, even the vanilla extract for another extract, if you have a vision. This is a super-flexible format, ready for your imagination to take hold!

PEPPERMINT PATTIES

Makes 12

Peppermint patties have the sneaky advantage of being a candy that's disguised as a mint, meaning you're completely justified in crushing them at any time of day or night. The brilliance of these choco discs is that their core is really a few simple ingredients, but jet-fueled by a killer use of extract. This recipe is a pretty spot-on patty dupe that's—shocking!—a great template for you to take beyond the walls of peppermint, because a patty is really the perfect anytime, anywhere, anywhy treat.

⇨ Sub in shortening for butter if you want to go vegan.

⇨ Sub in sweetened condensed milk for corn syrup, if needed.

⇨ Make sure you're using peppermint extract and not mint extract (mint will taste like toothpaste—peppermint will be more well rounded in its mintiness!).

⇨ Fancy chocolate is totally allowed here! Sub it in for chocolate chips if you have it and, va va voom, the classiness factor will be off the charts.

For the Patty Filling
4 tablespoons unsalted butter, soft
1/3 cup corn syrup
2 teaspoons peppermint extract

3 cups confectioners' sugar
1/4 teaspoon salt

For the Chocolate Shell
2 cups chocolate chips
2 teaspoons vegetable oil

1. **Make the patty filling:** In a medium bowl, with a sturdy spatula, combine the butter, corn syrup, and extract, mixing until smooth, about 30 seconds. Add the confectioners' sugar and salt, and mix until everything is combined and smooth, about 1 minute.

2. Divide the dough evenly into twelve 2- tablespoon-sized portions. Roll each portion into a ball, then flatten it with the palm of your hand to make a disc, reminiscent in size and shape of the candy itself. Transfer the discs to a plate, and freeze them for at least 10 minutes, until they're super cold. Line a half sheet pan with parchment paper, and set it aside.

3. **Make the chocolate shell:** In a medium heatproof bowl, in the microwave, gently melt the chocolate chips in the oil. Work in 30-second spurts, stirring with a sturdy heat-safe spatula in between blasts, until the mixture is smooth, 2–3 minutes.

4. Remove the patties from the freezer and, using a fork, dip each patty into the chocolate, coating it all around. Transfer the chocolate-coated patties to the prepared pan, and let them sit for 30 minutes, or until the chocolate shells harden (pop them into the fridge to chill for 5 minutes if they're taking too long). Store them in an airtight container in the fridge for up to 1 month.

BAKE CLUB

Swap standard chocolate chips for any other meltable chip out there (dark, milk, white, peanut butter, butterscotch, etc.).

Swap in Brown Butter (page 111) or any nut butter or spread for the butter.

Swap in any flavored extract you like: vanilla! strawberry! coconut! banana!

Bring some texture, personality, and fun to the mix. Add up to ¼ cup sprinkles (to make birthday patties!), cocoa powder (for chocolate-chocolate patties!), crushed mints and mini-pretzels (peppermint-bark patties!), or other textural (but very small—i.e., nearly pulverized) fun stuff to the patty filling in Step 1, or sprinkle them on the outside chocolate shell at the end of Step 4.

I've seen Almond Joy, strawberry Nilla, chocolate sugar cone, and lemon-coconut ditties from @alexandrajthomsen. And even orange-cream filling with crushed Orange Vanilla Cream M&M's over both white and dark chocolate shells from @massiemenandme.

CARAMEL APPLES

Makes 6

6 apples
6 wooden sticks or skewers

1 recipe Caramel Sauce
(page 21)

When the turtleneck sweaters come out and the leaf peeping begins, I like to go big on cheesy fall moments. Pumpkin patches. Seasonal beverages. Scarves that could be blankets. Play it cool, I do not. Caramel apples are high on the list of "leaning in" to fall and all its tacky traditions. Somehow reserved for the seasonal aisle or the gift shop, these sweet encased fruits are an easy at-home activity parlayed into an incredible snack.

⇨ I'm a fan of crisper, less sweet apples—Honeycrisps are my favorite—to eat and to coat in caramel (and more). But bring whatever apples you have (or prefer) to the table!

1. Pan-spray a half sheet pan, and set it aside. Rinse and dry the apples, washing away the waxy coating (which would prevent the caramel from sticking). Pull out the apples' stems, and replace them with sticks or skewers. Chill the apples in the fridge for 15 minutes. Fun fact: the caramel will stick more easily to a cold apple than to a room-temp one.

2. When the caramel has cooled slightly, dip one apple into the caramel, letting any excess drip off, then place it on the prepared pan to set entirely, which will take 30 minutes. Warm the caramel sauce slightly if it begins to get too thick or firm from the cold apples dipping into it. Alternatively, if your caramel sauce is too warm and therefore too thin to make a great caramel shell, cool it down in the fridge for 10 minutes, then try again. Let cool, then serve the apples, or wrap them in cello bags if you're in the gifting mood! Covered or wrapped at room temperature, the caramel apples will keep fresh for up to a week.

- DO YOU -
BAKE CLUB

To make caramel apple-pie apples, coat the apples in caramel and let them set for 3 minutes, until they are still sticky but not hardened. Roll the bottom quarter of your apples in a bowl of baked pie crust scraps (page 120).

@elainedarer rocks peanut-butter cookie crumbs, speculoos crumbs, and brilliant seasonal sprinkles. No two apples are the same, so why coat them like they are, right?!

PUPPY CHOW

Makes 5 cups, 1 big bowlful

½ cup chocolate chips
1 tablespoon unsalted
   butter

½ cup peanut butter
½ teaspoon vanilla extract

4–5 cups Corn Chex cereal

1¼ cups confectioners'
   sugar
Pinch of kosher salt

This layered and coated Ziploc bag brilliance is a top-notch snack, but the name just doesn't measure up. Depending on what neck of the woods you are from, you may know it as "muddy buddy" or "monkey munch," which aren't much better. Naming aside, because it's so easy, because the possibilities for flavor stories here are endless, my imagination ignites whenever I pull out a bowl to get going. Plus, you can scale it down and make an awesome late-night snack / dirty dessert secret whenever you want.

⇨ Fancy chocolate is totally allowed here! Sub it in for chocolate chips if you have it and, va va voom, the classiness factor will be off the charts.

⇨ In my very well-tested opinion, of all the Chex cereals, Corn Chex makes the best, most spirited base to help carry all other flavors.

1. In the microwave, in a large heatproof bowl, gently melt the chocolate chips and butter. Work in 30-second spurts, stirring with a sturdy heat-safe spatula in between blasts, until the mixture is smooth, 1–2 minutes.

2. Stir in the peanut butter and vanilla, and mix until they're fully incorporated, about 30 seconds.

3. Add 4 cups of cereal to the bowl, and stir thoughtfully, to coat the cereal fully, but not so aggressively that you're crushing it into smaller pieces. If plenty of the chocolate mixture remains on the sides and bottom of the bowl, add another ½ cup of cereal at a time until all is well coated and no chocolate mixture remains unspoken for.

4. Transfer the mixture to a Ziploc bag along with the confectioners' sugar and salt, seal it tightly, and party (toss in the air, dance around like a fool, whatever you've got to do) to coat the cereal fully.

5. Freeze or refrigerate your creation for 10–15 minutes to harden it. Serve it, or store at room temperature, in the same bag or a new airtight container (it's up to you), for up to a week or in the fridge or freezer for up to a month, though it's doubtful it will come close to lasting that long!

- DO YOU -
BAKE CLUB

@conscious_consequences swaps in Cookie Crisp cereal and pretzels, dusting everything in cinnamon–powdered sugar; @elainedarer makes a raspberry-lemonade-inspired puppy chow, swapping in white chocolate, omitting peanut butter, and using a raspberry-lemonade drink mix with her confectioners' sugar.

Current Favorite Puppy Chow Moves

Replace standard chocolate chips with any other meltable chip out there (dark, milk, white, peanut butter, butterscotch, etc.).

Swap the peanut butter with any other nut paste or fatty spread (almond! sunflower seed! Nutella! cookie butter!). It's important that this add-in not be too "wet," or it will add sog to your cereal (so jam, fudge sauce, caramel sauce, etc., are off the table).

Swap in any extract that drives your flavor story (lemon, banana, coconut, etc.), or omit it entirely if it doesn't bring you joy.

Heck, swap the Chex with any other cereal you choose! The more surface area and airy crunch the better, which is to say Cap'n Crunch or Cocoa Puffs work much, much better than Rice Krispies or cornflakes. While you're at it, swap in—partially or entirely—other dry, crunchy things, like saltines or Ritz cracker pieces, classic Milk Bar crumbs, Graham Crackers, or Brown Sugar Wafers (pages 37, 32), broken into smaller pieces.

Anything powdered and flavorful can be used as an outer coating or to enhance the confectioners' sugar—add some cocoa powder, or sprinkles, or cinnamon, or drink mix! You can even swap the powdered sugar with cake mix or brownie mix from the box.

ORANGESICLE

Kix + shortbread pieces + white chocolate + confectioners' sugar + orange drink mix or orange zest

PISTACHIO LEMON

Corn Chex + white chocolate + pistachio butter + lemon extract + confectioners' sugar + lemon drink mix or zest

FROSTED SUGAR COOKIE

Corn Chex + cookie crumbs + white chocolate + cookie butter + confectioners' sugar + pink sugar sprinkles

BIRTHDAY

Oyster crackers + white chocolate + vanilla extract + confectioners' sugar + rainbow sprinkles

CHOCOLATE BANANA NUTELLA

Cocoa Puffs + semisweet chocolate + Nutella + banana extract + confectioners' sugar + cocoa powder

CINNAMON BUTTERSCOTCH

Cheerios + butterscotch + white chocolate + confectioners' sugar + cinnamon

FROSTED YELLOW/LEMON CAKE

Corn Chex + white chocolate + yellow or lemon cake mix

CHOCOLATE BDAY

Cocoa Puffs + white chocolate + vanilla extract + confectioners' sugar + rainbow sprinkles + cocoa powder

ROCKY ROAD

Corn Chex + almond butter + butterscotch chips + confectioners' sugar

PB PRETZEL

Pretzels + peanut butter chips + peanut butter + vanilla extract + confectioners' sugar

- DO YOU -
BAKE CLUB

Swap the standard chocolate chips for any other meltable chip out there (dark, milk, white, peanut butter, butterscotch, etc.).

Nuts are just a starting point—bring any seed you please, or any fun thing you'd like to see dipped in caramel and chocolate beyond—mini-pretzels! mini- or maxi-marshmallows! Starlight candies! You get the gist . . .

TURTLES

Makes 18

Someone woke up with a sense of humor the morning these were invented: pecans covered in caramel and chocolate to make confections that look like turtles. Though we usually see these nutty candies regionally or seasonally, I personally think they make an incredible snack every day of the week. I mean, they're basically my ideal trail mix.

- -

⇨ If you want to make a vegan turtle, bring 1 can full-fat coconut milk and 1/3 cup sugar to a boil to dissolve the sugar and thicken the milk. Sub in 3/4 cup of this mixture for the sweetened condensed milk and unsalted butter.

⇨ If you don't have sweetened condensed milk, sub in 3 tablespoons light brown sugar, 1 tablespoon honey, and 2 tablespoons butter (making 5 tablespoons butter total) in its place in Step 1.

⇨ Fancy chocolate is totally allowed here! Sub it in for chocolate chips if you have it and, va va voom, the classiness factor will be off the charts.

- -

1/2 cup sugar

1/2 cup sweetened
condensed milk

1/2 cup water

3 tablespoons unsalted
butter

1 teaspoon vanilla extract

2 cups whole nuts

1/2 teaspoon kosher salt

1/2 cup chocolate chips

1. In a heavy-bottomed medium-sized saucepan, with a sturdy heat-safe spatula, combine the sugar, sweetened condensed milk, water, butter, and vanilla, and bring the ingredients to a boil over medium heat. Turn down the heat to low, and simmer the ingredients gently for 20 minutes, stirring every 5 minutes, until the mixture has taken on a warm caramel color, reduced by half, and thickened.

2. As the mixture heats up, heat the oven to 350°F. Spread out the nuts on an ungreased half sheet pan, and toast them in the oven for 5–10 minutes until they're fragrant. Cool them completely. On a new, pan-sprayed half sheet pan, arrange the nuts in clusters of 5–8, spacing the clusters about 2 inches apart.

3. When your saucepan mixture is ready, remove it from the heat and stir in the salt. Then carefully spoon it into 1-tablespoon pools over the nut clusters. If your caramel starts to cool down, return it to medium heat to warm up until it's just fluid enough for you to continue.

4. In a small heatproof bowl, in the microwave, gently melt the chocolate chips. Work in 30-second spurts, stirring with a sturdy, heat-safe spatula in between blasts until they're smooth, 1–2 minutes. Spread or drizzle the finished turtles with melted chocolate, and let them sit at room temperature, or pop them into the fridge to cool quickly, so the chocolate will set. In an airtight container at room temperature, turtles will keep fresh for up to a month.

TABLETOP
DESSERTS

Skillet Cookie   258

PB S'mores Bars   261

Cheesecake   262

Macarons   267

Payday Pie   270

Glazed Pumpkin Pie Bars   272

No-Churn Ice Cream   274

Chocolate Peanut Butter Crunch Pie   276

Pavlova   279

Chocolate Mirror Cake   281

Pretzel Swirl Brownies   285

Apple Cider Donut Bundt Cake   286

Ice Cream Roll Cake   289

Crème Brûlée   291

@alicekollinzas

@halibaking

@jessmakesfood

#bakeclub

@jessmakesfoods

@mister_stiffler

@danielletockerphoto

@bluebellflorals

@mburke4

In case you haven't picked it up by now, I believe in always prioritizing flavor over fuss, over fancy. This chapter is about desserts that are centerpieces in their own right—worthy of a dinner—nay, *dessert*—party. Recipes to have people over to marvel at before noshing. Sweets that get a great deal of oohs and aahs when they appear on the scene. Some require a longer time commitment, some a bit more technique, and some are just plain temperature-sensitive (hello, no-churn ice cream!). And—because I wouldn't be me if I weren't always attempting to turn others into ooey, gooey, not-too-stuffy dessert believers—some are really humble in their DNA, just plated in a way that makes others stop and give them the attention we all know they deserve. Just make sure you save room!

(P.S.: If you're trying to get even more dessert showstoppers into your life, here's a pro tip: any 8-by-8-inch recipe can go into a 9-inch round pan and immediately become fancy and tabletoppy.)

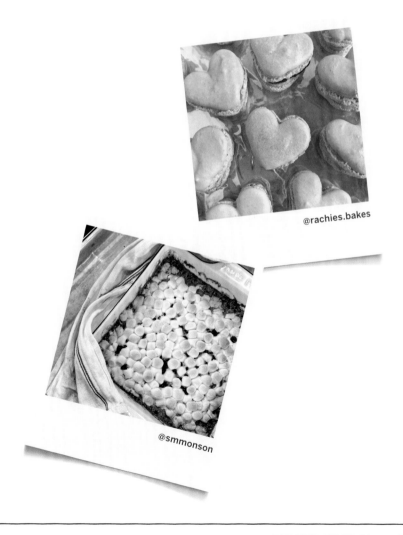

@rachies.bakes

@smmonson

SKILLET COOKIE

Makes 1 cookie, serving 8–10

Are you by any chance looking for an insanely gooey, nearly underbaked cookie when you're supposed to be looking for a gorgeous, photographable, formal dessert? Then do I have a cookie for you! Only, don't tell anyone how easy it is to bake a batch of cookie dough up in a skillet for the ultimate high/low effect. This tabletop treat is worthy of every party, including a PJ party, so frocks are by no means necessary here. Go ahead, slather it with ice cream if you're up for it, too.

➪ Milk powder will bring a secret depth of flavor and a slight chew (see page 5). If you don't have access to it, feel free to omit it.

➪ Preheat your grill or bonfire for a real summertime "baking" moment! Not all tabletop parties take place indoors.

➪ Any skillet from 8-inch to 12-inch will do here. If you're using a 12-inch, bake for 2 minutes less—using the same visual cues to clue doneness.

1 stick (8 tablespoons)
  unsalted butter, softened
2/3 cup light brown sugar
1/2 cup sugar

1 egg
1¼ teaspoons vanilla
  extract

1¼ cups flour
1 tablespoon milk powder
3/4 teaspoon baking soda
1/2 teaspoon kosher salt
1 cup chocolate chips

1. Heat the oven to 350°F with a seasoned 8-inch cast-iron skillet in it.

2. In a large bowl, using a sturdy spatula, mix together the butter and sugars, flexing your muscles for about 2 minutes, until they're fully combined. Add the egg and vanilla, and stir until the mixture is combined and fluffy, about 1 minute.

3. Measure the flour, milk powder, baking soda, and salt into the mixing bowl. Toss together only the dry ingredients on top with the spatula first, before truly stirring them into the wet ingredients below. Mix until everything is just combined. Stir in the chocolate chips.

4. Carefully remove the skillet from the heated oven, and spread the dough evenly in it, to the edges. Bake the dough-filled skillet at 350°F for 16–18 minutes, until the cookie is golden brown on top and just set in the center. Carefully remove the skillet from the oven, and let it cool on a rack or pot holder for 10 minutes before using a clean, sturdy heat-safe spatula to indent and "slice" warm wedges. Spoon or slather it with ice cream. Cover what's left of the skillet cookie (if anything!), still in the skillet, with plastic wrap, and store it at room temp for up to 5 days. Serve at room temp, or warm pieces anew as you want to serve them.

- DO YOU -
BAKE CLUB

Swap the chocolate chips for any single-flavor baking chip you have—or a combo.

Swap the vanilla extract for any other flavor you like.

Add up to 1½ cups other fun pantry items to bring your flavor story to life: I like to add 1 cup Cinnamon Toast Crunch and ½ cup mini-marshmallows, and swap in white chocolate chips.

Once it's cooled, drizzle the cookie with ⅓ cup melted chocolate chips mixed with 1 teaspoon neutral oil and up to ½ cup fun pantry items for an extra-WOW moment.

@AM_Beardsley drizzles hers with maple syrup for a breakfast take. @simplyscorching swirls in marshmallow fluff and chocolate chunks for a s'mores moment.

PB S'MORES BARS

Makes 9

"How many *new* ways can you find to celebrate s'mores?" I thought to myself a few years back. Turns out at least one more, because these bars have become a mainstay year-round in my home. Essentially large-format oven s'mores with a chocolate-crumb bottom that will knock your socks off and a grahammy/peanut-buttery middle, these bars bring a bit more sweet/salty/peanut-buttery energy to the classic trio.

⇨ Honestly, no notes 😄

For the Choco Bottom

3 tablespoons unsalted
　　butter, melted
¹⁄₄ cup cocoa powder
¹⁄₄ cup flour
¹⁄₃ cup sugar
¹⁄₄ teaspoon kosher salt

For the PB-Graham Middle

¹⁄₂ cup peanut butter,
　　softened
5 tablespoons unsalted
　　butter, melted
2 teaspoons vanilla extract

¹⁄₂ cup sugar
¹⁄₃ cup graham cracker
　　crumbs
¹⁄₂ teaspoon kosher salt

**For the Choco-
　Marshmallow Top**
¹⁄₂ cup chocolate chips
1¹⁄₂ cups mini-
　　marshmallows

1. Heat the oven to 375°F, and pan-spray an 8-by-8-inch baking pan.

2. **Make the choco bottom:** In a medium bowl, with a sturdy spatula, mix the melted butter with the cocoa powder, flour, sugar, and salt, and stir to combine them until a rich cocoa crumble forms, about 1 minute. Press this evenly into the base of the prepared pan.

3. **Make the PB-graham middle:** In a medium bowl, with a sturdy spatula, mix together the peanut butter, butter, and vanilla until the combination is smooth, about 30 seconds. Stir in the sugar, graham cracker crumbs, and salt, and mix to combine everything, about 30 seconds. Spread this middle evenly across the choco bottom.

4. **Make the choco-marshmallow top:** Sprinkle the chocolate chips evenly across the middle layer, then do the same with the mini-marshmallows. Bake at 375°F for 20 minutes, until your kitchen smells like a PB paradise and your mini-marshmallows have started to caramelize. Remove the pan from the oven, turn on the broiler, and dangle the pan below the heat source for 30–60 seconds if you want a little more of a campfire char on top.

5. Cool the s'mores completely in the pan before cutting them into three rows of three squares. Store these in an airtight container at room temp for up to 5 days, or in the fridge for up to 2 weeks.

CHEESECAKE

Makes 1 cheesecake, serving 10–12

There is a reason why there is a whole "factory" committed to this tangy, luxurious dessert. Cheesecake is the tabletop treat that does not fail: guests are always impressed by it, and no one can resist its cream-cheesy charms. Mixing the batter on a painfully low speed is half the secret to its luxurious density. And though deploying a water bath may feel MacGyver-level, the gentle hug it gives your cheesecake is key to a solid yet softly set filling—and you'll feel like a mad dessert-scientist when you add this move to your now fully loaded baking playbook.

⇨ Milk powder gives this recipe a luscious depth of flavor, omit if you don't have any.

⇨ Buy your graham cracker crumbs or make your own (page 37); 1½ cups of crumbs is about twelve full sheets of crackers ground down.

⇨ Sub a 9-inch cake pan with a 9- or 10-inch springform pan if you prefer. This recipe also scales down into smaller cheesecakes; just remember to adjust the baking time down, using the same visual cues to judge doneness.

⇨ If you have ANY doubt about the smoothness and density of your filling, pull out a fine-mesh sieve and strain the mixture to deflate it and separate out any tiny lumps of cream cheese.

⇨ Slice your cheesecake with a chef's knife, running it under warm water (or dunking it into a pitcher of warm water) and drying it between cuts.

For the Crust

1 stick unsalted butter

1½ cups graham cracker crumbs
¼ cup milk powder
¼ cup sugar

For the Filling

Four 8-ounce blocks cream cheese, at room temperature

1½ cups sugar
2 tablespoons flour

4 eggs
1 tablespoon vanilla extract

1. Place a half sheet pan in the oven on the middle rack, and heat the oven to 325°F.

2. **Make the crust:** Line a 9-inch cake pan with aluminum foil above the pan's edges, then pan-spray the foil—or pan-spray a 9-inch springform pan and wrap the bottom edges with foil. In a medium-sized heatproof bowl, melt the butter in 30-second spurts, stirring with a sturdy heatproof spatula between spurts, about 60 seconds total. Stir in the graham cracker crumbs, milk powder, and ¼ cup sugar until they're well combined. Transfer the mixture to the prepared baking pan and, with the palm of your hand and fingertips, press the mixture evenly across the surface and completely up the walls of your cake pan, about 2 inches. Set it aside.

3. **Make the filling:** In a stand mixer fitted with the paddle attachment, slowly paddle the cream cheese on low speed until it's smooth, scraping down the sides of the bowl and the paddle intermittently.

(···)

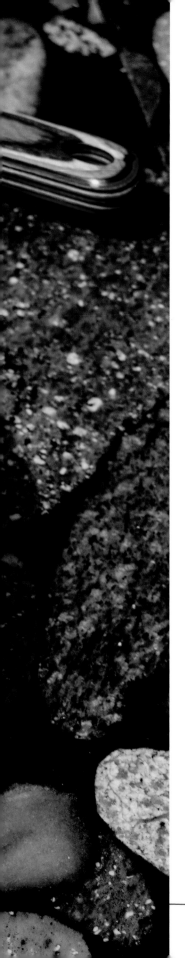

4. Paddle in the 1½ cups sugar a little at a time, continuing to mix on low speed, stopping to scrape down the sides of the bowl and the paddle intermittently. With the last addition of sugar, add the flour, too, to make sure it's evenly distributed.

5. Still on low speed, add the eggs one at a time and then the vanilla; continue to mix on low speed, stopping to scrape down the sides of the bowl and the paddle intermittently.

6. Gently transfer the filling mixture into your crust, and spread it evenly. Gently transfer the pan of cheesecake to the heated oven, and place it in the center of the sheet pan. Before closing the oven, fill the baking sheet just below its lip, just shy of 1 inch, with hot tap water, to create a "water bath." Gently close the oven door (so many "gently"s—I know!—but we want a gentle bake so as not to color or crack our luxurious cheesecake!).

7. Bake at 325°F for 90 minutes, until your cheesecake has set firmly in the center, confidently jiggles back at you when nudged, but has not taken on much color, if any at all. Add another 5–10 minutes, if needed, until you get this result. Turn the oven off, prop the door open, and let the cheesecake sit there for 10 minutes. This will allow it to cool down gently, so as to avoid any cracking.

8. Remove the cheesecake from the water bath and oven, and finish cooling it at room temperature for an hour before refrigerating it for the final cooling, an additional hour. (You want to cool it down as gently as you mixed and baked it!) Slice and serve it. Wrapped well in plastic or stored in an airtight container, cheesecake will keep fresh in the fridge for up to a week.

- DO YOU -
BAKE CLUB

Add up to ⅔ cup peanut butter, melted chocolate chips, or melted baking chips of any kind to the batter to flavor the cheesecake.

Add up to 2 teaspoons of some other extract to the batter to flavor the cheesecake.

Add up to ½ cup of smaller fun stuff bits (mini–chocolate chips, crushed candy cane pieces, toffee bits, etc.) to the batter to give the cheesecake texture and a different kind of personality.

I like my cheesecake as is, but feel free to serve it with jammy fruit (page 27), some flavored Whipped Cream (page 24), or a sweetened sour cream if you please.

- DO YOU -
BAKE CLUB

Make one giant macaron bottom and top, and serve it as a cake at your next celebration—I promise the crowd will WOW!

Use as much or as little food coloring as you like—less for a more muted, pastel moment, more for a color blast. We eat with our eyes first, so choose a color that tells the flavor story you're bringing.

Swap the frosting out for any filling—jams (pages 27, 28), Caramel Sauce (page 21), or Cream Cheese Frosting (page 117), etc.

MACARONS

Makes 12

2 egg whites, at room
   temperature
¼ cup sugar

½ cup almond flour
1 cup confectioners' sugar
Pinch of kosher salt

4 or 5 drops food coloring

1 recipe Any Flavor Frosting
   (page 269)

This is one of my favorite Bake Clubs, but I waited nearly two years to teach and share macarons. They're such a gorgeous format in their own right, and, though not super tricky to make, they're specific in what they need to be successful. Egg whites, sugar, almond flour, a great frosting, and a great attitude are all that stand between you and macaron glory. Oh, and a flavor story. Choose that first—it will help direct you as to the color(s) and filling(s) you'll need to bring your tabletop to life!

⇨ Room-temperature egg whites will whip more easily and successfully. And since they're the core of your macarons, take the time to temper your egg whites before you begin.

⇨ Make sure your almond flour is fresh and not rancid. Give it a smell and a taste—if it tastes like anything but a very, very mellow almond, grab a new bag. Store almond flour in an airtight container in the freezer. (This is my reco for all your baking nuts: you want them fresh and ready to do great work, and this keeps the guessing out of it.)

⇨ If you don't have a piping bag and tip, not to worry: a Ziploc bag with a hole snipped in the corner will do good work, too.

⇨ Google "macaron piping guide" and print two copies if you'll feel more comfortable with a template to hide below your parchment paper and trace over for perfectly sized macarons—that's what I did when I first started—after all practice makes perfect.

1. Stack two half sheet pans on top of each other. Line the top pan with parchment paper.

2. Make sure the bowl of your stand mixer is super clean and dry. Fit the mixer with the whisk attachment, and whip the egg whites on high speed until they're foamy, about 90 seconds. Slowly stream in the granulated sugar, and continue whisking on high speed until stiff, glossy peaks form, about 2 minutes.

3. In a small bowl, whisk together the almond flour, confectioners' sugar, and salt until they're combined, about 30 seconds. With a spatula, gently fold the almond mixture into the egg white mixture—tracing the spatula through the center of the bowl, pulling the mixture toward you, then tracing the sides of the bowl to scoop any unmixed almond mixture on top of the egg whites, repeating until both elements are fully incorporated, any white or nutty streaks having disappeared in full, and a slightly deflated but thick, sandy mixture remains.

(···)

4. Fold in the food coloring until you have a homogeneously colored thick, sandy mixture. Test the batter by lifting some up with the spatula, then dropping it back into the bowl. You are looking for the batter from above to disappear into the batter below in 10 seconds or so. If it is still holding shape rather than disappearing, continue folding the batter another minute or two and test again.

5. Transfer the batter to a piping bag fitted with a $1/2$-inch round tip, and thoughtfully pipe it into twenty-four $1^{1}/_{2}$-inch rounds on the top stacked sheet pan, leaving $1/2$ inch between them (the macarons don't run much). Tap the stacked baking sheets against the counter to remove any air bubbles, and let them sit out for 1 hour, to allow the surface of the batter to dry out—a classic characteristic of a macaron.

6. Heat the oven to 325°F, and bake for 10–12 minutes, until the macarons puff a tad at the bottom, creating a little "foot," maintain a matte flat top, and hollow out in the center, but do not take on much color. I like to rotate my macarons top to bottom and front to back halfway through, to ensure a consistent bake.

7. Cool the macarons completely on the baking sheets, then peel them off the parchment paper. Pair together those with the most consistent diameters. Sandwich the tops and bottoms together by spooning, piping, or spreading frosting onto one macaron, and topping with the other, using a little pressure to encourage the filling to peek out just to the edge. Macarons freeze amazingly well. Stored in an airtight container, they will keep fresh in the freezer for up to 1 month. I don't recommend storing them at room temp or in the fridge, because they start to lose their super-special texture.

Any Flavor Frosting

Makes 2 cups

1½ sticks (12 tablespoons)
unsalted butter, softened

2¼ cups confectioners'
sugar

¼ teaspoon salt

2 tablespoons milk

Food coloring (optional)

You didn't think I would take you this far and not give you my go-to recipe for frosting, malleable into any flavor idea you might dream up, did you?!

⇨ Sub in shortening or any vegan margarine for the butter, and alt milk for milk, if you're looking for a dairy-free moment.

⇨ Double, triple, quadruple this recipe for more macarons, layer cakes, or any other moment when you're craving MORE frosting in life.

1. In a stand mixer fitted with the paddle attachment, mix the butter, confectioners' sugar, and salt on low speed to combine them, about 1 minute. Turn off the mixer and, with a sturdy spatula, scrape down the sides of the bowl. Increase the mixer speed to medium, and whip until the mixture is super smooth, about 2 minutes. Scrape down the sides of the bowl anew.

2. Add the milk and, on medium speed, continue mixing until everything is combined and fluffy, about 1 minute. Add a drop or two of food coloring, if you want. In an airtight container, frosting will keep in the fridge for up to 2 weeks.

- DO YOU -
BAKE CLUB

For vanilla frosting, add in 1½ teaspoons vanilla extract with the milk.

For chocolate frosting, add ⅓ cup cocoa powder with the confectioners' sugar, and increase the milk to 3 tablespoons.

For strawberry frosting, reduce the confectioners' sugar to ½ cup and add ⅓ cup of Strawberry Jam (page 27).

For coffee frosting, reduce the confectioners' sugar to ½ cup, increase the milk to ¼ cup, and add in 1 teaspoon instant coffee powder with the milk.

Add in 1½ teaspoons any extract with the milk to make it that flavor.

Use as much or as little food coloring as you like—less for a more muted, pastel moment.

PAYDAY PIE

Makes 1 pie, serving 8–10

I had never had a Payday until I saw my husband, Will, pick one up. Because I'm the kind of partner who thinks she is entitled to half of what my counterpart is eating, I grabbed a bite. *How had I NEVER had a Payday before?!* I was hooked, and knew I had to translate this brilliant candy creation into a pie. Layers of buttery, flaky crust, a peanut-butter nougat in the center, and vanilla caramel on top holding roasted, salted peanuts in their place is not for the faint of heart, so I've saved it for last. It's the payday you've earned for rocking the recipes in this book!

1 recipe Pie Crust
(page 120), unfilled

1 recipe Peanut Butter
Nougat (page 228)

1¹/₂ cups roasted and
salted peanuts

1 recipe Caramel Sauce
(page 21)

1. Heat the oven to 375°F, and pan-spray a 10-inch pie dish.

2. Blind-bake your pie crust (bake the crust before it's filled) by forking tiny holes into the center of the crust. Put a coffee filter in the center, and fill it with dried rice or beans to weigh down the crust. Bake for 15 minutes, until the crust is golden brown all over. Carefully remove the beans and coffee filter, and bake for an additional 5–10 minutes, until the base of the pie has dried out and colored slightly. Cool the crust completely at room temperature.

3. Spread the peanut butter nougat evenly into the cooled pie shell.

4. Sprinkle the peanuts evenly across the surface of the nougat.

5. Pour the caramel sauce atop the peanuts, allowing it to hug between the nuts and glaze the surface of them all. Chill the pie in the fridge for 1 hour, to ensure that all the elements are set. Slice and serve it! In an airtight container in the fridge, the pie will keep fresh for up to 1 week.

- DO YOU -
BAKE CLUB

Swap the peanuts and peanut butter for any nut you please. I'm partial to a hazelnut moment . . . maybe even some Nutella in place of the peanut butter for a chocolatey peekaboo.

GLAZED PUMPKIN PIE BARS

Makes 9

I love a format that is a crowd pleaser and can carry me through seasons. Plus, you know me, I'm not getting fussy unless I need to. Making a pie-crust-and-crumb mixture without having to labor over the rolling, chilling, crimping, and baking is my flex here—leaving me more time to conceive of the flavor and filling. I can't wait to see how you pie it up on your terms.

⇨ Bake this in a circular form in a greased pie pan, for the same time and at the same temperature.

For the Pie Crust and Crumbs

1²/₃ cups flour
3 tablespoons sugar
1¹/₂ teaspoons cinnamon
¹/₂ teaspoon kosher salt

9 tablespoons unsalted butter, melted

For the Pumpkin Filling

1¹/₄ cups pumpkin purée
¹/₃ cup sugar
1 egg
¹/₂ teaspoon vanilla extract
¹/₂ teaspoon kosher salt

For the Glaze

1¹/₂ cups confectioners' sugar
1 tablespoon milk

1. Heat the oven to 350°F, and pan-spray an 8-by-8-inch pan.

2. **Make the pie crust and crumbs:** In a medium bowl, with a sturdy spatula, stir together the flour, sugar, cinnamon, and salt until they're combined, about 15 seconds. Stir in the melted butter, mixing just until everything is combined, forming rocky clusters. Using your hands, press 1¹/₄ cups of the mixture into the bottom of the prepared pan, smooshing to make an even layer that fills it to the corners plus a ¹/₄-inch brim. Set the remaining mixture aside for the top.

3. **Make the pumpkin filling:** In a small bowl, whisk together the pumpkin, sugar, egg, vanilla, and salt, stirring to combine, about 30 seconds. Pour the filling over the crust, and spread it evenly over the surface.

4. Scatter (don't press) the remaining crumbs on top of the pumpkin to make a loose, crumby top layer.

5. Bake at 350°F for 25–30 minutes, until the crumb topping is golden brown (think the color of your favorite pie crust once it's baked). Depending on the oven, I may place my pan closer to the top heating coil for the last 10 minutes if the color change doesn't happen on its own.

6. **Make the glaze:** In a small bowl, whisk the confectioners' sugar and milk together, mixing until the combination is smooth, about 30 seconds. Cover the bowl and set it aside. Cool the bars before cutting into three rows of three squares before drizzling the glaze atop and serving them. If you've got a crowd willing, I highly recommend serving these bars warm with a scoop of ice cream on top (my mom's favorite). Wrapped in plastic or stored in an airtight container at room temperature, these bars, amazingly, get better with age, up to 5 days. I love a good pie bar for breakfast, myself. Keep the party going the morning after!

- DO YOU -
BAKE CLUB

Omit the cinnamon in the crust and crumbs if you like.

Swap the pumpkin filling for any Fruit Jam (page 27) OR Caramel Sauce (page 21) with 1 cup nuts (think pecans! walnuts! slivered almonds!).

Omit the glaze, or flavor it with 1 teaspoon extract or 2 tablespoons cocoa powder, based on your flavor story and vision.

@massiemenandme swaps in gooey apples to get comfy-cozy, and @ausome86 swaps in Strawberry Jam (page 27). @bluebellflorals bakes hers in a 9-inch round pan for a deceptively easy pie moment.

NO-CHURN ICE CREAM

Makes about 1½ pints, serving 4

1 cup heavy cream

One 14-ounce can
   sweetened condensed
   milk

1 teaspoon vanilla extract

½ teaspoon kosher salt

Why DON'T we make more ice cream at home? My hunch is, we're all thinking the same thing: "I'd love to, only I don't have an ice cream machine, and those suckers are big/expensive/complicated." Well, what if I told you you don't need one? Ice cream is delicious, sweet dairy aerated and frozen at the same time (what we refer to as churning). This recipe just separates the two parts: whipping air into cream (whipped cream), then freezing it. No machine, no problem.

- -

1. In a large bowl, whip the cream to medium peaks.

2. Gently whisk in the sweetened condensed milk, vanilla, and salt; then transfer the mixture to a more storable, scoopable container, like a loaf pan or a quart container. Keep this in the freezer for 3–4 hours, until the entire mixture is frozen through. In an airtight container in the freezer, your ice cream will keep creamy and delicious for up to 1 month.

- DO YOU -
BAKE CLUB

Swap in any extract you like.

Swap in any Choose Your Flavor Whipped Cream (unwhipped) (page 24).

Make a fruity flavor: remove ½ cup sweetened condensed milk and add ½ recipe Fruit Jam (page 27) to bring some fresh notes in—strawberry! blueberry! peach!—removing or swapping vanilla extract if it doesn't fit your flavor story.

Make a chocolate-fudge ice cream: remove ½ cup sweetened condensed milk and add in 1 recipe Fudge Sauce (page 22).

Make a brownie-batter ice cream: remove ½ cup sweetened condensed milk and add in 1 recipe brownie-batter Fudge Sauce (page 22) (½ cup sugar, ¼ cup milk, 4 tablespoons unsalted butter, 6 tablespoons cocoa powder).

Mix in up to 1 cup of fun pantry stuff that tells your flavor story before you transfer your mixture to the freezer.

Plus it up into a sundae bar with DIY Pantry Cones (page 43), Chocolate Shell (page 44), Sprinkles (page 40), and more!

CHOCOLATE PEANUT BUTTER CRUNCH PIE

Makes 1 pie, serving 8–10

4 cups Rice Krispies

⅓ cup coconut oil

1 cup peanut butter

2¼ cups confectioners'
sugar

1 teaspoon kosher salt

1 tablespoon peanut butter

1 cup chocolate chips

When we're having people over, I always ask my husband, whom I deem my culinary creative director (I have too many ideas, I just need him to decide and commit for me!), what to make. Without fail, he says THE PIE, which means this pie. (When I ask him what I should wear, he always says, "A jumpsuit.") Quick, timeless, and always a winner is how I'd describe both.

⇨ This gem is coincidentally gluten-free and vegan (if you're using vegan chocolate chips)—so a FULL-ON crowd pleaser!

⇨ Swap the peanut butter for whatever crunchy, honey-nut, or alt butter you enjoy most when snacking or desserting.

⇨ I love prepping several of these pies in advance and storing them in the freezer, so there's always one ready to serve or bring with.

1. Pan-spray a 10-inch pie dish and set aside.

2. In a large heavy-bottomed saucepan, over medium heat, toast the rice cereal until it is a fragrant and deep golden brown, tossing intermittently with a sturdy heat-safe spatula, about 3 minutes. Remove the pan from the heat, and set it aside.

3. In a large microwave-safe bowl, melt the coconut oil in the microwave in 30-second spurts until it's liquid, about 60 seconds. Stir in 1 cup of the peanut butter, and mix with a sturdy spatula until it's smooth, about 30 seconds. Add in the toasted rice cereal, confectioners' sugar, and salt, and stir until everything is well combined, about 60 seconds.

4. Pour the mixture into the prepared pan, and press down firmly with the spatula to ensure a flat, solid layer all around. Pop it into the freezer to begin chilling.

5. In a microwave-safe medium bowl, melt 1 tablespoon of peanut butter and the chocolate chips together in the microwave in 30-second spurts, stirring with a sturdy heat-safe spatula after each spurt, until smooth, about 60 seconds. Pour this chocolate/peanut-butter mixture over the top of the pie, and spread it into a smooth layer all around.

6. Freeze the pie for 30–40 minutes, or until it's firm to the touch. Slice and serve it out of the fridge or freezer. In an airtight container the pie will keep fresh for up to 1 week at room temp, two weeks in the fridge, and up to 1 month in the freezer.

- DO YOU -
BAKE CLUB

Layer this into an 8-by-8-inch pan or mini–pie shells. You could even use the filling to make a crunchy filling for Peppermint Patties (page 244) or Black Bottom Cupcakes (page 183).

Use ¼ cup of the melted chocolate/peanut-butter mixture in Step 5 to thinly coat the bottom and edges of the pie shell to create a chocolate "crust," then pour the rest on top to coat it, as instructed.

Add extra crushed peanuts to the melted chocolate top with the salt for an extra WOW moment.

PAVLOVA

Makes 1, serving 8–10

A meringue that's super crunchy on the outside, super chewy on the inside, with a marshmallow-like filling, the pavlova is a stunner. It's not a dessert of my childhood, but I've fallen deeply in love with it in my older age—ha. I'm a HUGE fan of serving it with the more tart curds and creams, and when it's in season, with really, really fresh fruit. The pavlova is easily made with everyday ingredients and gluten-free, making it a "company is calling" triple threat.

⇨ Take those yolks and go to Curd town (page 55), or Crème Brûlée it up another night (page 291). Just remember to store them with a film of plastic on top in an airtight container so they don't dry out.

⇨ Room-temperature egg whites will whip more easily and successfully. And since they're the core of a pavlova, take the time to temper your egg whites before you begin.

⇨ Swap the lemon juice for white vinegar or apple cider vinegar or rice wine vinegar, steering clear of any deeper vinegars (sherry, balsamic) unless you like the idea of their playing a role in the flavor of your pavlova.

⇨ Scale this recipe up or down based on crowd size or number of egg whites you have on hand.

⇨ Whatever you do, keep meringues away from humidity or moisture—that would ruin the crunch of this delight!

6 egg whites, at room temperature

1 teaspoon kosher salt

3/4 cup confectioners' sugar

2/3 cup sugar

2 teaspoons vanilla extract
1 1/2 teaspoons lemon juice

1 recipe (Any) Fruit Curd (page 55) or Choose Your Flavor Whipped Cream (page 24)
2 cups berries or other bite-sized fresh fruit pieces

1. Heat the oven to 350°F, and pan-spray a half sheet pan.

2. In the bowl of a stand mixer fitted with the whisk attachment, whip the egg whites on high speed until they're fluffy and foamy, about 2 minutes. Sprinkle in the salt, and whisk for an additional 1 minute, until the salt disappears and the whites stiffen slightly. Add the confectioners' sugar, and beat until the mixture is glossy and medium peaks form, about 1 minute. Sprinkle in the sugar, and continue beating for 1 minute. Add the vanilla and lemon juice, and continue whisking until super-stiff peaks form, about 5 minutes.

3. Spoon or spatula the mixture into a 12-inch round on the prepared pan, using your spreading tool to create a giant nest, purposefully leaving some swooshes and swirl-like peaks on the top and sides (drama is everything for the texture and look of the finished dessert).

(···)

4. Place the pan in the oven, immediately turn the heat down to 300°F, and bake for 90 minutes. Turn off the oven, and keep the door closed with the pan of pavlova inside, allowing it to cool in the oven completely, about an hour; this will create a lightly colored, crisp, nearly cracked crust that feels dry to the touch.

5. Just before serving, spread curd or whipped cream into the center and not quite to the edges of the pavlova (leaving some meringue bare for a "crust" effect), then top this with fresh fruit. Serve immediately. If you have any pavlova left over, it will keep fresh in an airtight container for up to 5 days, staying every bit as tasty, but becoming chewy.

- DO YOU -
BAKE CLUB

Swap in light brown sugar or dark brown sugar for a moodier-flavored (and -colored) tabletop delight.

Fill her up with one of my new personal favorites, yogurt whipped cream (page 25), then adorn it with super-ripe fruit (never underestimate the power of a fragrant strawberry) or Fruit or Citrus Jam (pages 27, 28).

@timross41

CHOCOLATE MIRROR CAKE

Makes 1 cake, serving 8–10

Mirror, mirror, on the chocolate cake, how'd you get so glamorous? In all my time working in the kitchens of fine-dining restaurants, this beauty always blew me away the most, not just for its looks, but for the simplicity of the ingredients that create its impossibly shiny, nearly glittery, mirrored chocolate glaze effect. And you know I wouldn't bring it to the table if it wasn't an absolute knockout in the flavor department. It is for the "More is more, I eat the fudge sauce off an ice cream sundae first" crowd.

⇨ Read up on Blooming Gelatin on page 48.

¼ cup + ⅔ cup water
4 teaspoons (1½ packets)
  gelatin powder

1 cup sugar
1 cup cocoa powder
Pinch of kosher salt

⅔ cup heavy cream

1 recipe Chocolate Mayo
  Cake (page 184), baked
  and cooled

1. Bloom the gelatin: Measure ¼ cup water in a small bowl, then sprinkle the gelatin across the surface so all the powder is wet. Let it sit for 2–3 minutes, until it's bouncy and hydrated.

2. Off heat, in a heavy-bottomed medium-sized saucepan, whisk the sugar, cocoa powder, and salt together. Add the remaining ⅔ cup of water and the cream, whisking it in a little at a time until the mixture is smooth. Turn on the heat to medium-low, and gently stir the mixture around. As it warms and slowly comes to a boil, which will take about 2 minutes, the mixture will become more and more fluid, the cocoa powder will hydrate and deepen in color, and the sugar will dissolve. Remove the mixture from the heat. Gently whisk in the bloomed gelatin, and stir until it has dissolved and the mixture is smooth and glossy, about 30 seconds. You want a consistently smooth and fluid mixture, which is why we're using a whisk, but want to be careful not to aerate the mixture, creating unwanted bubbles.

3. Strain the mixture through a fine-mesh sieve into a medium bowl. Tap the bowl on the counter to surface and pop any bubbles.

4. Cover the bowl of glaze with a clean towel or plastic wrap, and let it cool on the countertop for 1 hour. Clean the fine-mesh sieve, grab another medium bowl, and strain the glaze again, removing any impurities or film that would fog up your mirror. Cover it anew, and let it sit for 1 hour. Clean the fine-mesh sieve, and strain one last time into a clean medium bowl. (While you're waiting and skimming, make and cool the cake.)

(⋯)

5. Invert the cooled chocolate cake onto a wire rack with a half sheet pan below. Starting at the bull's-eye center, confidently pour the glaze onto the cake in steadily expanding circles until the glaze hits the edges, being careful not to use all the glaze at once. You want one thick stream and coat (rather than a thin drizzle). If the sides are not fully coated, pour more glaze down the sides.

6. Quickly thereafter, gently move the cake to a plate. Once it's transferred, it will take the glaze 15 minutes to fully set before the cake is ready to be sliced (though you can take longer to slice and serve it if you like!). Use a clean chef's knife to slice the cake, dipping it into or running it under warm water between cuts for perfect pieces.

7. At room temperature, with a dome over it (I use an upside-down bowl) and nothing directly touching the glaze, the cake will keep fresh for up to 5 days.

- DO YOU -
BAKE CLUB

Swap out the Chocolate Mayo Cake for any other 9-inch cake you like. This glaze works just as well to cover a pound cake, cupcake, or layered cake—just remember, the glaze's mirror is maximized by large, flat surface areas. Check out @katia .mazierremax's mirrored Bundt!

- DO YOU -

BAKE CLUB

Take it to the next level. Two of my favorite moves:

Layer brownie batter, then a layer of Caramel Sauce (page 21), then the pretzel batter for a caramel-pretzel-brownie moment.

Add 1 teaspoon peppermint extract to the brownie batter, and drizzle melted white chocolate and crushed candy canes on top, for a brilliant peppermint-bark moment.

PRETZEL SWIRL BROWNIES

Makes 9

Brownies were one of the first box mixes I took on as an aspiring home baker. I'd add any and every combo I could dream up, testing what did and didn't work to my delight—and my mom's poor depleted snacking pantry's chagrin. The one combo I could never find the right balance of was the salty, sweet, moody wonderfulness of chocolate and pretzel. It wasn't until decades later that I realized I could make a pretzel "blondie" batter and swirl it with a brownie batter—the perfect blend of chocolate and pretzel, in brownie form.

⇨ Mini-pretzels have the maximum surface area for pretzel flavor. If you don't have mini-pretzels, larger pretzels also work.

For the Pretzel Batter

2 cups mini-pretzels

1 stick unsalted butter, softened
2/3 cup light brown sugar
1/4 cup sugar

1 egg

1/4 cup flour
1/2 teaspoon kosher salt
1/4 teaspoon baking powder

For the Brownie Batter

4 tablespoons (1/2 stick) unsalted butter
2/3 cup chocolate chips

1/2 cup sugar

1 egg
3/4 teaspoon vanilla extract

1/3 cup flour
1/4 teaspoon kosher salt

1. Heat the oven to 350°F, and pan-spray an 8-by-8-inch baking dish.

2. In a food processor, grind 2 cups of pretzels down into 3/4 cup pretzel "flour."

3. **Make the pretzel batter:** In a large bowl, using a sturdy spatula, mix together the butter and sugars until they are fully combined, about 1 minute. Add the egg, and stir until it's combined, about 30 seconds. Measure the ground pretzel "flour," the other flour, salt, and baking powder into the mixing bowl. Toss together only the dry ingredients on top with the spatula first, before truly stirring them into the wet ingredients below. Mix until everything is just combined. Set this pretzel batter aside.

4. **Make the brownie batter:** In the microwave, in a medium-sized heatproof bowl, melt the butter and chocolate chips together, working in 30-second spurts, stirring with a sturdy heat-safe spatula in between blasts, until the mixture is smooth, about 90 seconds.

5. Switch mixing tools: Whisk in the sugar, stirring until it's combined, about 30 seconds. Whisk in the egg and vanilla, and stir until the mixture is smooth and glossy, about 30 seconds.

6. Measure the flour and salt into the mixing bowl. Switch back to the spatula, and toss together only the dry ingredients on top first, before truly stirring them into the wet ingredients below. Mix until everything is just combined.

7. Spatula some of the brownie batter, then some of the pretzel batter repeatedly into the prepared pan so you get a brilliant mix of the two throughout. Drag a dinner knife a few times around once the batters are distributed, to swirl them. Bake at 350°F for 20–25 minutes, until the pretzel filling has set (the brownie batter will still have a little shine). Cool it before slicing it with a plastic knife. At room temperature, covered with a lid or plastic wrap, the brownies will keep fresh for 1 week.

APPLE CIDER DONUT BUNDT CAKE

Makes 1 cake, serving 12

We've all been there: You got a dozen apple cider donuts because you were really feeling that "I pulled out my cable knit sweater for THIS perfect day" feeling. But your eyes were bigger than your belly. Enter this stunner, literally: your sad day-old donuts used for Bundt cake perfection. Made in the style of bread pudding, this simple recipe never lets a well-intended nosh sesh go to waste. Recycling never tasted so good.

⇨ Scale this recipe up or down, based on the number of donuts or cake pan size you have. No one gets mad at an individually sized ACDBC!

½ cup sugar

3 eggs

¾ cup milk

¾ cup apple cider

⅓ cup heavy cream

1 teaspoon vanilla extract

½ teaspoon kosher salt

10–12 day-old apple cider donuts (about 2 pounds total)

Cinnamon sugar (page 106), for top

1. Heat the oven to 350°F, pan-spray a 12-cup Bundt pan, and lightly dust it with flour to coat the crevices.

2. In a large bowl, whisk together the sugar, eggs, milk, apple cider, cream, vanilla, and salt, mixing until everything is smooth and combined, about 1 minute.

3. Break up the donuts by hand into bite-sized pieces, and add them to the bowl. Ditch the whisk for a sturdy spatula, and stir the donut pieces into the liquid below to coat them completely. Let the mixture sit for 10 minutes so the donut pieces completely absorb the liquid.

4. Pour the mixture into the prepared pan, and bake at 350°F for 50 minutes. The mixture will puff, rise, and caramelize, setting into a freshly baked cake with some donut pieces still prevalent.

5. Let the cake cool in the pan at room temperature for 30 minutes, then invert the pan onto a plate to release the cake. While it's still warm, sprinkle the cinnamon sugar over the top (the humidity will act as a glue to the granules). Cool the cake fully, or slice it and serve it warm. In an airtight container, it will keep fresh for up to 5 days at room temperature or in the fridge for up to 2 weeks.

- DO YOU -
BAKE CLUB

Take the donut show on the road—swap in any flavor of day-old store-bought donut (hello, chocolate!) and any flavored liquid (coffee!) for the apple cider.

Heck, use whatever is left from your last adventure in Old-Fashioned Donuts (page 114)!

Swap the cinnamon sugar for any other flavored sugar—maybe a little fudge sauce drizzle if you're taking the chocolate-donut/coffee suggestion?!

ICE CREAM ROLL CAKE

Makes 1 cake, serving 10–12

The marriage of ice cream and cake is one for the dessert history books. In this recipe, these two all-stars come together to make one mega-dessert that proves teamwork makes the dream work. Rolling ice cream and cake together, then coating them in fudge sauce—no one gets mad at that. This cake takes on seasons, flavors, and textures to your heart's desire, creating magic in the moment.

⇨ If you can get your hands on the extra-dark version of your average grocery store cocoa powder, it works wonders here, both in color and depth of flavor.

4 eggs, whites and yolks
  separated
1/2 cup sugar

4 tablespoons unsalted
  butter, melted
1/4 cup sugar

2 tablespoons milk
2 teaspoons vanilla extract

1/2 cup flour
1/3 cup cocoa powder
  + more to sprinkle on
  parchment
1 teaspoon baking powder
1/2 teaspoon kosher salt

2 pints ice cream

1 recipe Fudge Sauce
  (page 22)

1. Heat the oven to 350°F, pan-spray a half sheet pan, line it with parchment paper, and then pan-spray the parchment paper, too.

2. In a stand mixer with the whisk attachment, whip the egg whites on medium-high speed until soft peaks form. On low speed, slowly sprinkle in 1/2 cup sugar, then turn the speed up to high and continue whisking until you achieve glossy, medium-stiff peaks, with a little droop when you pull the mixture away from itself and turn it upside down, 3–4 minutes.

3. In a separate large bowl, whisk together the melted butter, the remaining 1/4 cup sugar, and the yolks, mixing aggressively to combine and aerate them, about 1 minute. Whisk in the milk and vanilla, and stir to combine, about 30 seconds. Ditch the whisk and grab a sturdy spatula.

4. Measure the flour, cocoa powder, baking powder, and salt into the mixing bowl. Toss together only the dry ingredients on top with the spatula first, before truly stirring them into the wet ingredients below. Mix until everything is just combined.

5. Take a heaping spatula-full (about 1/2 cup) of egg whites and mix it into the chocolate mixture until it disappears and the chocolate is lighter. Then spatula in the remainder of the egg whites, and carefully mix the two together, folding the egg in— or tracing the spatula through the center of the bowl, pulling the mixture toward you, then tracing the sides of the bowl to scoop any unmixed chocolate mixture on top of the egg whites, repeating until the egg whites are fully incorporated, any white streaks having disappeared in full, and only a lighter chocolate mixture remains.

(···)

6. Spread the batter thinly and evenly on the prepared pan, and bake at 350°F for 10 minutes. The cake will pouf in height and start to pull back from the sides of the pan. Remove it from the oven, and immediately flip the hot pan upside down onto a new piece of parchment paper, sprinkled lightly with cocoa powder to prevent sticking. Carefully but quickly, peel off the bottom layer of parchment that the cake baked on, then roll the warm cake up lengthwise into a tight log. Let it cool completely at room temperature in this log shape for 10 minutes. Pull the 2 pints of ice cream from the freezer to temper for 10 minutes, making it more spreadable.

7. Gently unroll the cooled cake, and spread the ice cream evenly over the surface, then roll the cake back up, placing the seam side down to keep the roll intact. Place it on a wire rack, and pop it into the freezer to chill for 10 minutes, to keep the ice cream frozen.

8. Ensure that the fudge sauce is in a pourable state, warming it slightly if it's not, then pour it evenly over the surface of the log. Slice it and serve it! In an airtight container in the freezer, the cake will keep for up to 1 month.

- DO YOU -
BAKE CLUB

Swap in the Carrot Cake recipe (page 176) as is—or remove the cinnamon and shredded carrots and add 1 teaspoon vanilla extract, if you're looking for more of a vanilla base cake.

Swap fudge sauce for Caramel Sauce (page 21) if you like.

@alicekollinzas swaps freshly whipped flavored cream (page 24) for the ice cream, creating a lighter, dreamier cake.

@elainedarer doubles down on big flavor by covering her cake in Chocolate Shell (page 44).

CRÈME BRÛLÉE

Makes 6

Long before ASMR was an acronym, we knew it as the moment when your tiny little demitasse spoon made contact with the brittle caramel on top of a crème brûlée. This is why crème brûlée is a mainstay on dessert menus everywhere—it just scratches every itch. Don't let this fancy dessert fool you—you can master it in your own home for the final course. And once you go crème brûlée, you never go back.

- -

⇨ This recipe calls for 2 cups heavy cream. Don't skimp!

⇨ The vanilla bean is what sets a great crème brûlée apart from a good one :) but sub ½ teaspoon vanilla paste or 1 teaspoon vanilla extract, if you want.

⇨ Splurge for a blowtorch (twenty dollars–ish online) to ensure that lust-worthy hard-crack top.

⇨ Get your nougat on with those leftover egg whites (page 228)!

⇨ This recipe calls for a hand or immersion blender, a worthy kitchen investment that acts as a blender, homogenizer, food processor, and more—one of my favorite tools. You can also use a standard blender, but be sure to blend on the lowest possible speed to ensure minimal bubbles.

⇨ Divide your brûlée mixture across smaller ramekins or put it into one larger ramekin, adjusting the bake time down or up as needed, adhering to the visual cues to gauge doneness.

1 cup heavy cream
¼ cup milk
1 vanilla bean, split
  lengthwise

4 egg yolks
¾ cup sugar + more for top
Pinch of kosher salt

1 cup heavy cream, cold

- -

1. Heat the oven to 325°F, and position one rack in the middle, making sure there are no racks above it.

2. In a heavy-bottomed medium-sized saucepan, over medium heat, bring 1 cup cream, the milk, and the vanilla to a near boil.

3. While the mixture is heating, in a separate medium bowl, whisk the yolks, sugar, and salt to combine, then slowly and gently pour this into the warm, creamy mixture while whisking gently, being careful not to pour too much in at once (you don't want to scramble the yolks!); this "tempers" or slowly raises the temperature of the egg yolk mixture.

4. Pour the warm mixture into a medium bowl. Add the remaining cup of cold heavy cream and, on the lowest speed possible, blend the two together with a hand blender. You want a confident, homogeneous mixture but not a bubbly one—think dense and creamy.

(···)

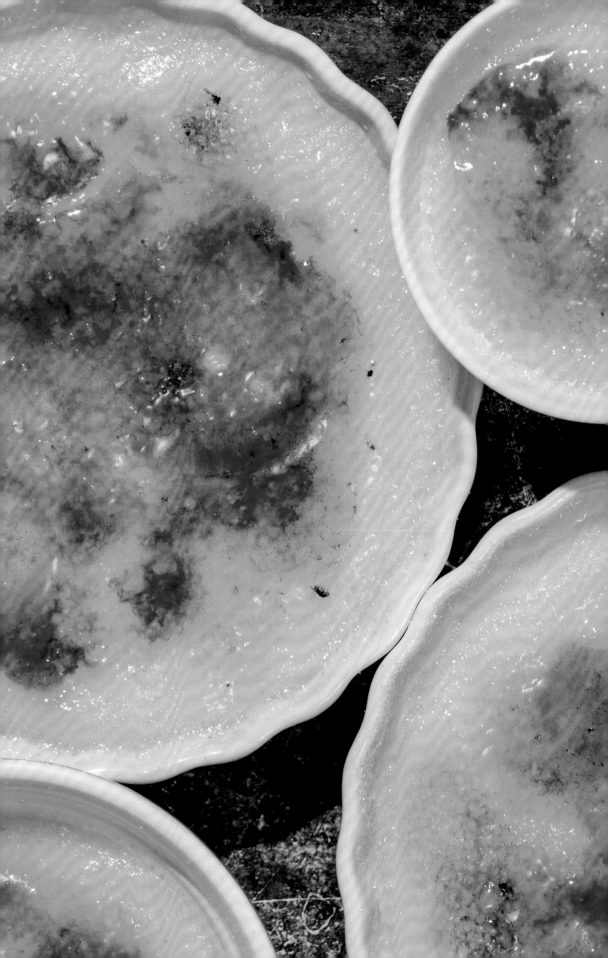

5. Strain the mixture into a bowl, and if there are bubbles, tap the bowl on the countertop aggressively to surface and pop them. Straining multiple times also helps, as does draping a sheath of plastic wrap over the surface of any bubbles.

6. Place six individual 6-ounce ramekins into a 9-by-13-inch pan. Pour the crème brûlée base equally among the ramekins. Carefully carry the pan to the oven, and place it gently onto the center rack. Pour warm tap water into the pan, to cover the bases of your ramekins, with as much water as the pan can hold without spilling over.

7. Bake at 325°F for 30–40 minutes, or until the edges of the custard are set but the bull's-eye center is still a bit loose when you nudge it. Gently remove the water-and-brûlée-filled pan from the oven, and cool the contents of the pan (your crèmes brûlées will continue baking) until the water is temperate enough so you can grab the ramekins with your bare hands, about 1 hour. Transfer the ramekins to the fridge to cool and set the contents completely, at least 2 hours.

8. Right before serving, remove the brûlées from the fridge and paper-towel-dry the surface of each if there is any condensation. Sprinkle just enough sugar to cover the surface of each, inverting each ramekin to let any excess fall off into a small bowl.

9. Torch with confidence. Fire up your torch, and move it thoughtfully across the sugared surface. The sugar will melt into a clear, then light-golden state. Take it further, until it's a deep golden amber. (This ensures a deep caramel flavor and hard crack when you serve it up immediately after!) Bring your torch closer to the sugar if not much is happening; take it farther from your sugar if it's caramelizing too quickly or unevenly.

10. Serve immediately, the hard-crack top waits for no one and will dissolve into a sugar syrup 5–10 minutes after you torch it.

- DO YOU -
BAKE CLUB

Use flavored heavy cream (unwhipped) (page 24) to make your crème brûlée one of a kind.

Omit the vanilla bean from the recipe if it doesn't make sense with your new flavor story.

SHOUTOUTS

From Christina

To Lexy Bloom, for believing in this project (and us) to the moon and beyond. EVERYONE needs a guardian angel in life and you are ours. Our creative spirits adore you. All the other parts of us do, too.

To Tom Pold, our beloved, insanely dependable cookbook partner in crime—one who loves the weeds and Thanksgiving Croissants as much as we do. You help us see the stickiness in all that we do, and do a fantastic job pretending to be humored by our harebrained ideas, recipes, lingo, and ways of working. You deserve a gold medal.

To the rest of the incredible team at Knopf for shepherding this project forward! That includes you, sweet Shubhani, for your tireless work in design—making these glossy pages feel worn and welcome and loved while also new and full of infinite possibility.

To Kim Witherspoon for always, ALWAYS stepping up to the plate fearlessly with us. You are legend, friend, and confidant. Sixteen years in and we never, ever have to explain ourselves, you just GET IT.

To Chip Kidd for seeing in us what has always been and inspiring and driving our most proud cover. Working with you is the least chill we've ever been—you're THAT cool.

To Henry Hargreaves and Rana Düzyol for the hospitality, strong coffee, killer playlists, and BEAUTIFUL photos. Every cookbook is partly an excuse to create with you.

To Noah Dallemand for carrying the torch of goodness, calm, and hilarity of our beloved Martine. Your help, killer taste, and hand modeling made this book great. We love you (and her) every single day.

To the Lone Bellow—Zach Williams, Brian Elmquist, Kanene Pipkin, and team, including Julian Dorio and more! Thank you for being all of the things our ears want to hear any time of day, for being peer-pressured into eating and holding things for photos and BIG shoutout to our girl, Kanene, for being all the threats—she's got pipes, she's got looks, she moms . . . and yes, she has pastry skills. Those croissants!!!

To Hilly, our incredible partner in all things delicious and beautiful. Your calm, your preparation, your eye, and your taste are so, so powerful. We are lucky to call you teammate. Thank you for going on this ride with us.

To the Milk Bar team for the love, support, inspiration, and extra flour, sugar, and salt I reupped on shamelessly when grocery stores ran bare.

To Rachies, President of Bake Club Merch for sure, Stylist to the bright blue skies and all good things above, you are my favorite reason to make friends as a grown up. Thank you for your up-for-anything spirit and your prowess in the kitchen and behind a camera. Having you be a part of this book in such a big way is a testament to why Bake Club exists and the sticky, joyful thing it does for us all.

To Bake Clubbers, to our incredible guests and friends over the years and for many more to come. You come alive in these pages, you give us a reason to be. You take care of one another, you make this place better, you make life worth living, far beyond the bounds of baking.

To my Mom, Greta! And Grandma and Nonna Trudy, my baking heroes for teaching me how to join clubs, start clubs, burn things, drop things, clean them up, and laugh. You remind me day in and day out that turning on the oven creates all the purpose one might need, good day or bad.

To Will for cheering me on all the while damning all the desserts taunting you from the kitchen.

To Frankie and Sonny for hiding so peacefully as I tinkered and toiled as you grew in my belly and eventually came out and wailed from BabyBjörns in front of all my Bake Club Friends.

To Butter, for being a part of every single Bake Club, even though I still haven't received that signed waiver for you for your name and likeness. You slept through most 2:00 pms, so maybe the legalese is irrelevant.

And to Shannon Salzano for trading places with me driver's seat to passenger's seat and back in a jalopy, pedal to the metal down an unpaved road leading to heck knows where. Why you trust me and show up so big and bright every single moment is still beyond me, but I promise to never, ever let you down. Thank you for believing in all that we create together. You are brilliant and brilliance.

From Shannon

To my mother, Carroll, for teaching me the magic of dessert and the importance of joy. To my father, Patrick, for never questioning what I would do with my English degree he worked so hard to pay for. To my husband, Gage, for telling me everything I bake tastes great, even when it is burnt to heck. And to Christina Tosi, for making my life an adventure.

@willguidara

@lynne.must.exercise

@__kathleen.kelly__

#bakeclub

INDEX

Page numbers in *italics* indicate photographs

A

almond flour
  Lemon Crinkle Cookies, *96*, 97
  Macarons, *266*, 267
Almond Popcorn, Salted Dark Chocolate–, 226
Apple Cider Donut Bundt Cake, 286, *287*
apples
  Caramel Apples, 246, *247*
  Cinnamon Apple (Marshmallow Treats), 213

B

Babycakes, Lemon Honey Ginger, 179, *180*
Bagels, *126*, 127, *128*
Bake Club, origins, 1–2
baking powder and baking soda, about, 5
Banana Pudding, 52
bar cookies *see also* brownies
  Bugle Bars, *72*, 73
  Chewy Granola Bars, 216, *217*
  Chewy Oat Bars, 78, *79*
  Glazed Pumpkin Pie Bars, 272, *273*
  Lemon Bars, 88, *89*
  PB S'mores Bars, *260*, 261
  Sunshine Bars, 84, *85*
basics *see* DIY Pantry
beverages *see* drinks
Birthday Blondies, *76*, 77
biscuits
  Biscuits, 124, *125*
  cheddar-chive biscuit (variation of Biscuits), 124
Black Bottom Cupcakes, *182*, 183
blender, about, 9
Blondies, Birthday, *76*, 77
blueberries
  Blueberry Pie (Marshmallow Treats), 213
  Blueberry Muffin Bundt Cake, 186, *187*

bread
  Bagels, *126*, 127, *128*
  Brioche, 147, *148*
  Buns, *144*, 145
  cheesy flaky bread (variation of Flaky Bread), 153
  Easy, Can't Mess It Up Bread, 140, *141*
  English Muffins, 130, *131*
  Flaky Bread, 152, *153*
  Flaky Bread, how-to photographs, *153*
  Flour Tortillas, *150*, 151
  garlicky flaky bread (variation of Flaky Bread), 153
  Pita, 154, *155*
  Popovers, 166, *167*
  scallion pancakes (variation of Flaky Bread), 153
breakfast
  Bagels, *126*, 127, *128*
  Biscuits, 124, *125*
  Brown Butter Chocolate Chip Muffins, 110, *111*
  Cinnamon Buns with Brown Sugar Goo, *116*, 117
  Cinnamon Toast Cereal, 106, *107*
  Crepes, *112*, 113
  Croissants, *132*, 133
  English Muffins, 130, *131*
  Granola, 38
  kitchen sink quiche (variation of Quiche), 123
  Old-Fashioned Donuts, 114, *115*
  Quiche, 120, *121, 122, 123*
  Silver Dollar Pancakes, *108*, 109
Brioche, 147, *148*
brown butter
  Brown Butter Chocolate Chip Muffin Bundt Cake (variation of Blueberry Muffin Bundt Cake), 186
  Brown Butter Chocolate Chip Muffins, 110, *111*
  how to make, 111
Brown Sugar Wafers, *30*, 32
brownies *see also* bar cookies
  Birthday Blondies, *76*, 77
  brownie batter no-churn ice cream (variation of No-Churn Ice Cream), 274
  Brownie Cake, 188, *189, 190*
  Brownies as You Like, 74, *75*

fudge brownie sauce (variation of Fudge Sauce), 22
  Pretzel Swirl Brownies, *284*, 285
Bugle Bars, *72*, 73
Bundt cake
  Apple Cider Donut Bundt Cake, 286, *287*
  Blueberry Muffin Bundt Cake, 186, *187*
  Butter Chocolate Chip Muffin Bundt Cake (variation of Blueberry Muffin Bundt Cake), 186
Buns, *144*, 145
butter *see also* butter, compound; peanut butter
  about, 4
  Brown Butter Chocolate Chip Muffins, 110, *111*
  brown butter, how to make, 111
  homemade, 16
butter, compound
  about, 16
  Cinnamon Sugar Butter, 19
  Coffee Butter, 19
  Curry Butter, 19
  Fancy Butter, 16, *17*
  Kimchi Butter, 19
  Mustard Butter, 19
  Old Bay Butter, 19
  Salt and Pepper Butter, 19
  Strawberry Jam Butter, 19
Butterscotch Pudding, 52

C

cakes *see also* Cheesecake
  Apple Cider Donut Bundt Cake, 286, *287*
  Black Bottom Cupcakes, *182*, 183
  Blueberry Muffin Bundt Cake, 186, *187*
  Brownie Cake, 188, *189, 190*
  cake recipes, scaling up or down, 178
  Carrot Cake Marshmallow Rolls, 176, *177*
  Chocolate Mayo Cake, 184, *185*
  Chocolate Mirror Cake, 281, *282, 283*

Ice Cream Loaf Cake, 196, *197*
Ice Cream Roll Cake, *288*, 289
Lemon Honey Ginger
    Babycakes, 179, *180*
Lemon Loaf, 191, *192*
Maple Sheet Cake, *194*, 195
Peaches and Cream Upside
    Down Cake, 203, *204*
Skillet Cookie, 258, *259*
Skillet Veggie Cake, *198*, 199
Sprite Cake, 200, *201*
candy
    Breakfast Fudge, 237
    Fudge, 234, *235, 236*
    Gummy Bears, *232*, 233
    Malted Marshmallow
        Chocolate Fudge, 237
    PB Cups, 221, *222*
    Peanut Butter Nougat, 228,
        229, 230
    Peppermint Patties, 244, *245*
    Pop Rocks, 218, *219*
    Rocky Road Fudge, 237
    Soft Caramels, 50, *51*
    Toffee, *60*, 61
    Trail Mix Fudge, 237
    Turtles, *252*, 253
caramel *see also* Toffee
    Caramel Apples, 246, *247*
    Caramel Popcorn, 226
    Caramel Sauce of Your
        Dreams, *20*, 21
    Payday Pie, 270, *271*
    Soft Caramels, 50, *51*
carrots
    Carrot Cake Marshmallow
        Rolls, 176, *177*
    Sunshine Bars, 84, *85*
cereal
    Breakfast Fudge, 237
    Chewy Granola Bars, 216, *217*
    Cinnamon Toast Cereal, 106,
        107
    Maple Pecan Crispies, 82, *83*
    Puppy Chow, 248, *249*
    What's-in-Your-Pantry
        Marshmallow Cookies,
        80, 81
cheese
    cheddar-chive biscuit
        (variation of Biscuits),
        124
    Cheddar–Old Bay Popcorn,
        226
    Cheese Fondue, *164*, 165
    cheesy flaky bread (variation
        of Flaky Bread), 153
    Ham and Cheese Puffs, *168*,
        169
    kitchen sink quiche (variation
        of Quiche), 123
    Quiche, 120, *121, 122, 123*
Cheesecake, 262, *263, 264*
Cherry Pie (Marshmallow Treats),
    213
Chewy Granola Bars, 216, *217*
Chewy Oat Bars, 78, *79*
chocolate
    about, 5

Breakfast Fudge, 237
brownie batter no-churn ice
    cream (variation of No-
    Churn Ice Cream), 274
Brownie Cake, 188, *189, 190*
Brownies as You Like, 74, *75*
Chocolate Banana Nutella
    (Puppy Chow), 250
chocolate fudge no-churn ice
    cream (variation of No-
    Churn Ice Cream), 274
Chocolate Mayo Cake, 184, *185*
Chocolate Mirror Cake, 281,
    282, 283
Chocolate Peanut Butter
    Crunch Pie, 276, *277*
Chocolate Pudding, 52
Chocolate Shell, 44, *44, 45*
Chocolate Wafers, *31*, 33
Fudge, 234, *235, 236*
fudge brownie sauce
    (variation of Fudge
    Sauce), 22
Fudge Sauce, 22, *23*
Go-To Chocolate Chip Cookies,
    67, *68*
Hot Chocolate, 58
Inside Out PB Cup Fudge, 237
Malted Marshmallow
    Chocolate Fudge, 237
Mint Cookies and Cream
    Fudge, 237
PB Cups, 221, *222*
PB S'mores Bars, *260*, 261
Puppy Chow, 248, *249*
Rocky Road Fudge, 237
Salted Dark Chocolate–
    Almond Popcorn, 226
Super Chocolate Cookies,
    90, 91
Trail Mix Fudge, 237
Chocolate Shell, 44, *44, 45*
Choose Your Flavor Whipped
    Cream, 24
cinnamon
    Cinnamon Buns with Brown
        Sugar Goo, *116*, 117
    Cinnamon Sugar Butter, 19
    Cinnamon Sugar Kettle Corn,
        226
    Cinnamon Toast Cereal, 106,
        107
citric acid
    Pop Rocks, 218, *219*
    Sour Patch Kids (variation of
        Gummy Bears), 233
citrus
    Citrus Jam, 28, *29*
    Frosted Yellow/Lemon Cake
        (Puppy Chow), 250
    Lemon Bars, 88, *89*
    Lemon Crinkle Cookies, *96*, 97
    Lemon Honey Ginger
        Babycakes, 179, *180*
    Lemon Ice, 240, *241*
    Lemon Loaf, 191, *192*
    Lemon–Olive Oil Popcorn, 226
    Pistachio Lemon (Puppy
        Chow), 250

Sprite Cake, 200, *201*
Sprite Glaze, 202
Sunshine Bars, 84, *85*
coconut
    Coconut Oatmeal Cookies,
        86, 87
    Coconut Pudding, 52
    Chewy Granola Bars, 216, *217*
Coffee Butter, 19
compound butter *see* butter,
    compound
condensed milk *see* sweetened
    condensed milk
Cones, Ice Cream, *42*, 43
cookies *see also* bar cookies;
    brownies
    Brown Sugar Wafers, *30*, 32
    Chocolate Wafers, *31*, 33
    Coconut Oatmeal Cookies,
        86, 87
    cookie cutters, about, 9
    cookie dough, scaling up or
        down, 99
    cookie scoop, about, 9
    Frosted Gingersnaps, 100, *101*
    Go-To Chocolate Chip Cookies,
        67, *68*
    Macarons, *266*, 267
    Maple Pecan Crispies, 82, *83*
    Mint Chip Sammies, 92, *93, 94*
    PB-Pretzel Freezer Cookies,
        242, 243
    Skillet Cookie, 258, *259*
    Sugar Cookies, 98, *99*
    Super Chocolate Cookies,
        90, 91
    The Biscuits, 70, *71*
    What's-in-Your-Pantry
        Marshmallow Cookies,
        80, 81
Cream, Whipped, Choose Your
    Flavor, 24
Crème Brûlée, 291, *292*
crepes *see also* pancakes
    crepe fillings (sweet and
        savory), 112
    Crepes, *112*, 113
Crinkle Cookies, Lemon, *96*, 97
croissants
    Croissants, *132*, 133
    croissants, how-to
        photographs, 135
    Croissants, Stuffing, 170, *171*
Cupcakes, Black Bottom, *182*, 183
Curd, (Any) Fruit, 55
Curry Butter, 19
cutout cookies
    Brown Sugar Wafers, *30*, 32

D

decorating *see* glazes; frostings
    and fillings; Sprinkles
desserts *see also* cakes; pies and
    tarts; pudding
    Cheesecake, 262, *263, 264*
    Crème Brûlée, 291, *292*
    Pavlova, *278*, 279

Ice Cream Loaf Cake, 196, *197*
Ice Cream Roll Cake, *288*, 289
...

DIY Pantry
    Any Flavor Glaze, 34
    (Any) Fruit Curd, 55
    Banana Pudding, 52
    Brown Sugar Wafers, *30*, 32
    Butterscotch Pudding, 52
    Caramel Sauce of Your
        Dreams, *20*, 21
    Chocolate Pudding, 52
    Chocolate Shell, 44, *44, 45*
    Chocolate Wafers, *31*, 33
    Choose Your Flavor Whipped
        Cream, 24
    Cinnamon Sugar Butter, 19
    Citrus Jam, 28, *29*
    Coconut Pudding, 52
    Coffee Butter, 19
    Curry Butter, 19
    Fancy Butter, 16, *17*
    Fruit Jam, 27
    Fudge Sauce, 22, *23*
    Graham Crackers, 37
    Granola, 38
    Hot Chocolate, 58
    Ice Cream Cones, *42*, 43
    Kimchi Butter, 19
    Marshmallows, *46*, 47, *49*
    Mustard Butter, 19
    Old Bay Butter, 19
    Pudding, 52
    Rice Pudding, 52
    Ricotta (homemade), 56
    Salt and Pepper Butter, 19
    Soft Caramels, 50, *51*
    Sprinkles, 40, *41*
    Strawberry Jam Butter, 19
    Toffee, *60*, 61
donuts
    Apple Cider Donut Bundt
        Cake, 286, *287*
    Old-Fashioned Donuts, 114,
        115
    pumpkin spice donuts
        (variation of Old-
        Fashioned Donuts),
        115
drinks
    Hot Chocolate, 58

E

Easy, Can't Mess It Up Bread,
    140, *141*
eggs, about, 4
English Muffins, 130, *131*
equipment
    about, 8–9
    blender, 9
    bowls, 8
    cookie cutters, 9
    measuring cups/spoons, 8
    pan, half-sheet, 8
    pans, baking, 9
    parchment paper, 8
    pots/pans/skillets, 9
    rolling pin, 9
    sieve, 9
    spatula, heat-safe, 8

F

Fancy Butter, 16, *17*
fillings *see* frostings and fillings
Flaky Bread, 152, *153*
    how-to photographs, *153*
flatbreads
    Flaky Bread, 152, *153*
    Flour Tortillas, *150*, 151
    Pita, 154, *155*
flour, about, 4
Fluffernutter (Marshmallow
    Treats), 213
Fondue, Cheese, *164*, 165
Frosted Gingersnaps, 100, *101*
frostings and fillings *see also*
    glazes
    Any Flavor Frosting, 269
    (Any) Fruit Curd, 55
    Caramel Sauce of Your
        Dreams, *20*, 21
    Cream Cheese Frosting, 117
    Mint Filling, *95*, 95
    Pudding, 52
    Ricotta (homemade), 56
fruit
    Blueberry Muffin Bundt Cake,
        186, *187*
    Caramel Apples, 246, *247*
    Citrus Jam, 28, *29*
    Crepes, *112*, 113
    fruity no-churn ice cream
        (variation of No-Churn
        Ice Cream), 274
    Lemon Bars, 88, *89*
    Lemon Crinkle Cookies, *96*, 97
    Lemon Honey Ginger
        Babycakes, 179, *180*
    Lemon Ice, 240, *241*
    Lemon Loaf, 191, *192*
    Pavlova, *278*, 279
    Peaches and Cream Upside
        Down Cake, 203, *204*
    Pistachio Lemon (Puppy
        Chow), 250
    Sprite Cake, 200, *201*
    Sunshine Bars, 84, *85*
fudge
    Breakfast Fudge, 237
    Fudge, 234, *235, 236*
    fudge brownie sauce (variation
        of Fudge Sauce), 22
    Fudge Sauce, 22, *23*
    Inside Out PB Cup Fudge, 237
    Malted Marshmallow
        Chocolate Fudge, 237
    Mint Cookies and Cream
        Fudge, 237
    Rocky Road Fudge, 237
    Trail Mix Fudge, 237

G

garlicky flaky bread (variation of
    Flaky Bread), 153
Gazillionaire Energy
    (Marshmallow Treats),
    213

gelatin
    blooming, 48
    Chocolate Mirror Cake, 281,
        282, 283
    Gummy Bears, *232*, 233
    Marshmallows, *46*, 47, *49*
Gingersnaps, Frosted, 100, *101*
Glazed Pumpkin Pie Bars, 272,
    273
glazes *see also* frostings and
    fillings
    Any Flavor Glaze, 34
    Frosted Glaze, 101
    Mirror Glaze, 281
    Sprite Glaze, 202
    Sunny Glaze, 85
gluten-free
    Caramel Apples, 246, *247*
    Chewy Granola Bars, 216,
        217
    Chewy Oat Bars, 78, *79*
    Chocolate Peanut Butter
        Crunch Pie, 276, *277*
    Chocolate Shell, 44, *44, 45*
    Crème Brûlée, 291, *292*
    Fudge, 234, *235, 236*
    Granola, 38
    Gummy Bears, *232*, 233
    Lemon Crinkle Cookies, *96*, 97
    Lemon Ice, 240, *241*
    Macarons, *266*, 267
    Marshmallow Treats, *210*, 211,
        212
    Marshmallows, *46*, 47, *49*
    Pavlova, *278*, 279
    PB Cups, 221, *222*
    Peanut Butter Nougat, 228,
        229, 230
    Peppermint Patties, 244,
        245
    Pop Rocks, 218, *219*
    Potato Chips, *214*, 215
    Pudding, 52
    Puppy Chow, 248, *249*
    Soft Caramels, 50, *51*
    Turtles, *252*, 253
Go-To Chocolate Chip Cookies,
    67, *68*
graham crackers
    Cheesecake, 262, *263, 264*
    Graham Cracker Toffee, *238*,
        239
    Graham Crackers, 37
    PB S'mores Bars, *260*, 261
granola
    Chewy Granola Bars, 216,
        217
    Granola, 38
Gruyère cheese
    Cheese Fondue, *164*, 165
    Ham and Cheese Puffs, *168*,
        169
Gummy Bears, *232*, 233

H

Ham and Cheese Puffs, *168*, 169
Hot Chocolate, 58

I

ice cream and ices
    brownie batter no-churn ice cream (variation of No-Churn Ice Cream), 274
    chocolate fudge no-churn ice cream (variation of No-Churn Ice Cream), 274
    fruity no-churn ice cream (variation of No-Churn Ice Cream), 274
    Ice Cream Cones, *42*, 43
    Ice Cream Loaf Cake, 196, *197*
    Ice Cream Roll Cake, *288*, 289
    Lemon Ice, 240, *241*
    No-Churn Ice Cream, 274, *275*
ices *see* ice cream and ices
ingredients
    about, 4–6
    baking powder and baking soda, 5
    butter, 4
    chocolate, 5
    eggs, 4
    extracts, 5
    flour, 4
    milk, 5
    milk powder, 5
    oil, 5
    sugar, 4
    yeast, 5
Inside Out PB Cup Fudge, 237
icing *see* frostings and fillings; glazes

J

jam *see also* Curd; (Any) Fruit
    Citrus Jam, 28, *29*
    Fruit Jam, 27
    Strawberry Jam Butter, 19

K

Kettle Corn, Cinnamon Sugar, 226
Kimchi Butter, 19
kitchen sink quiche (variation of Quiche), 123

L

layer cake
    Chocolate Mayo Cake, 184, *185*
lemon
    Lemon Bars, 88, *89*
    Lemon Crinkle Cookies, *96*, 97
    Lemon Honey Ginger Babycakes, 179, *180*
    Lemon Ice, 240, *241*
    Lemon Loaf, 191, *192*
    Lemon–Olive Oil Popcorn, 226
loaf, bread
    Brioche, 147, *148*
    Easy, Can't Mess It Up Bread, 140, *141*

loaf cakes
    Ice Cream Loaf Cake, 196, *197*
    Lemon Honey Ginger Babycakes, 179, *180*
    Lemon Loaf, 191, *192*

M

Macarons, *266*, 267
Malted Marshmallow Chocolate Fudge, 237
maple syrup
    Granola, 38
    Maple Pecan Crispies, 82, *83*
    Maple Sheet Cake, *194*, 195
marshmallow
    Blueberry Pie (Marshmallow Treats), 213
    Carrot Cake Marshmallow Rolls, 176, *177*
    Cherry Pie (Marshmallow Treats), 213
    Cinnamon Apple (Marshmallow Treats), 213
    Fluffernutter (Marshmallow Treats), 213
    Gazillionaire Energy (Marshmallow Treats), 213
    Malted Marshmallow Chocolate Fudge, 237
    Marshmallows, *46*, 47, *49*
    PB S'mores Bars, *260*, 261
    Rocky Road Fudge, 237
    Strawberry Corn (Marshmallow Treats), 213
    Strawberry Shortcake (Marshmallow Treats), 213
    What's-in-Your-Pantry Marshmallow Cookies, *80*, 81
Mayo Cake, Chocolate, 184, *185*
meringue
    Pavlova, *278*, 279
milk *see also* sweetened condensed milk
    about, 5
    milk powder, about, 5
mint
    Mint Chip Sammies, 92, *93, 94*
    Mint Cookies and Cream Fudge, 237
    Mint Filling, *95*, 95
    Peppermint Patties, 244, *245*
Mirror Cake, Chocolate, 281, *282, 283*
molasses
    Frosted Gingersnaps, 100, *101*
    Malted Marshmallow Chocolate Fudge, 237
muffins
    Blueberry Muffin Bundt Cake, 186, *187*
    Brown Butter Chocolate Chip Muffins, 110, *111*
Mustard Butter, 19

N

No-Churn Ice Cream, 274, *275*
Nougat, Peanut Butter, 228, *229, 230*
nuts
    Maple Pecan Crispies, 82, *83*
    Nut (or Seed) Butter, 230
    Payday Pie, 270, *271*
    Rocky Road Fudge, 237
    Trail Mix Fudge, 237
    Turtles, *252*, 253

O

oats
    Chewy Oat Bars, 78, *79*
    Coconut Oatmeal Cookies, *86*, 87
    Granola, 38
oil, about, 5
Old Bay Butter, 19
Old-Fashioned Donuts, 114, *115*
orange
    Citrus Jam, 28, *29*
    Gummy Bears, *232*, 233
    Sunshine Bars, 84, *85*

P

pans
    baking, about, 9
    half-sheet, about, 8
pancakes *see also* crepes
    Silver Dollar Pancakes, *108*, 109
pantry *see* ingredients; DIY Pantry
parchment paper, about, 8
pastries *see also* pies and tarts
    Biscuits, 124, *125*
    Cinnamon Buns with Brown Sugar Goo, *116*, 117
    Croissants, *132*, 133
    Ham and Cheese Puffs, *168*, 169
    Macarons, *266*, 267
    Old-Fashioned Donuts, 114, *115*
    Stuffing Croissants, 170, *171*
Pavlova, *278*, 279
Payday Pie, 270, *271*
PB Cups, 221, *222*
PB S'mores Bars, *260*, 261
PB-Pretzel Freezer Cookies, *242*, 243
Peaches and Cream Upside Down Cake, 203, *204*
peanut butter
    Chocolate Peanut Butter Crunch Pie, 276, *277*
    Fluffernutter (Marshmallow Treats), 213
    Inside Out PB Cup Fudge, 237
    Payday Pie, 270, *271*
    PB Cups, 221, *222*
    PB Pretzel (Puppy Chow), 250

PB S'mores Bars, *260*, 261
PB-Pretzel Freezer Cookies, *242*, 243
Peanut Butter Nougat, 228, *229, 230*
peanuts
  Payday Pie, 270, *271*
Pecan, Maple, Crispies, 82, *83*
Peppermint Patties, 244, *245*
pies and tarts
  Chocolate Peanut Butter Crunch Pie, 276, *277*
  kitchen sink quiche (variation of Quiche), 123
  Payday Pie, 270, *271*
  Quiche, 120, *121, 122, 123*
Pita, 154, *155*
pizza
  Pizza, 156, *158, 159*
  Simple Pizza Sauce, 160
popcorn
  Caramel Popcorn, 226
  Cheddar–Old Bay Popcorn, 226
  Cinnamon Sugar Kettle Corn, 226
  Lemon–Olive Oil Popcorn, 226
  Popcorn, *224*, 225
  Salted Dark Chocolate–Almond Popcorn, 226
Popovers, 166, *167*
Pop Rocks, 218, *219*
Potato Chips, *214*, 215
pots/pans/skillets, about, 9
pretzels
  PB Pretzel (Puppy Chow), 250
  PB-Pretzel Freezer Cookies, *242*, 243
  Pretzel Swirl Brownies, *284*, 285
  Pretzels, Soft, 161, *162, 163*
pudding
  Banana Pudding, 52
  Butterscotch Pudding, 52
  Chocolate Pudding, 52
  Coconut Pudding, 52
  Pudding, 52
  Rice Pudding, 52
Puffs, Ham and Cheese, *168*, 169
Pumpkin Pie Bars, Glazed, 272, *273*
pumpkin spice donuts (variation of Old-Fashioned Donuts), 115
Puppy Chow
  Birthday (Puppy Chow), 250
  Chocolate Banana Nutella (Puppy Chow), 250
  Chocolate BDay (Puppy Chow), 250
  Cinnamon Butterscotch (Puppy Chow), 250
  Frosted Sugar Cookie (Puppy Chow), 250
  Frosted Yellow/Lemon Cake (Puppy Chow), 250
  Orangesicle (Puppy Chow), 250

PB Pretzel (Puppy Chow), 250
Pistachio Lemon (Puppy Chow), 250
Puppy Chow, 248, *249*
Rocky Road (Puppy Chow), 250

Q

quiche
  kitchen sink quiche (variation of Quiche), 123
  Quiche, 120, *121, 122, 123*

R

Rice Krispies
  Chocolate Peanut Butter Crunch Pie, 276, *277*
  Maple Pecan Crispies, 82, *83*
  Marshmallow Treats, *210*, 211, *212*
Rice Pudding, 52
Ricotta (homemade), 56
Rocky Road
  Fudge, 237
  Puppy Chow, 250
Roll Cake, Ice Cream, *288*, 289

S

S'mores Bars, PB, *260*, 261
Salt and Pepper Butter, 19
Salted Dark Chocolate–Almond Popcorn, 226
sandwich cookies *see also* cookies; frostings and fillings
  Macarons, *266*, 267
  Mint Chip Sammies, 92, *93, 94*
Sauce, Simple Pizza, 160
sauces, sweet *see also* glazes
  Caramel Sauce of Your Dreams, *20*, 21
  Chocolate Shell, 44, *44, 45*
  fudge brownie sauce (variation of Fudge Sauce), 22
  Fudge Sauce, 22, *23*
scallion pancakes (variation of Flaky Bread), 153
Sheet Cake, Maple, *194*, 195
Silver Dollar Pancakes, *108*, 109
Skillet Cookie, 258, *259*
Skillet Veggie Cake, *198*, 199
snacks
  Birthday (Puppy Chow), 250
  Blueberry Pie (Marshmallow Treats), 213
  Breakfast Fudge, 237
  Caramel Apples, 246, *247*
  Caramel Popcorn, 226
  Cheddar–Old Bay Popcorn, 226
  Cherry Pie (Marshmallow Treats), 213

Chewy Granola Bars, 216, *217*
Chocolate Banana Nutella (Puppy Chow), 250
Chocolate BDay (Puppy Chow), 250
Cinnamon Apple (Marshmallow Treats), 213
Cinnamon Butterscotch (Puppy Chow), 250
Cinnamon Sugar Kettle Corn, 226
Fluffernutter (Marshmallow Treats), 213
Frosted Sugar Cookie (Puppy Chow), 250
Frosted Yellow/Lemon Cake (Puppy Chow), 250
Fudge, 234, *235, 236*
Gazillionaire Energy (Marshmallow Treats), 213
Graham Cracker Toffee, *238*, 239
Granola, 38
Gummy Bears, *232*, 233
Inside Out PB Cup Fudge, 237
Lemon–Olive Oil Popcorn, 226
Malted Marshmallow Chocolate Fudge, 237
Marshmallow Treats, *210*, 211, *212*
Mint Cookies and Cream Fudge, 237
Orangesicle (Puppy Chow), 250
PB Cups, 221, *222*
PB Pretzel (Puppy Chow), 250
Peanut Butter Nougat, 228, *229, 230*
Peppermint Patties, 244, *245*
Pistachio Lemon (Puppy Chow), 250
Popcorn, *224*, 225
Pop Rocks, 218, *219*
Potato Chips, *214*, 215
Puppy Chow, 248, *249*
Rocky Road (Puppy Chow), 250
Rocky Road Fudge, 237
Salted Dark Chocolate–Almond Popcorn, 226
Strawberry Corn (Marshmallow Treats), 213
Strawberry Shortcake (Marshmallow Treats), 213
Trail Mix Fudge, 237
Turtles, *252*, 253
soft ball (stage) sugar
  cooking to soft ball stage, how to, 220
  Marshmallows, *46*, 47, *49*
  Peanut Butter Nougat, 228, *229, 230*
  Pop Rocks, 218, *219*
Soft Caramels, 50, *51*
Soft Pretzels, 161, *162, 163*

Sprinkles, 40, *41*
Sprite Cake, 200, *201*
storage containers, about, 8
strawberries
　　Strawberry Corn
　　　　(Marshmallow Treats),
　　　　213
　　Strawberry Jam Butter, 19
　　Strawberry Shortcake
　　　　(Marshmallow Treats),
　　　　213
Stuffing Croissants, 170, *171*
Sugar Cookies, 98, *99*
sugar *see also* soft ball (stage)
　　sugar
　　about, 4
Sunny Glaze, 85
Sunshine Bars, 84, *85*
Super Chocolate Cookies, *90*, 91
sweetened condensed milk
　　brownie batter no-churn ice
　　　　cream (variation of No-
　　　　Churn Ice Cream), 274
　　Bugle Bars, *72*, 73
　　chocolate fudge no-churn ice
　　　　cream (variation of No-
　　　　Churn Ice Cream), 274
　　fruity no-churn ice cream
　　　　(variation of No-Churn
　　　　Ice Cream), 274
　　Fudge, 234, *235, 236*
　　Graham Cracker Toffee, *238*,
　　　　239
　　No-Churn Ice Cream, 274, *275*
　　Soft Caramels, 50, *51*
　　Turtles, *252*, 253

T

Toffee, *60*, 61
Toffee, Graham Cracker, *238*, 239
Tortillas, Flour, *150*, 151
Trail Mix Fudge, 237
Turtles, *252*, 253

U

Upside Down Cake, Peaches and
　　Cream, 203, *204*

V

Vegan
　　Chocolate Peanut Butter
　　　　Crunch Pie, 276, *277*
　　Chocolate Shell, 44, *44, 45*
　　Granola, 38
　　Lemon Ice, 240, *241*
　　Marshmallows, *46*, 47, *49*
　　Pop Rocks, 218, *219*
　　Potato Chips, *214*, 215

W

wafers
　　Brown Sugar Wafers, *30*, 32
　　Chocolate Wafers, *31*, 33
What's-in-Your-Pantry
　　　　Marshmallow Cookies,
　　　　80, 81

Whipped Cream, Choose Your
　　Flavor, 24

Y

yeast
　　about, 5
　　Bagels, *126*, 127, *128*
　　Brioche, 147, *148*
　　Buns, *144*, 145
　　Cinnamon Buns with
　　　　Brown Sugar Goo,
　　　　116, 117
　　Croissants, *132*, 133
　　Easy, Can't Mess It Up
　　　　Bread, 140, *141*
　　English Muffins, 130, *131*
　　Pita, 154, *155*
　　Pizza, 156, *158, 159*
　　Soft Pretzels, 161, *162, 163*
　　working with, 119

Z

Ziploc
　　Macarons, *266*, 267
　　PB Cups, 221, *222*
　　Puppy Chow, 248, *249*
　　Toffee, *60*, 61
　　What's-in-Your-Pantry
　　　　Marshmallow Cookies,
　　　　80, 81

When we started Bake Club (originally Baking Club IYKYK),
we dreamed up this simple membership card—something we
could send out to anyone and everyone who signed up, proof of
our commitment to the come-one-come-all spirit. Not one to
back down from a good branding moment, we pulled in some of
the words my dear friend Jason Polan handcrafted for a previous
baking project and channeled the energy of his beloved Taco Bell
Drawing Club. I think of Jason every time I wield my laminated
Bake Club card, and now I hope you will too. Write your name,
cut it out, own your spot! And above all else, welcome!

@jasonpolan

www.BakeClub.com

Christina Tosi is the two-time James Beard Award—winning chef and the owner of Milk Bar, which has bakery locations across the country, an online care package business, and products in the aisles of the grocery store. She served as a judge on Fox's *MasterChef Junior*, as the host of Netflix's *Bake Squad*, and was featured in the hit Netflix docuseries *Chef's Table: Pastry*. She is the author of the *New York Times* best seller *All About Cookies*, as well as *All About Cake*, *Momofuku Milk Bar*, *Milk Bar Life*, *Milk Bar: Kids Only*, *Dessert Can Save the World*, and for children, *Every Cake Has a Story* and *Just the Right Cake*.

Shannon Salzano is a *New York Times* best-selling author and a hospitality industry veteran. A graduate of Northern Illinois University's literature and communications program, Shannon spent half a decade in editorial publishing before making the pivot to hospitality. She served as the creative director to Chicago's lauded Girl & the Goat restaurant empire for five years under Chef Stephanie Izard. In Shannon's role as director of special projects at Milk Bar, she has executed dozens of brand partnerships, co-founded Bake Club, and oversees brand voice.